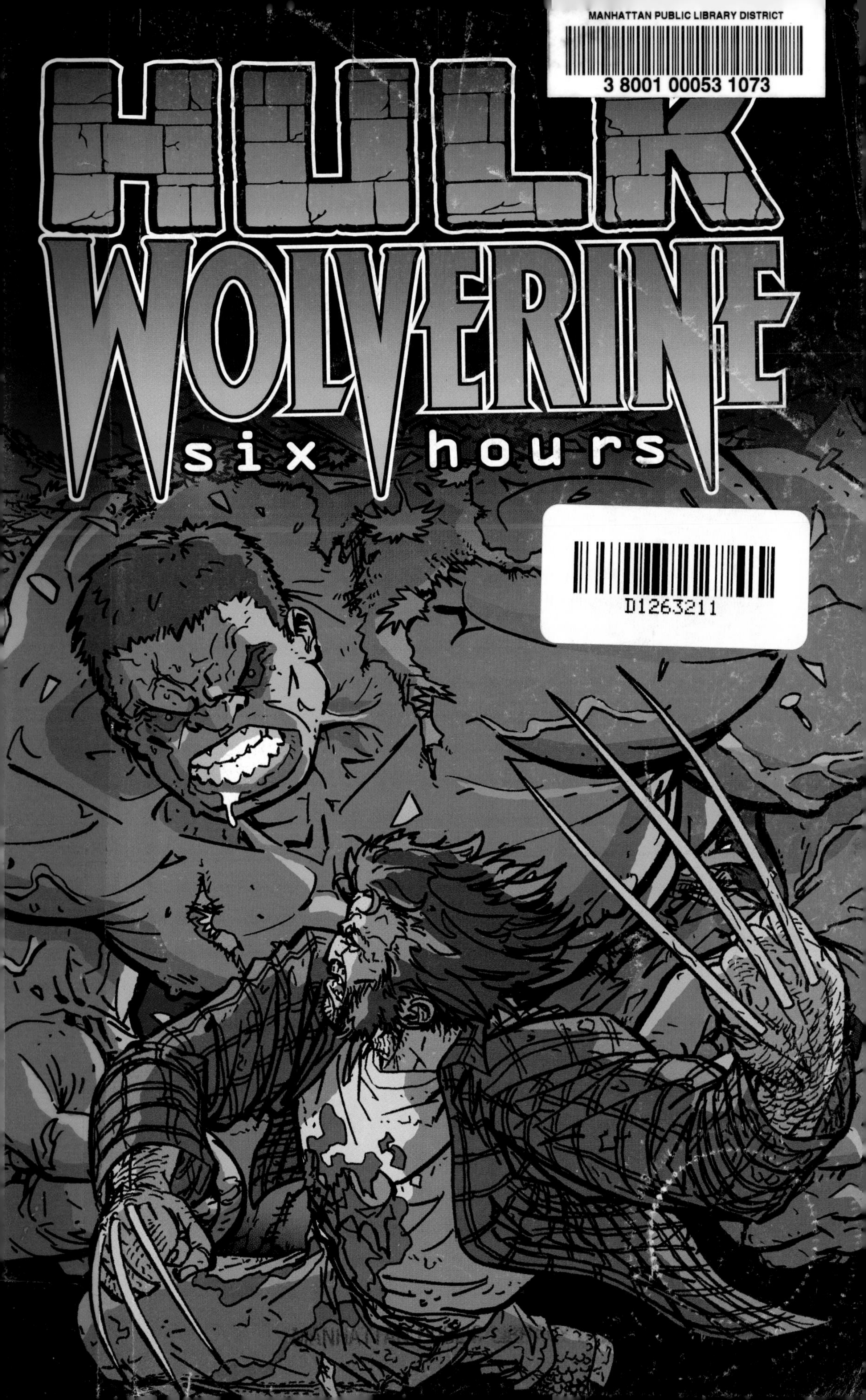
HULK
WOLVERINE
six hours

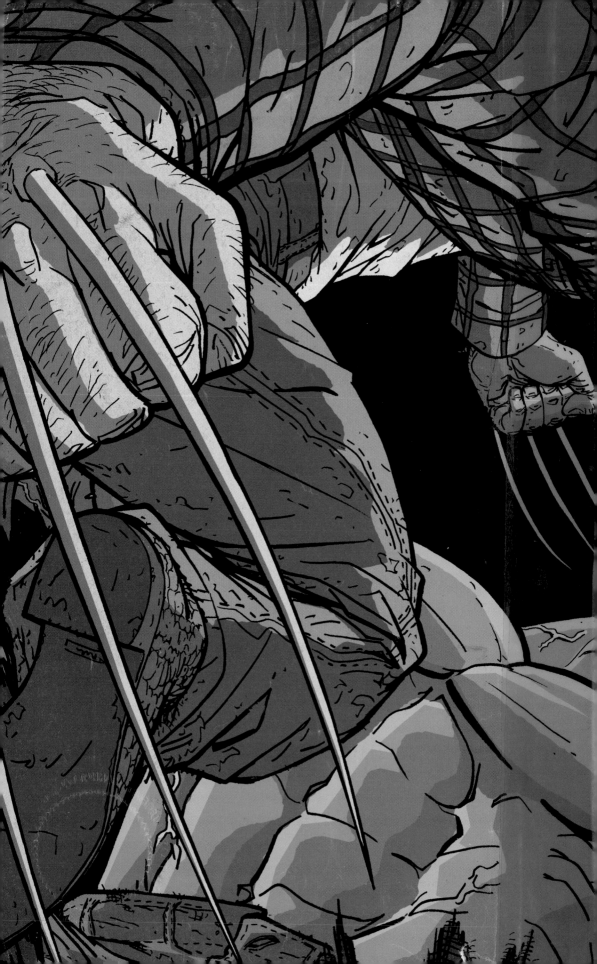

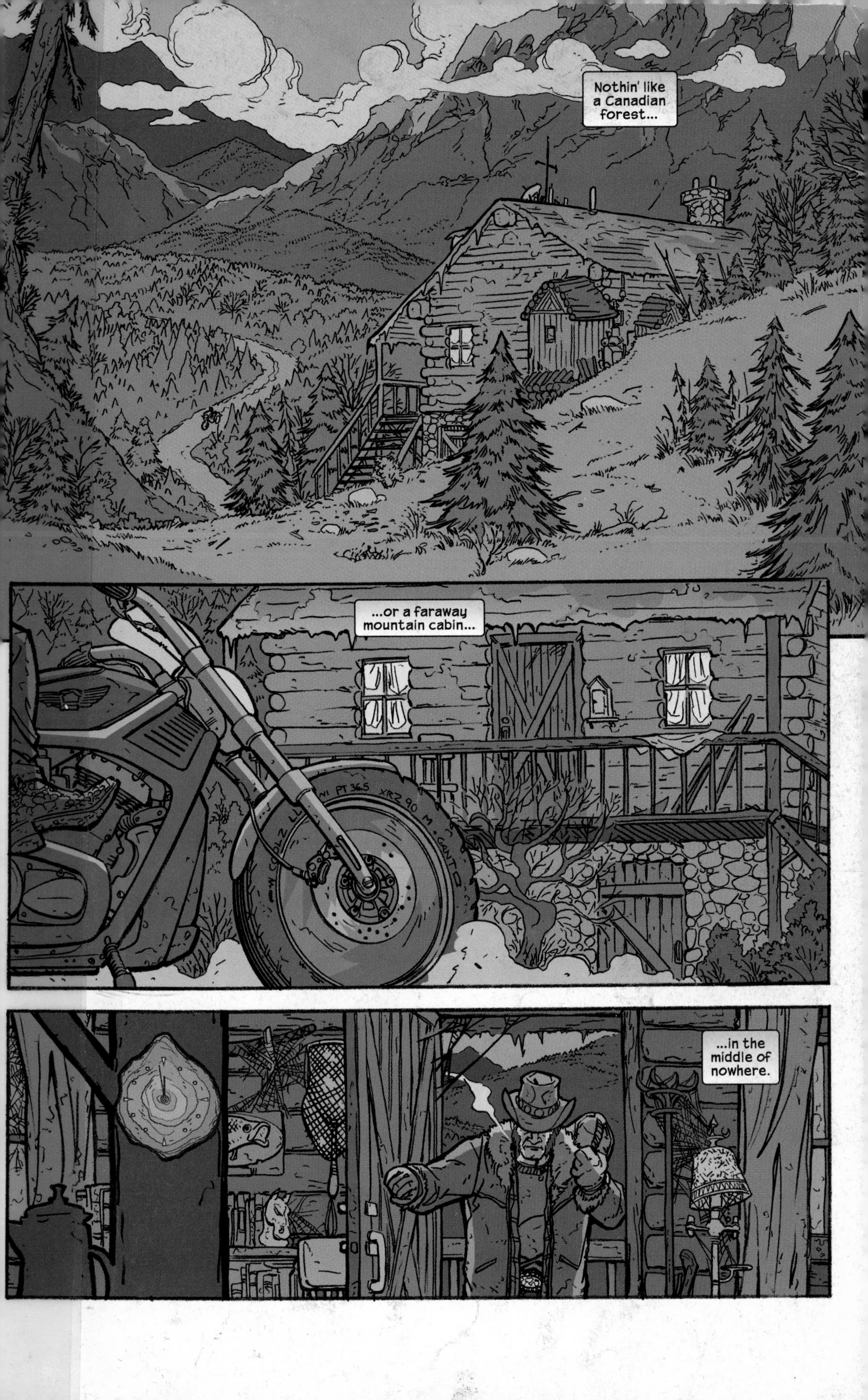
Nothin' like a Canadian forest...
...or a faraway mountain cabin...
...in the middle of nowhere.

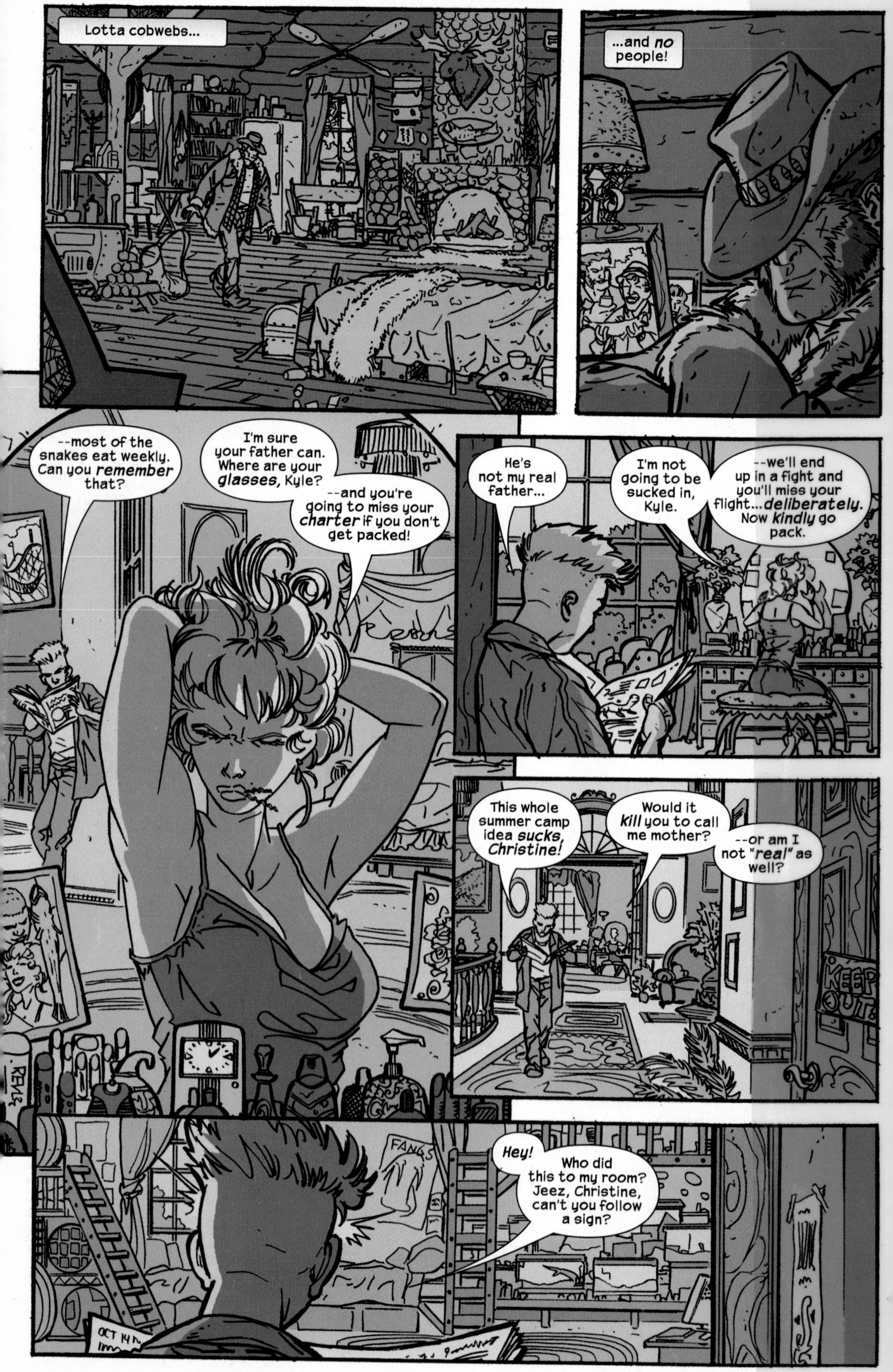
Lotta cobwebs...
...and *no* people!
--most of the snakes eat weekly. Can you *remember* that?
I'm sure your father can. Where are your *glasses,* Kyle?
--and you're going to miss your *charter* if you don't get packed!
He's not my real father...
I'm not going to be sucked in, Kyle.
--we'll end up in a fight and you'll miss your flight...*deliberately.* Now *kindly* go pack.
This whole summer camp idea *sucks, Christine!*
Would it *kill* you to call me mother?
--or am I not "*real*" as well?
KEEP OUT!
FANGS
Hey! Who did this to my room? Jeez, Christine, can't you follow a sign?

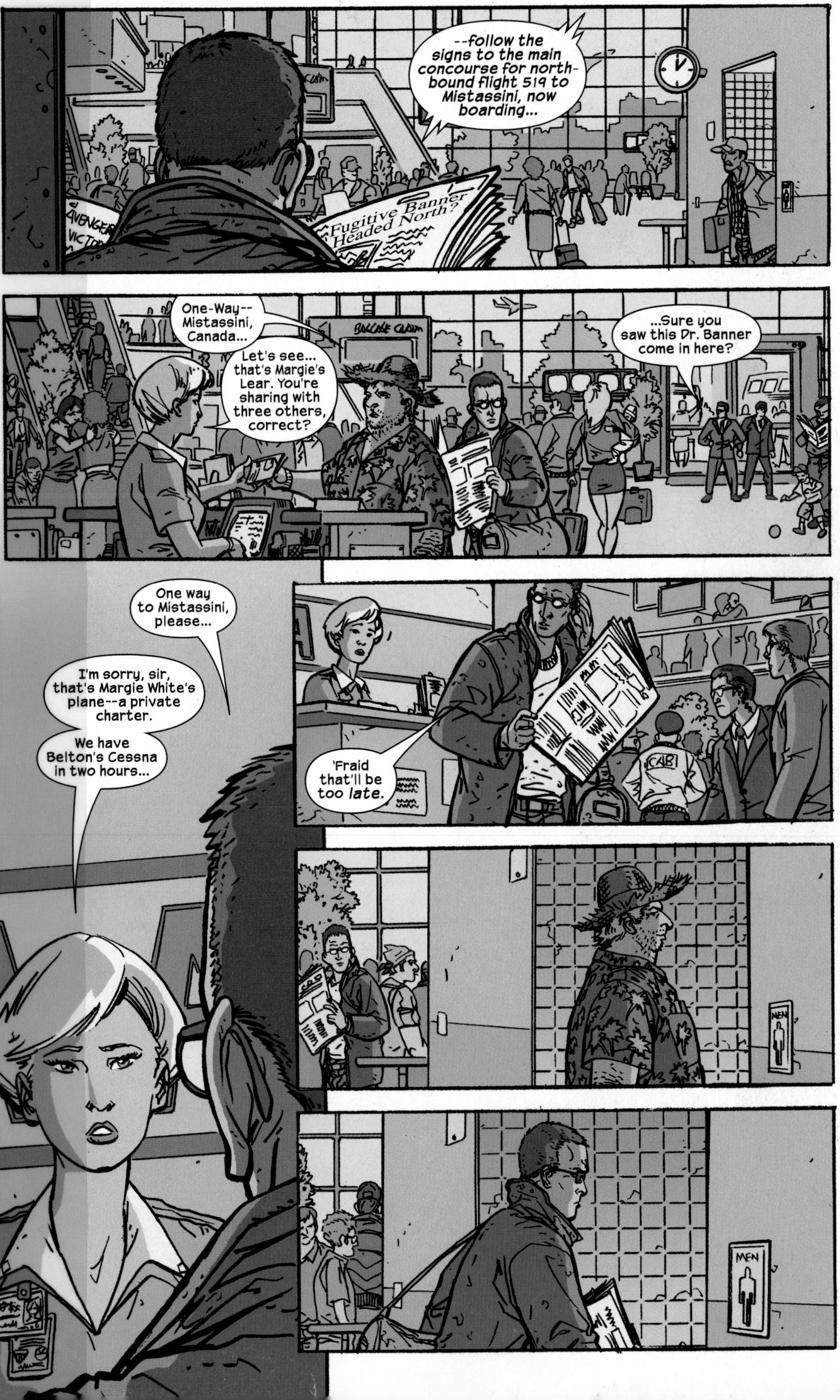

--follow the signs to the main concourse for north-bound flight 519 to Mistassini, now boarding...
Fugitive Banner Headed North?
AVENGER
VICTO
One-Way-- Mistassini, Canada...
Let's see... that's Margie's Lear. You're sharing with three others, correct?
...Sure you saw this Dr. Banner come in here?
One way to Mistassini, please...
I'm sorry, sir, that's Margie White's plane--a private charter.
We have Belton's Cessna in two hours...
'Fraid that'll be too *late*.
CAB
MEN
MEN

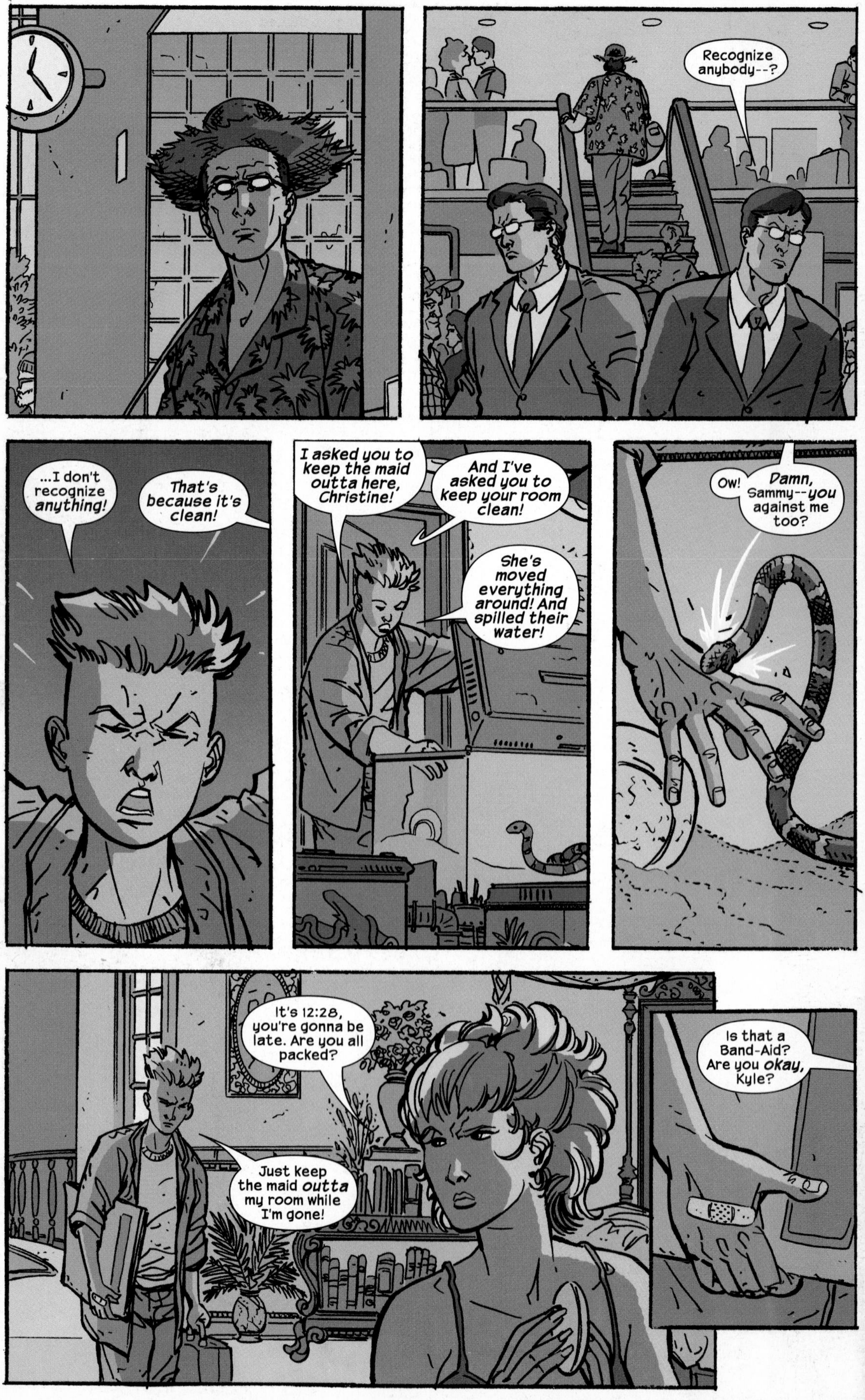
Recognize anybody--?
...I don't recognize anything!
That's because it's clean!
I asked you to keep the maid outta here, Christine!
And I've asked you to keep your room clean!
She's moved everything around! And spilled their water!
Ow!
Damn, Sammy--you against me too?
It's 12:28, you're gonna be late. Are you all packed?
Just keep the maid outta my room while I'm gone!
Is that a Band-Aid? Are you okay, Kyle?

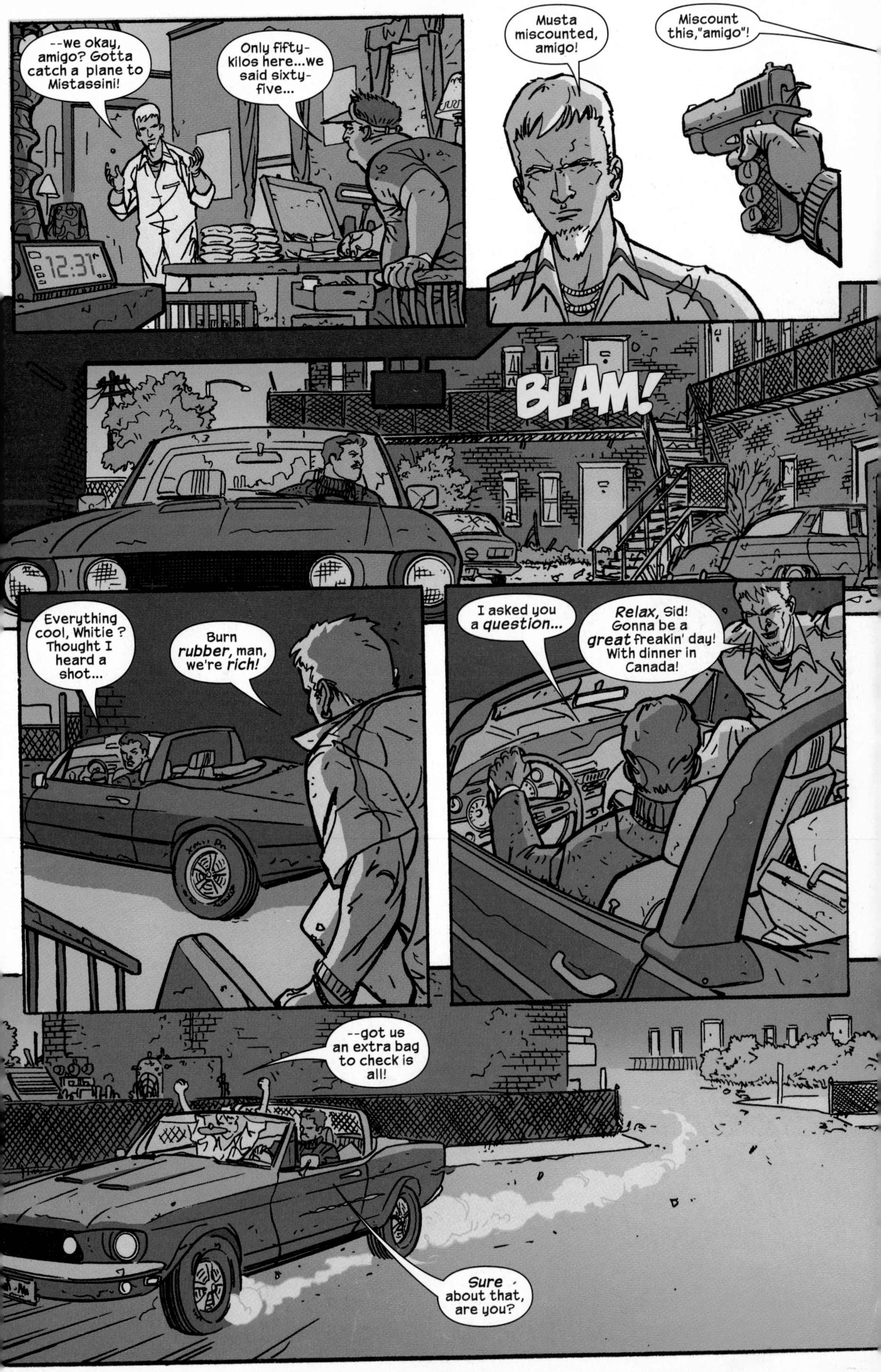
--we okay, amigo? Gotta catch a plane to Mistassini!
Only fifty-kilos here...we said sixty-five...
12:31
Musta miscounted, amigo!
Miscount this,"amigo"!
BLAM!
Everything cool, Whitie ? Thought I heard a shot...
Burn *rubber*, man, we're *rich!*
I asked you a *question*...
Relax, Sid! Gonna be a *great* freakin' day! With dinner in Canada!
--got us an extra bag to check is all!
Sure about that, are you?

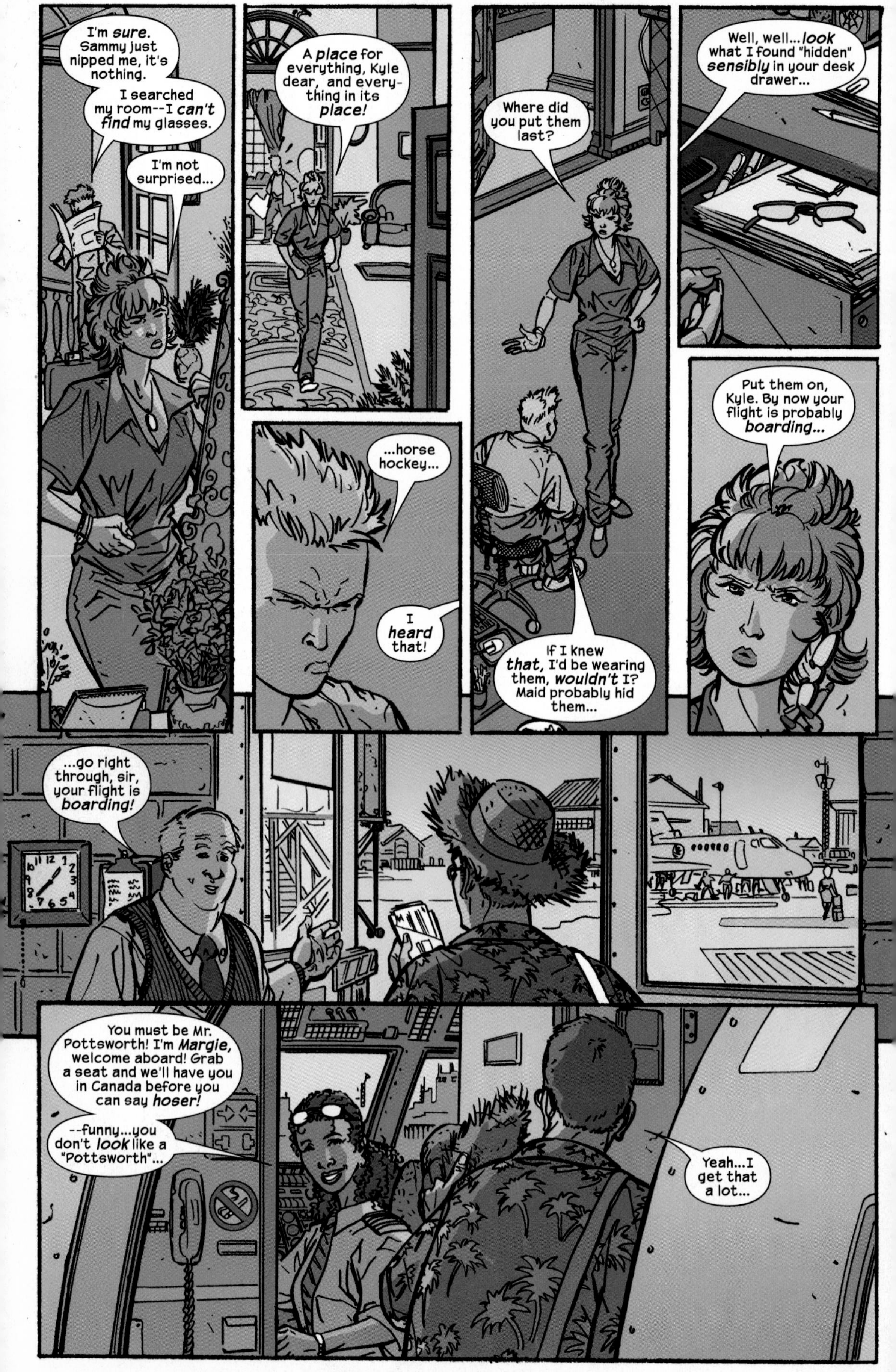
I'm sure. Sammy just nipped me, it's nothing.
I searched my room--I can't find my glasses.
I'm not surprised...
A place for everything, Kyle dear, and everything in its place!
Where did you put them last?
Well, well...look what I found "hidden" sensibly in your desk drawer...
...horse hockey...
I heard that!
If I knew that, I'd be wearing them, wouldn't I? Maid probably hid them...
Put them on, Kyle. By now your flight is probably boarding...
...go right through, sir, your flight is boarding!
You must be Mr. Pottsworth! I'm Margie, welcome aboard! Grab a seat and we'll have you in Canada before you can say hoser!
--funny...you don't look like a "Pottsworth"...
Yeah...I get that a lot...

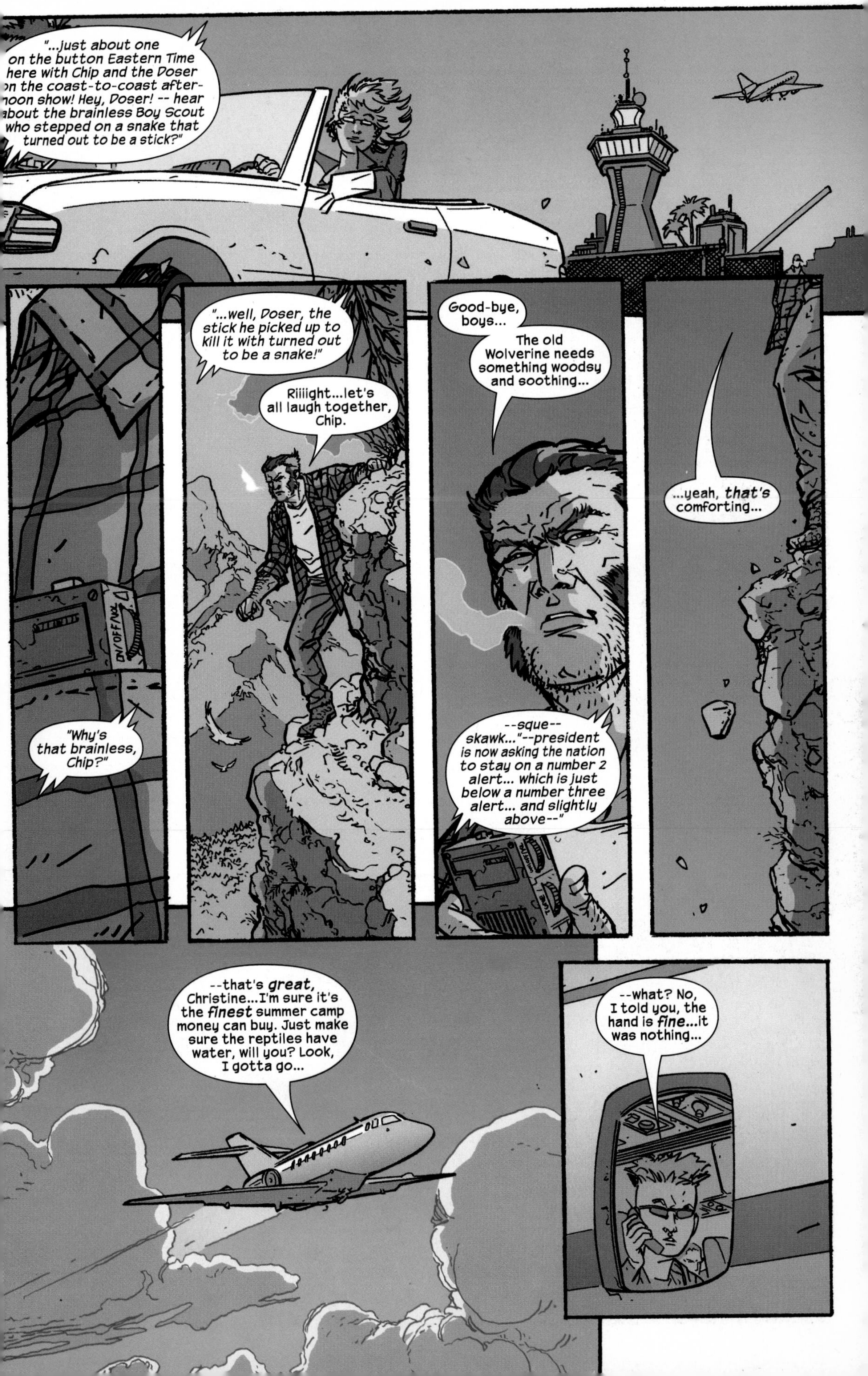
"...just about one on the button Eastern Time here with Chip and the Doser on the coast-to-coast after-noon show! Hey, Doser! -- hear about the brainless Boy Scout who stepped on a snake that turned out to be a stick?"
"Why's that brainless, Chip?"
"...well, Doser, the stick he picked up to kill it with turned out to be a snake!"
Riiiight...let's all laugh together, Chip.
Good-bye, boys...
The old Wolverine needs something woodsy and soothing...
--sque-- skawk..."--president is now asking the nation to stay on a number 2 alert... which is just below a number three alert... and slightly above--"
...yeah, that's comforting...
--that's great, Christine...I'm sure it's the finest summer camp money can buy. Just make sure the reptiles have water, will you? Look, I gotta go...
--what? No, I told you, the hand is fine...it was nothing...

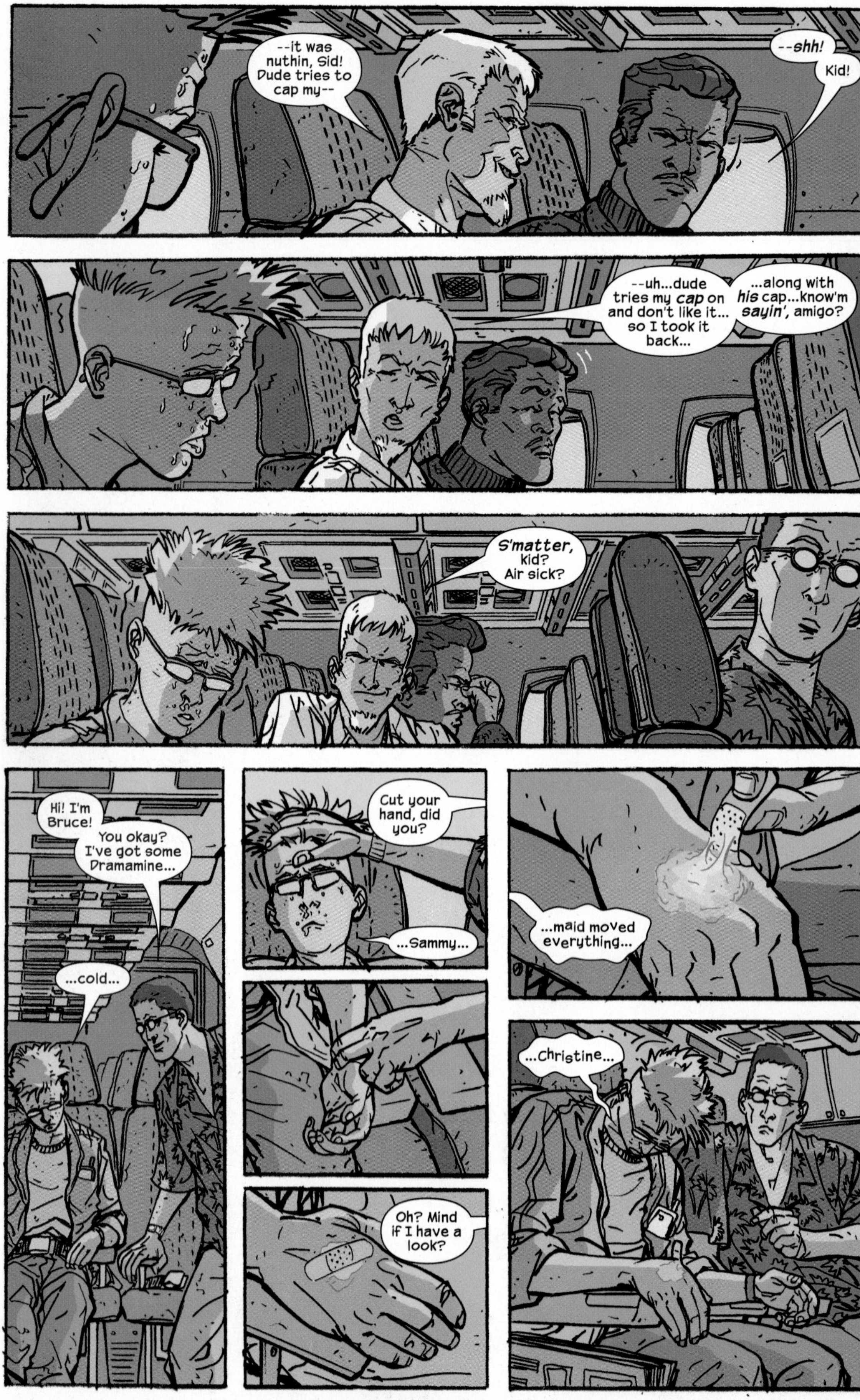

--it was nuthin, Sid! Dude tries to cap my--
--shh!
Kid!
--uh...dude tries my cap on and don't like it... so I took it back...
...along with his cap...know'm sayin', amigo?
S'matter, kid? Air sick?
Hi! I'm Bruce!
You okay? I've got some Dramamine...
...cold...
Cut your hand, did you?
...Sammy...
Oh? Mind if I have a look?
...maid moved everything...
...Christine...

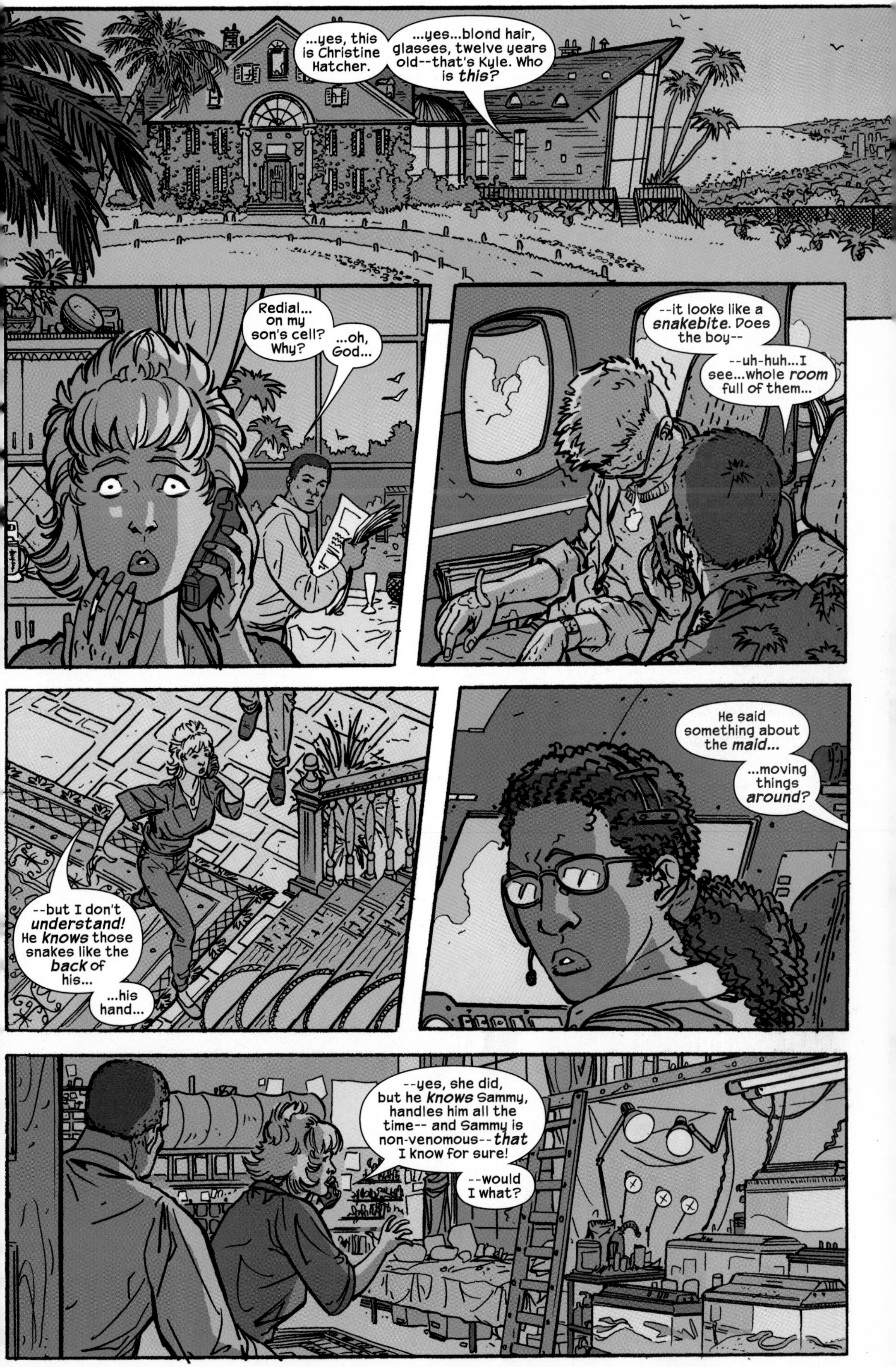

...yes, this is Christine Hatcher.
...yes...blond hair, glasses, twelve years old--that's Kyle. Who is *this?*
Redial... on my son's cell? Why?
...oh, God...
--it looks like a *snakebite.* Does the boy--
--uh-huh...I see...whole *room* full of them...
--but I don't *understand!* He *knows* those snakes like the *back* of his...
...his hand...
He said something about the *maid...*
...moving things *around?*
--yes, she did, but he *knows* Sammy, handles him all the time-- and Sammy is non-venomous--*that* I know for sure!
--would I what?

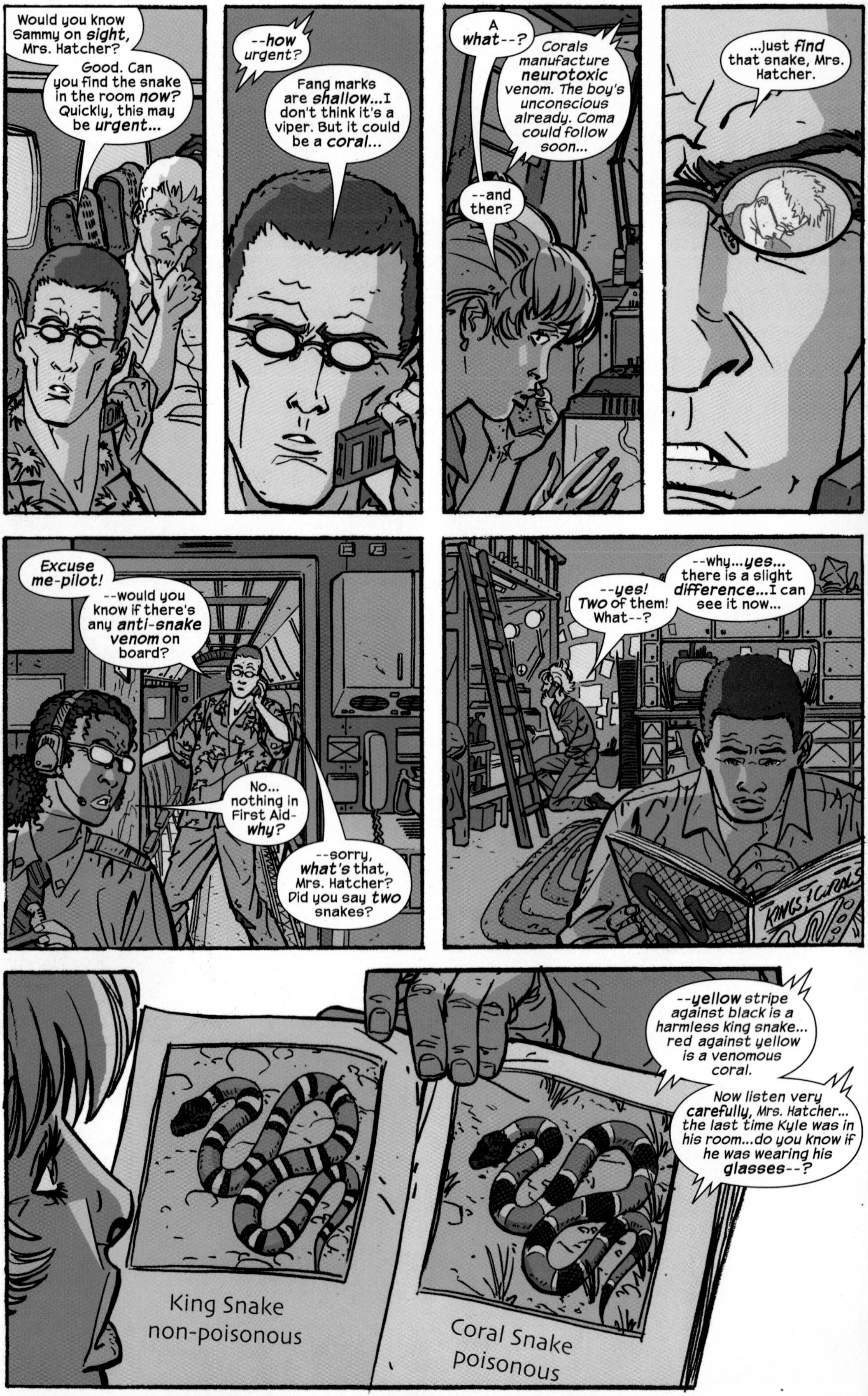
Would you know Sammy on sight, Mrs. Hatcher?
Good. Can you find the snake in the room now? Quickly, this may be urgent...
--how urgent?
Fang marks are shallow...I don't think it's a viper. But it could be a coral...
A what--?
Corals manufacture neurotoxic venom. The boy's unconscious already. Coma could follow soon...
--and then?
...just find that snake, Mrs. Hatcher.
Excuse me-pilot!
--would you know if there's any anti-snake venom on board?
No... nothing in First Aid- why?
--sorry, what's that, Mrs. Hatcher? Did you say two snakes?
--yes! Two of them! What--?
--why...yes... there is a slight difference...I can see it now...
KINGS & CORALS
--yellow stripe against black is a harmless king snake... red against yellow is a venomous coral.
Now listen very carefully, Mrs. Hatcher... the last time Kyle was in his room...do you know if he was wearing his glasses--?
King Snake non-poisonous
Coral Snake poisonous

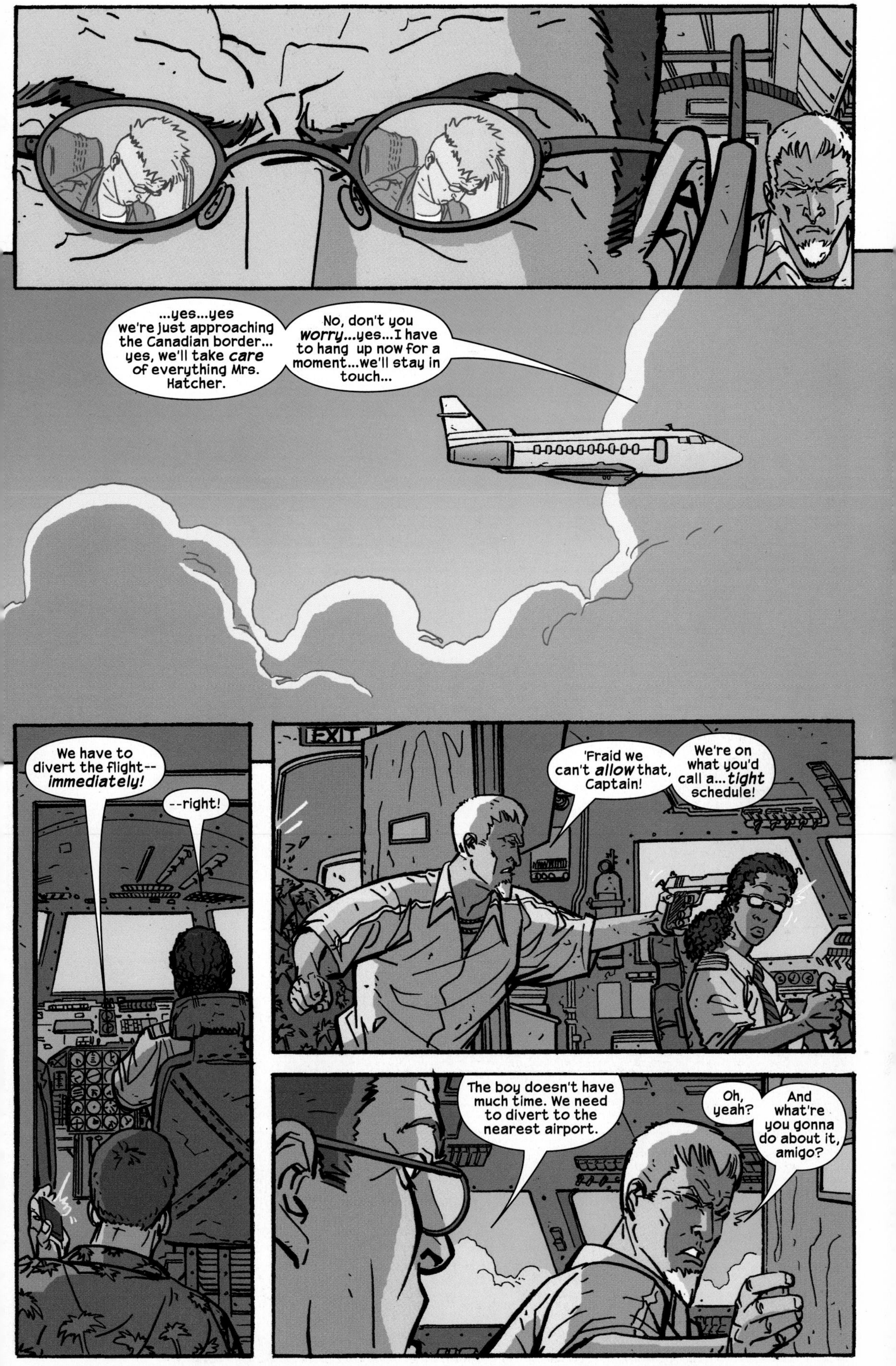
...yes...yes we're just approaching the Canadian border... yes, we'll take care of everything Mrs. Hatcher.
No, don't you worry...yes...I have to hang up now for a moment...we'll stay in touch...
We have to divert the flight-- immediately!
--right!
'Fraid we can't allow that, Captain!
We're on what you'd call a...tight schedule!
The boy doesn't have much time. We need to divert to the nearest airport.
Oh, yeah?
And what're you gonna do about it, amigo?

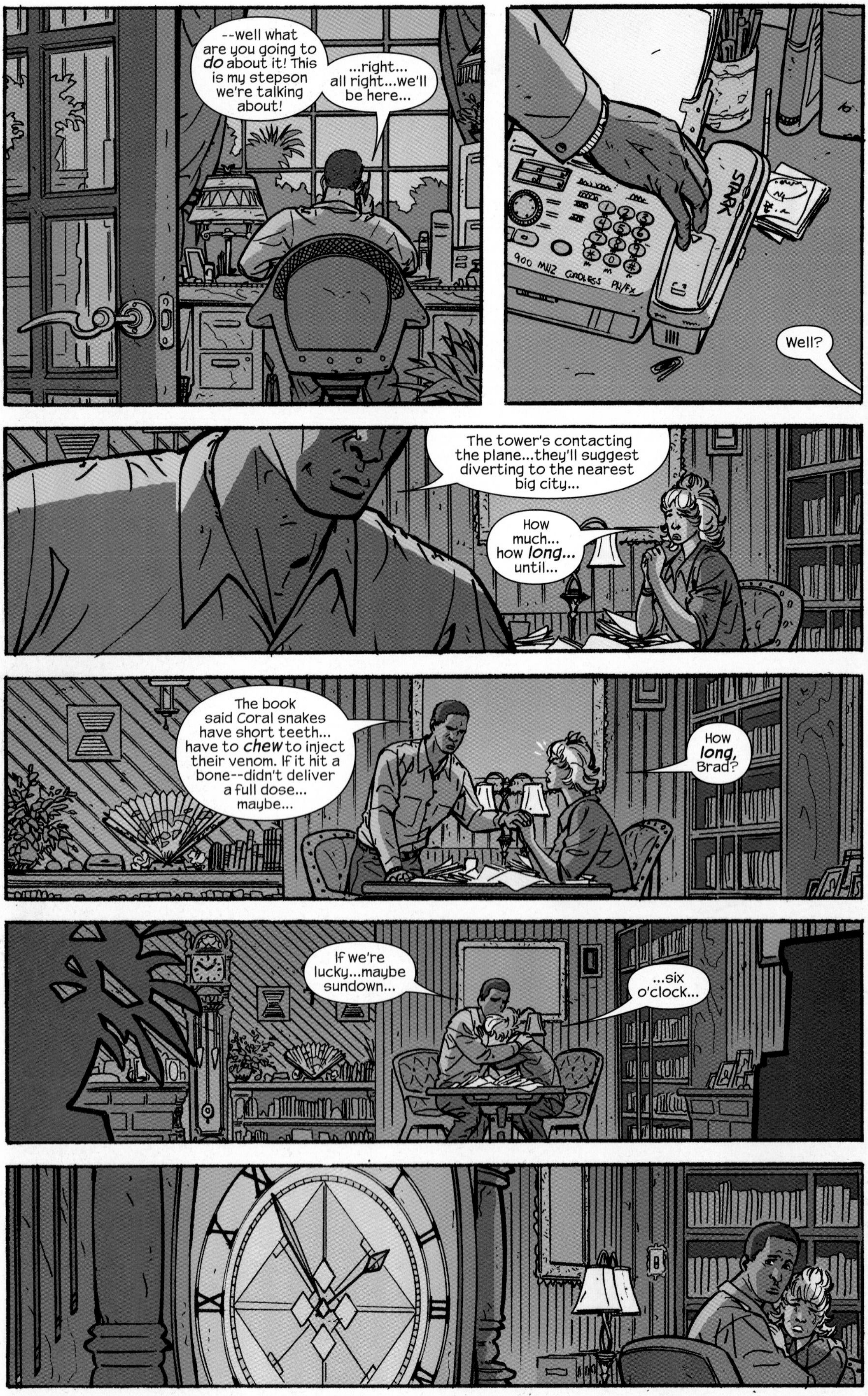
--well what are you going to do about it! This is my stepson we're talking about!
...right... all right...we'll be here...
STARK
900 MHZ CORDLESS PH/FX
Well?
The tower's contacting the plane...they'll suggest diverting to the nearest big city...
How much... how long... until...
The book said Coral snakes have short teeth... have to chew to inject their venom. If it hit a bone--didn't deliver a full dose... maybe...
How long, Brad?
If we're lucky...maybe sundown...
...six o'clock...

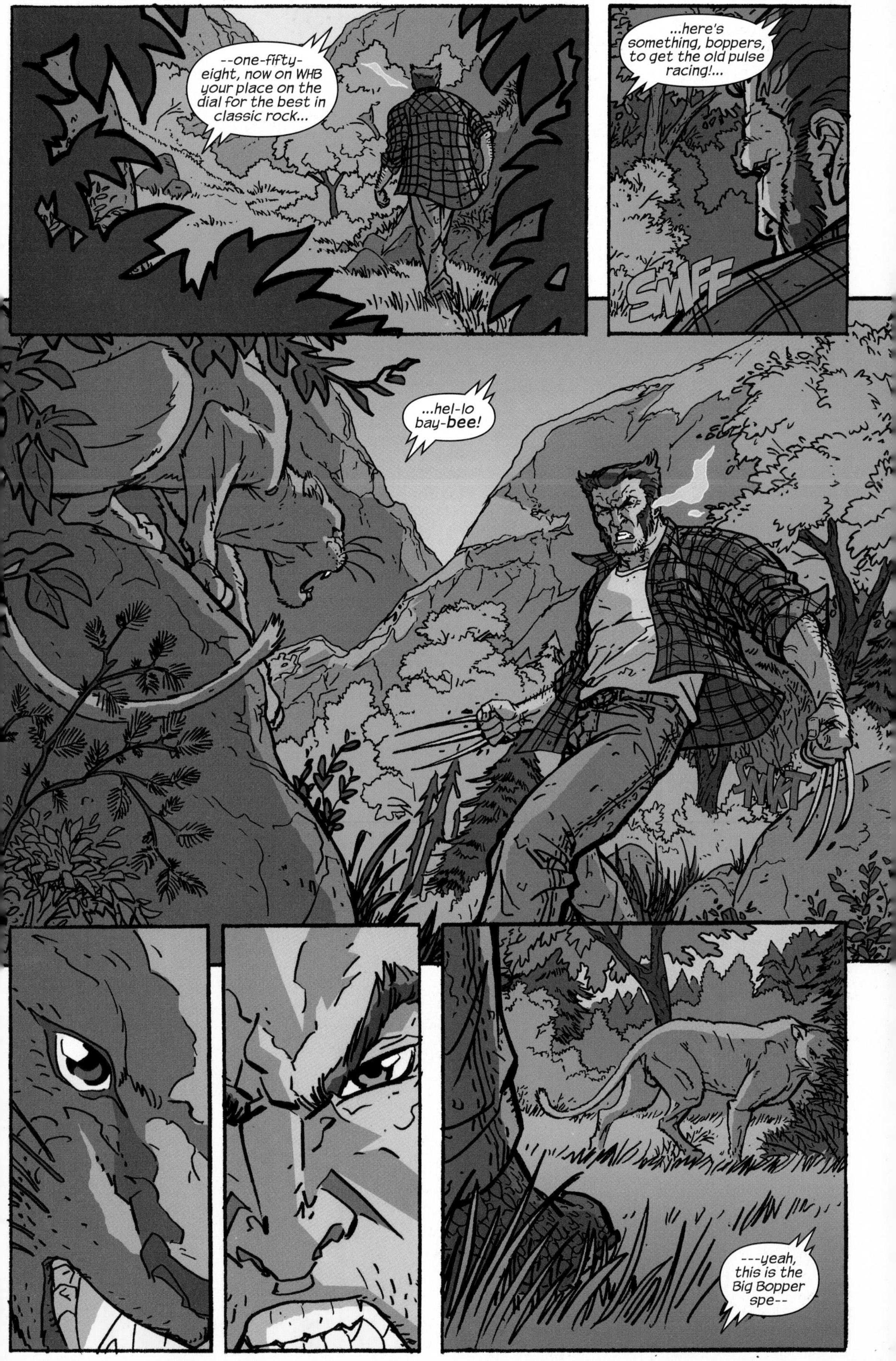
--one-fifty-eight, now on WHB your place on the dial for the best in classic rock...
...here's something, boppers, to get the old pulse racing!...
SNIFF
...hel-lo bay-bee!
SNKT
---yeah, this is the Big Bopper spe--

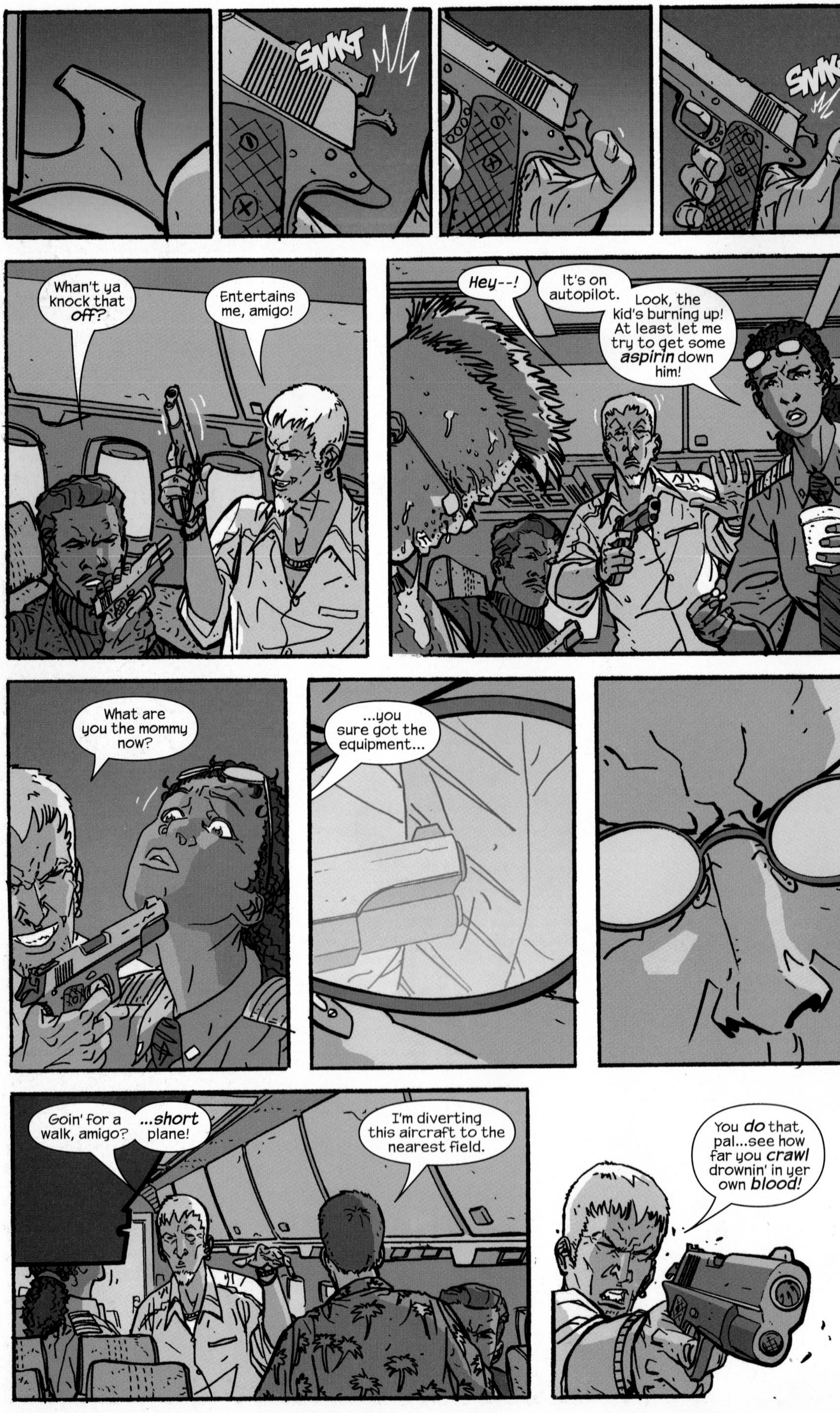
SNIKT
SNIKT
Whan't ya knock that off?
Entertains me, amigo!
Hey--!
It's on autopilot.
Look, the kid's burning up! At least let me try to get some aspirin down him!
What are you the mommy now?
...you sure got the equipment...
Goin' for a walk, amigo?
...short plane!
I'm diverting this aircraft to the nearest field.
You do that, pal...see how far you crawl drownin' in yer own blood!

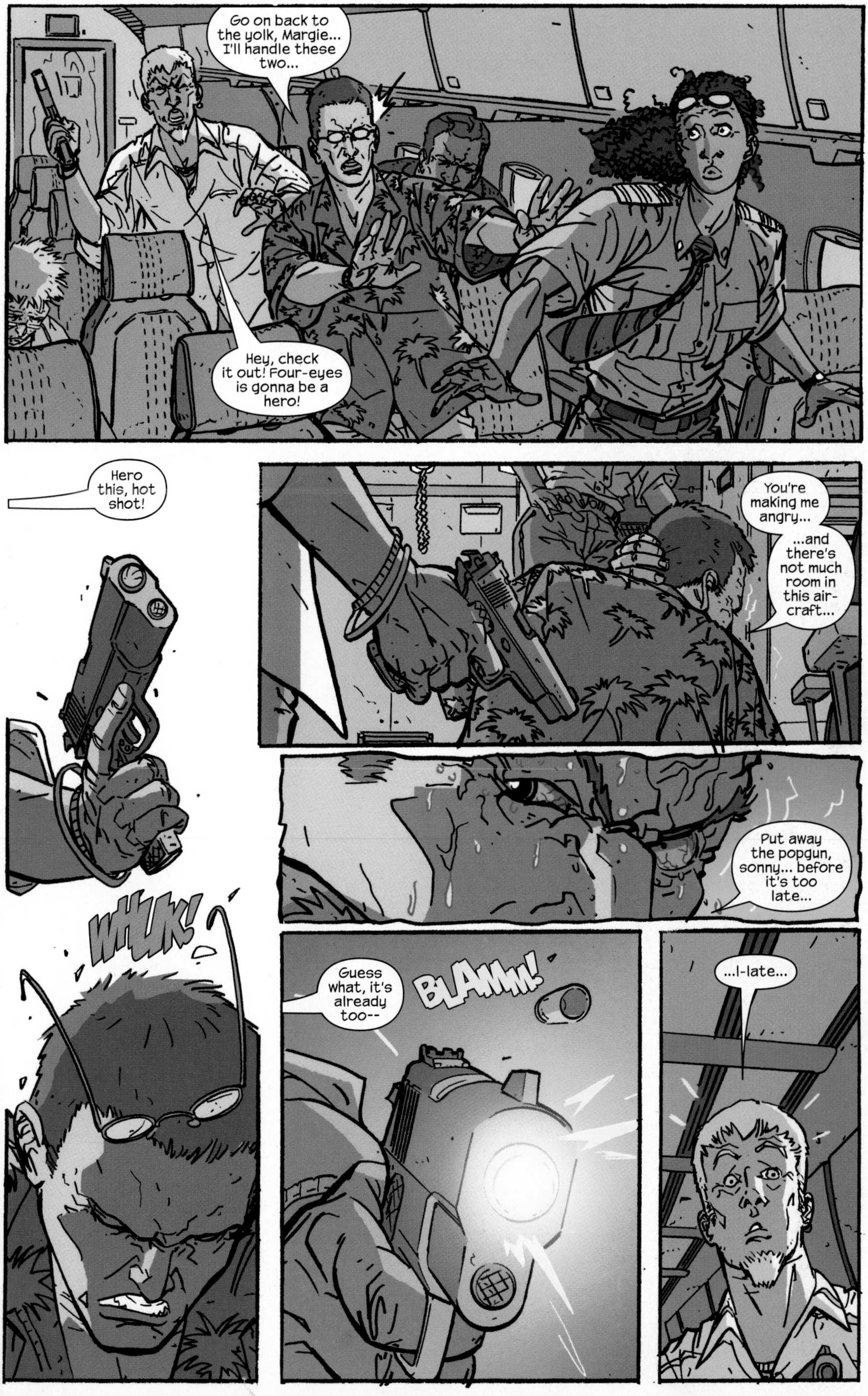
Go on back to the yolk, Margie... I'll handle these two...
Hey, check it out! Four-eyes is gonna be a hero!
Hero this, hot shot!
You're making me angry...
...and there's not much room in this aircraft...
Put away the popgun, sonny... before it's too late...
WHUK!
Guess what, it's already too--
BLAMMM!
...l-late...

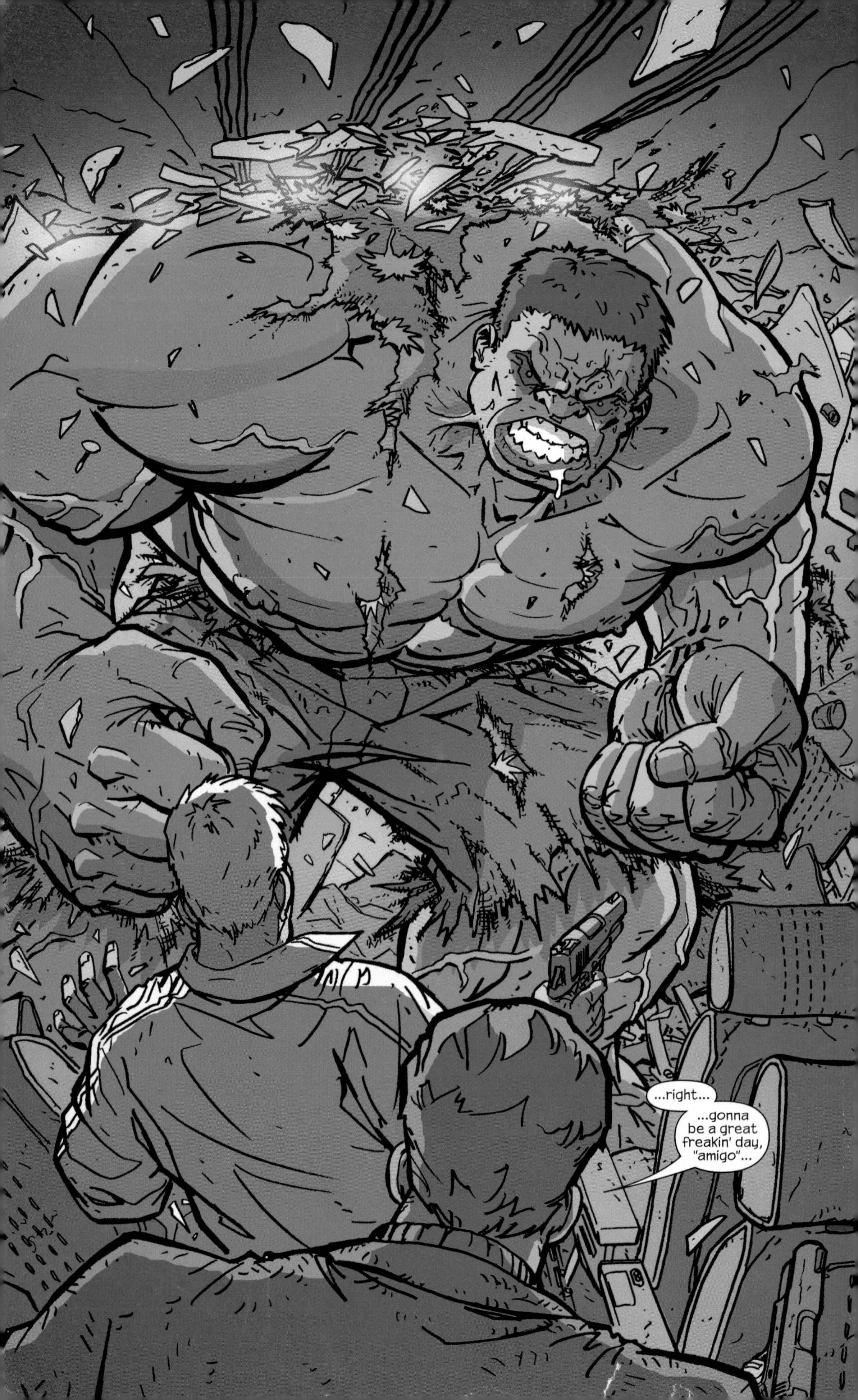
...right...
...gonna be a great freakin' day, "amigo"...

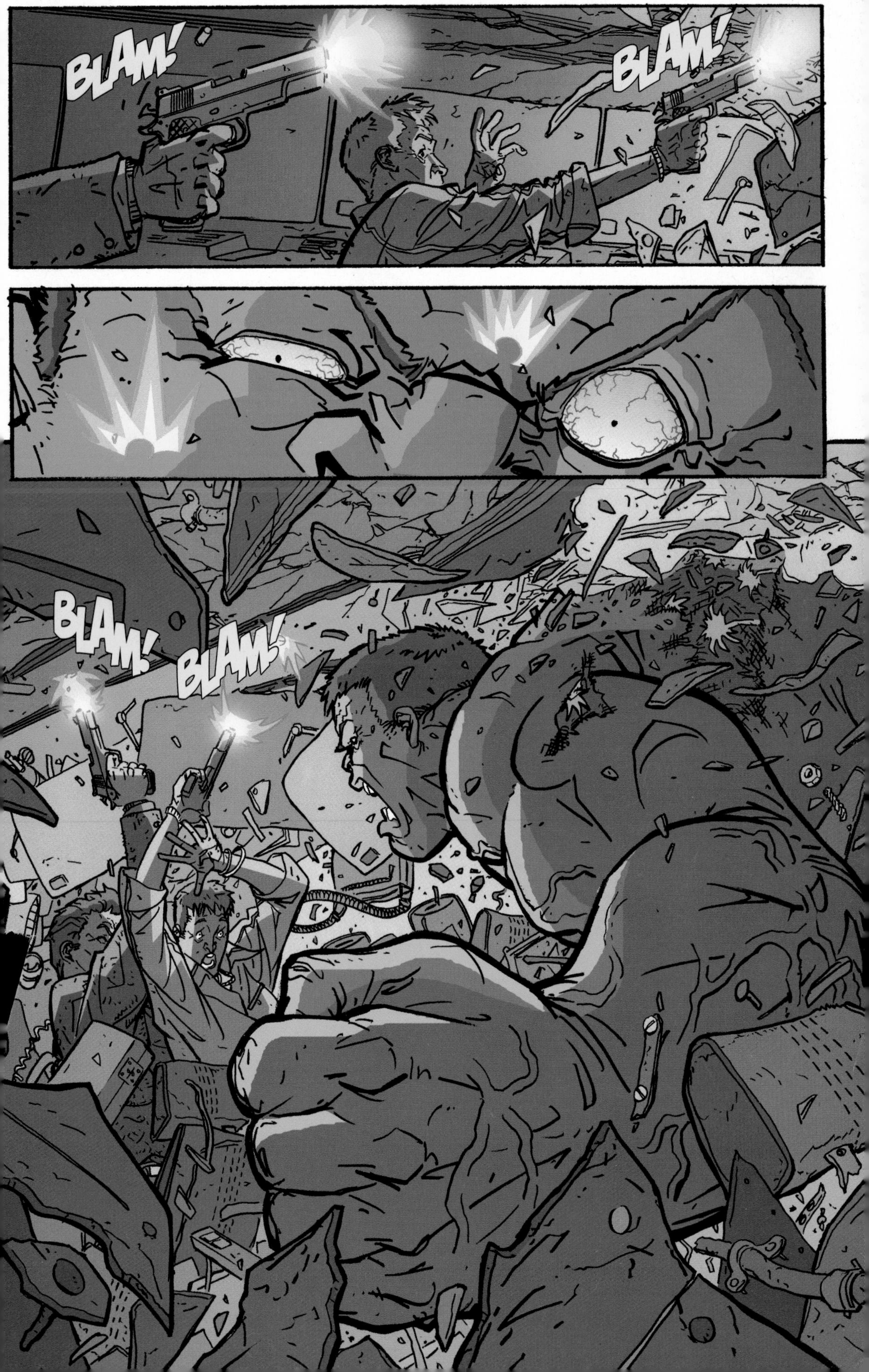
BLAM!
BLAM!
BLAM!
BLAM!

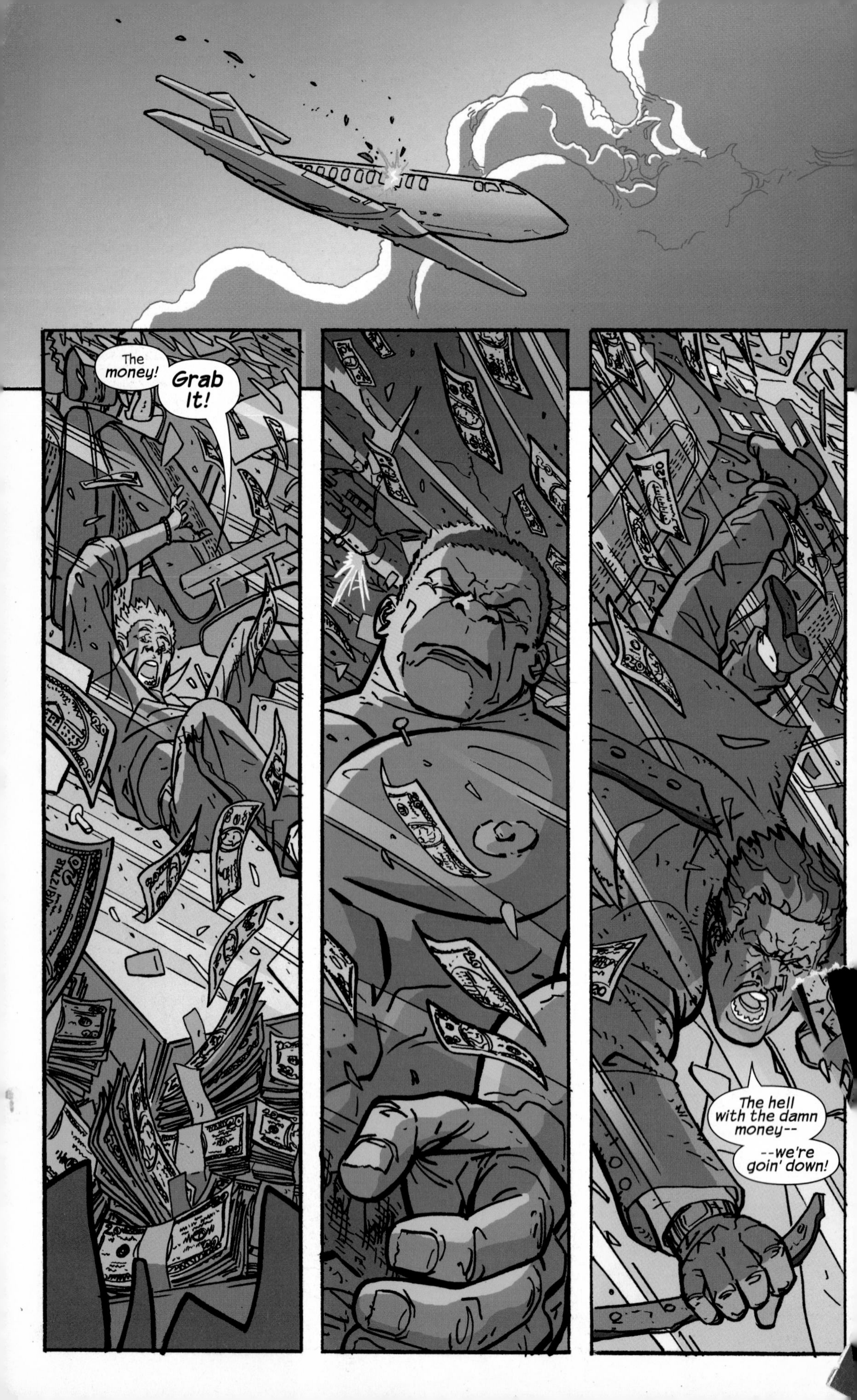
The money!
Grab It!
The hell with the damn money--
--we're goin' down!

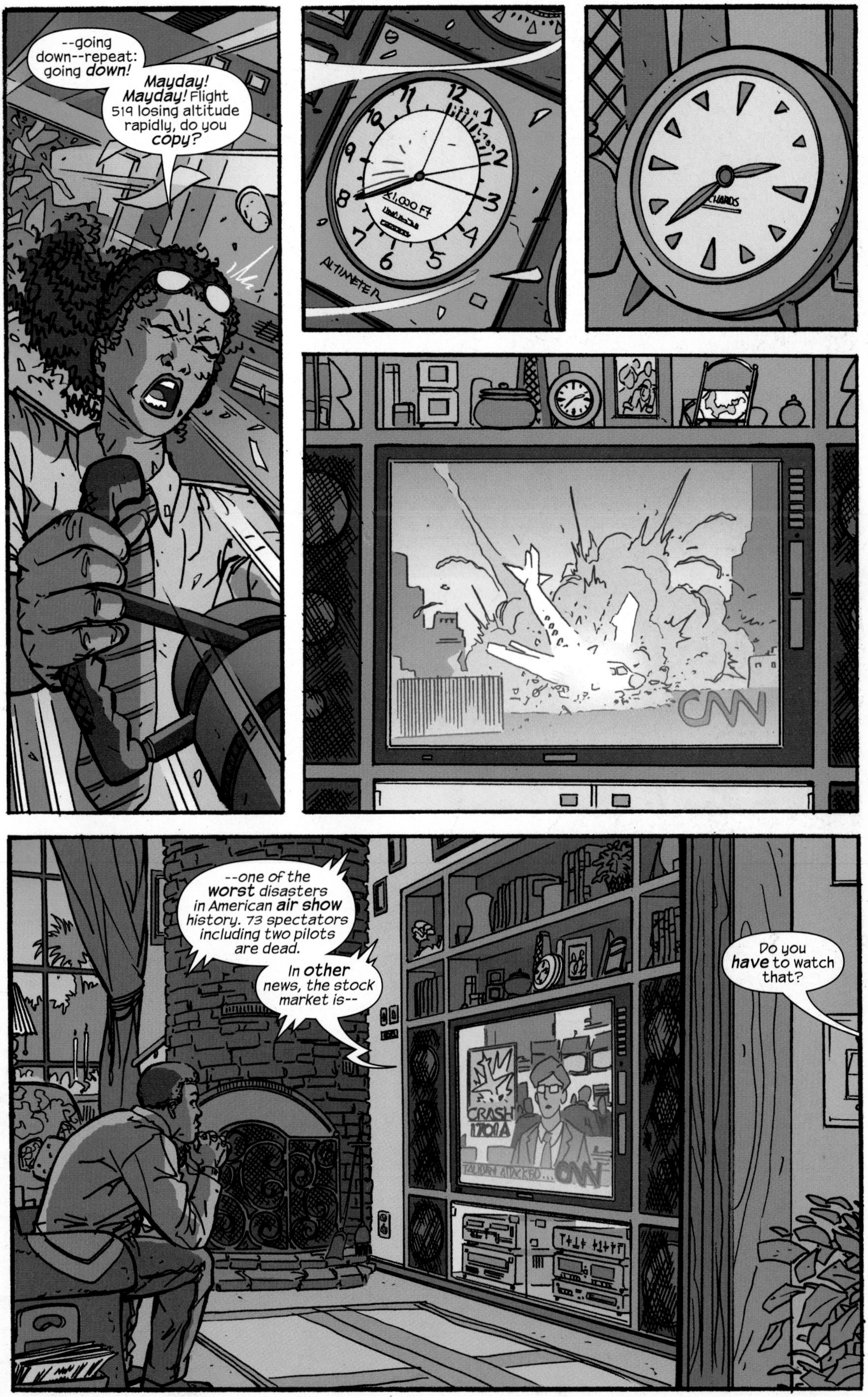

--going down--repeat: going **down!**
Mayday! Mayday! Flight 519 losing altitude rapidly, do you **copy?**
ALTIMETER
CNN
--one of the **worst** disasters in American **air show** history. 73 spectators including two pilots are dead.
In **other** news, the stock market is--
CRASH
CNN
Do you **have** to watch that?

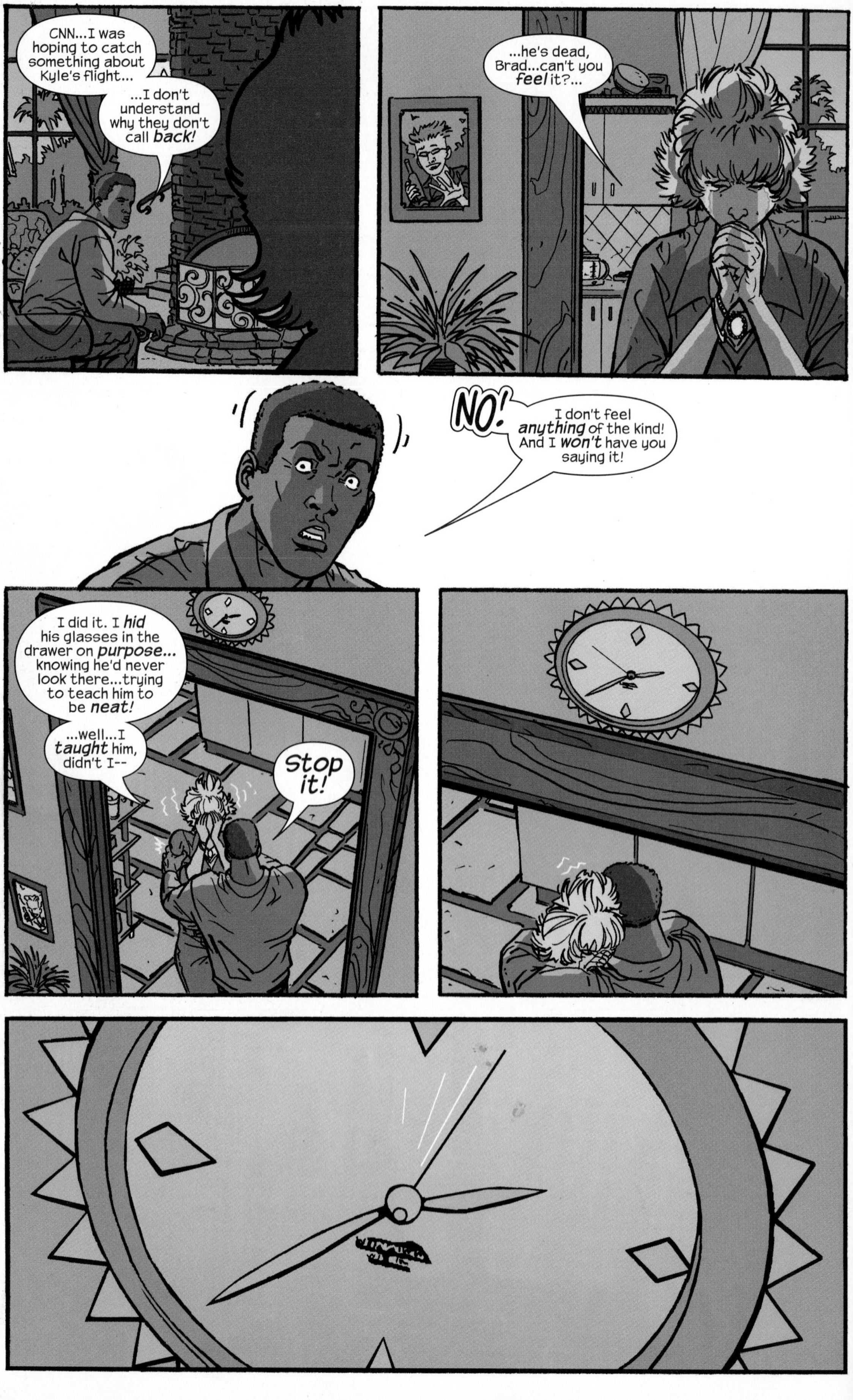
CNN...I was hoping to catch something about Kyle's flight...
...I don't understand why they don't call back!
...he's dead, Brad...can't you feel it?...
NO!
I don't feel anything of the kind! And I won't have you saying it!
I did it. I hid his glasses in the drawer on purpose... knowing he'd never look there...trying to teach him to be neat!
...well...I taught him, didn't I--
Stop it!

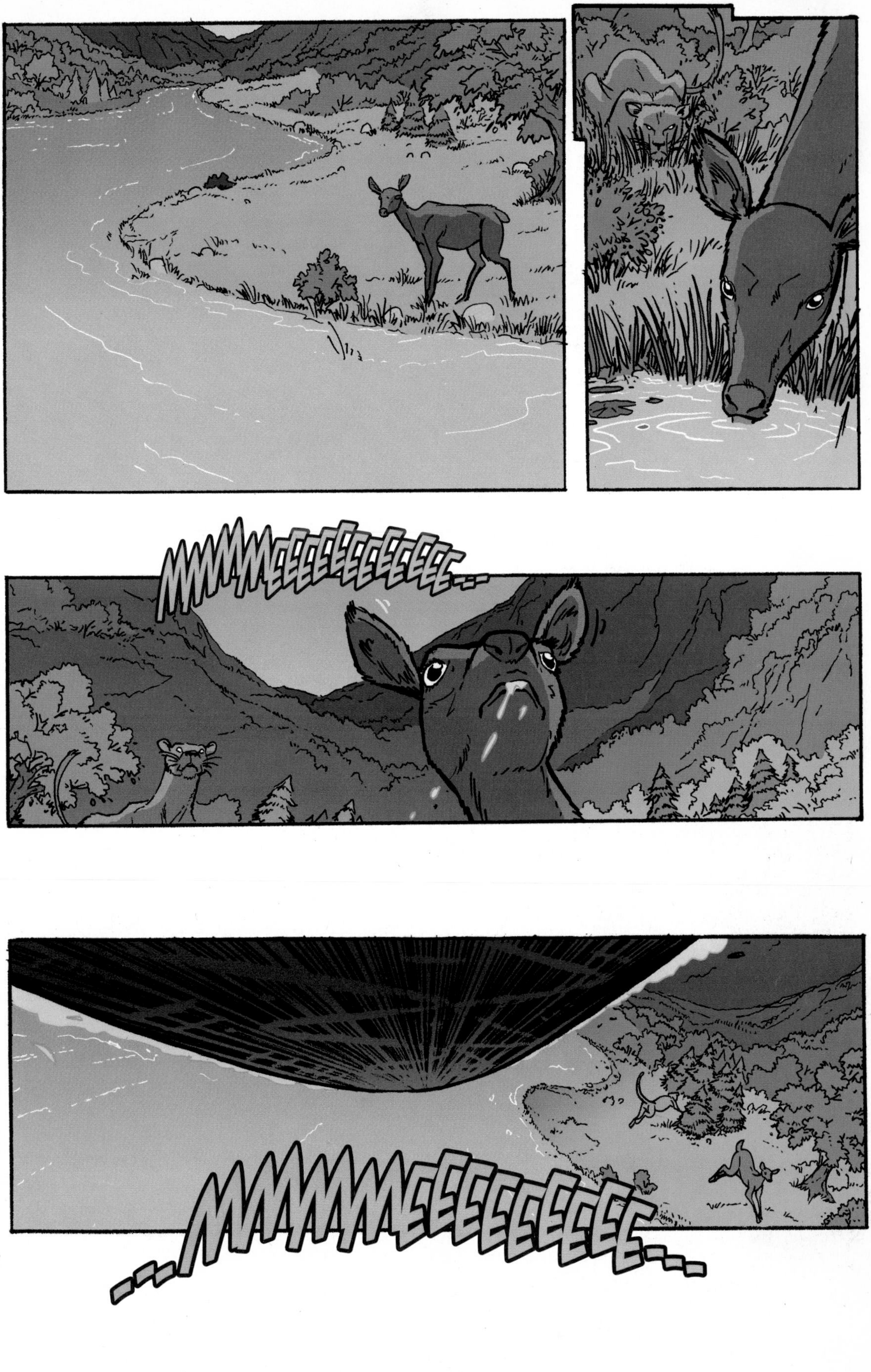
MMMMEEEEEEEEEEE---
---MMMMMEEEEEEEEE---

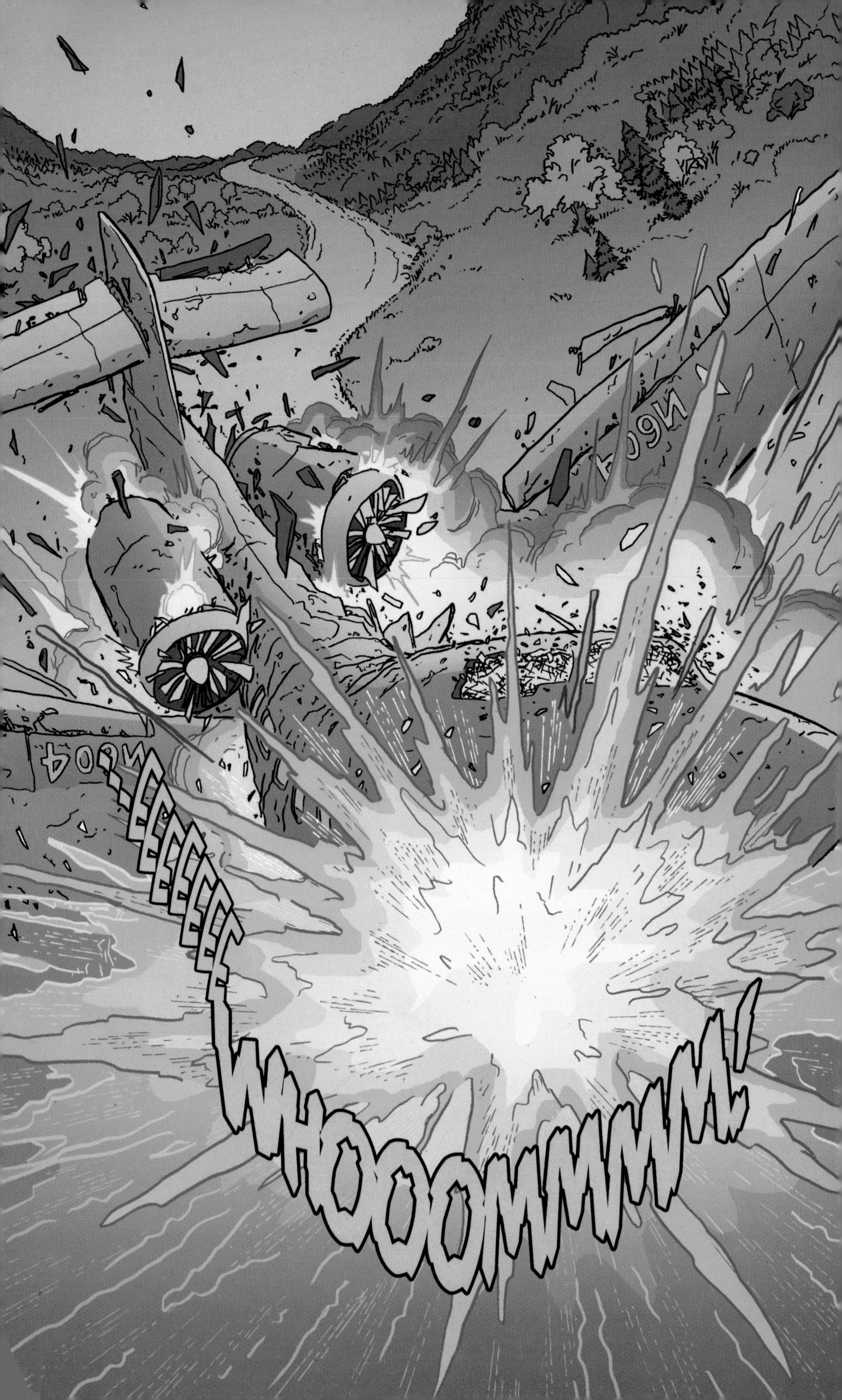
..EEEEEEEWHOOOMMMM!

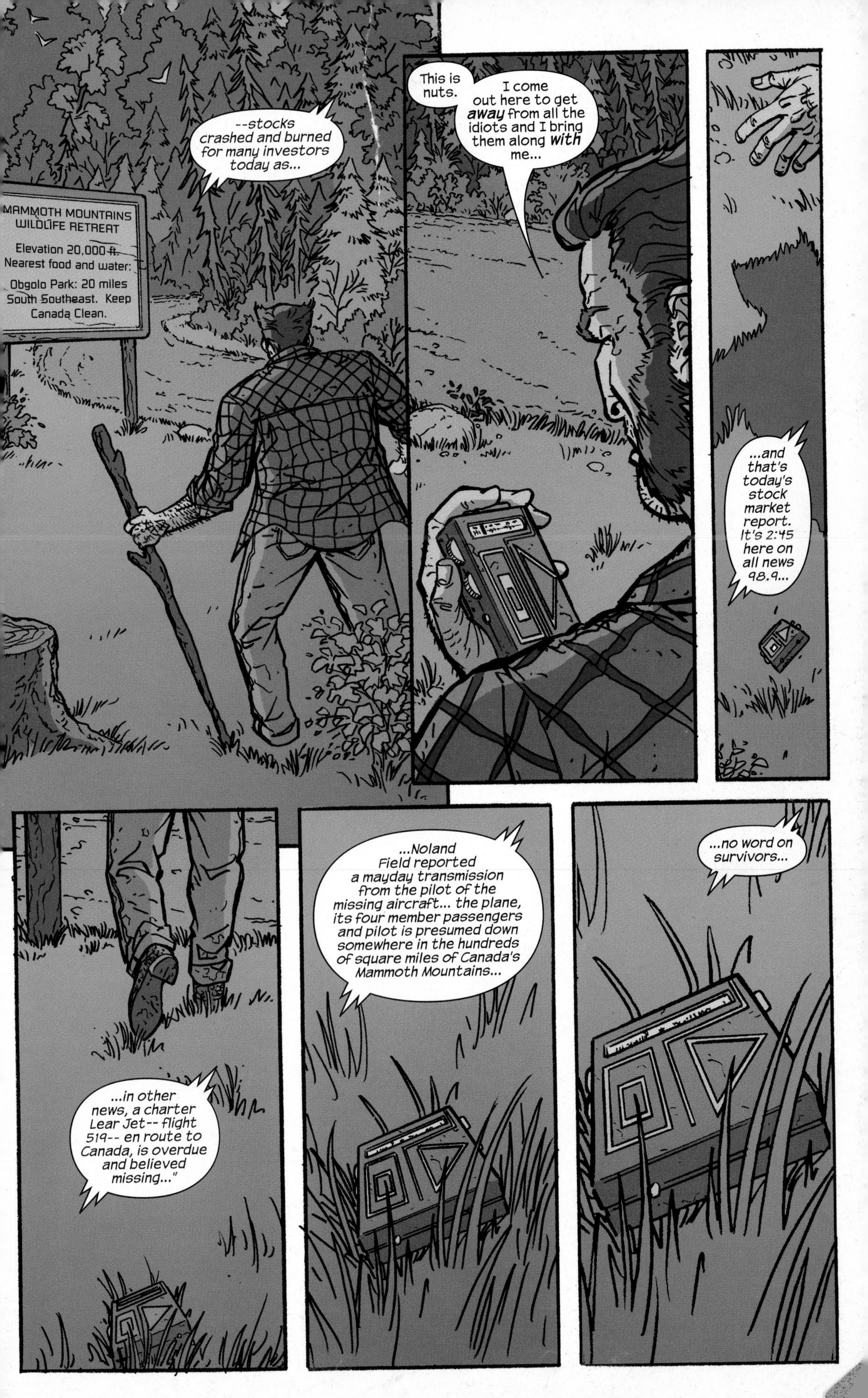
MAMMOTH MOUNTAINS WILDLIFE RETREAT
Elevation 20,000 ft. Nearest food and water:
Obgolo Park: 20 miles South Southeast. Keep Canada Clean.
--stocks crashed and burned for many investors today as...
This is nuts.
I come out here to get away from all the idiots and I bring them along with me...
...and that's today's stock market report. It's 2:45 here on all news 98.9...
...in other news, a charter Lear Jet-- flight 519-- en route to Canada, is overdue and believed missing..."
...Noland Field reported a mayday transmission from the pilot of the missing aircraft... the plane, its four member passengers and pilot is presumed down somewhere in the hundreds of square miles of Canada's Mammoth Mountains...
...no word on survivors...

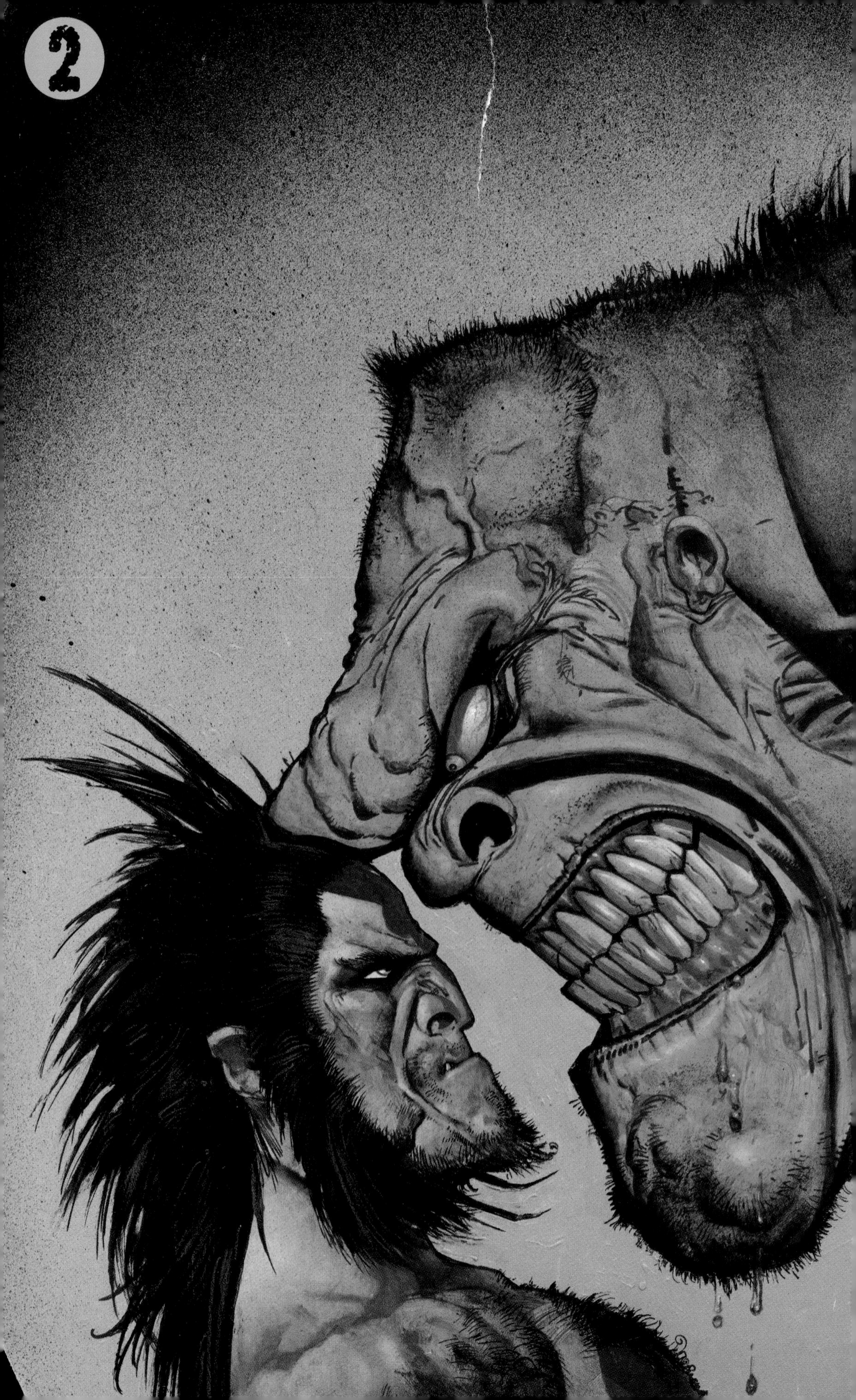
2

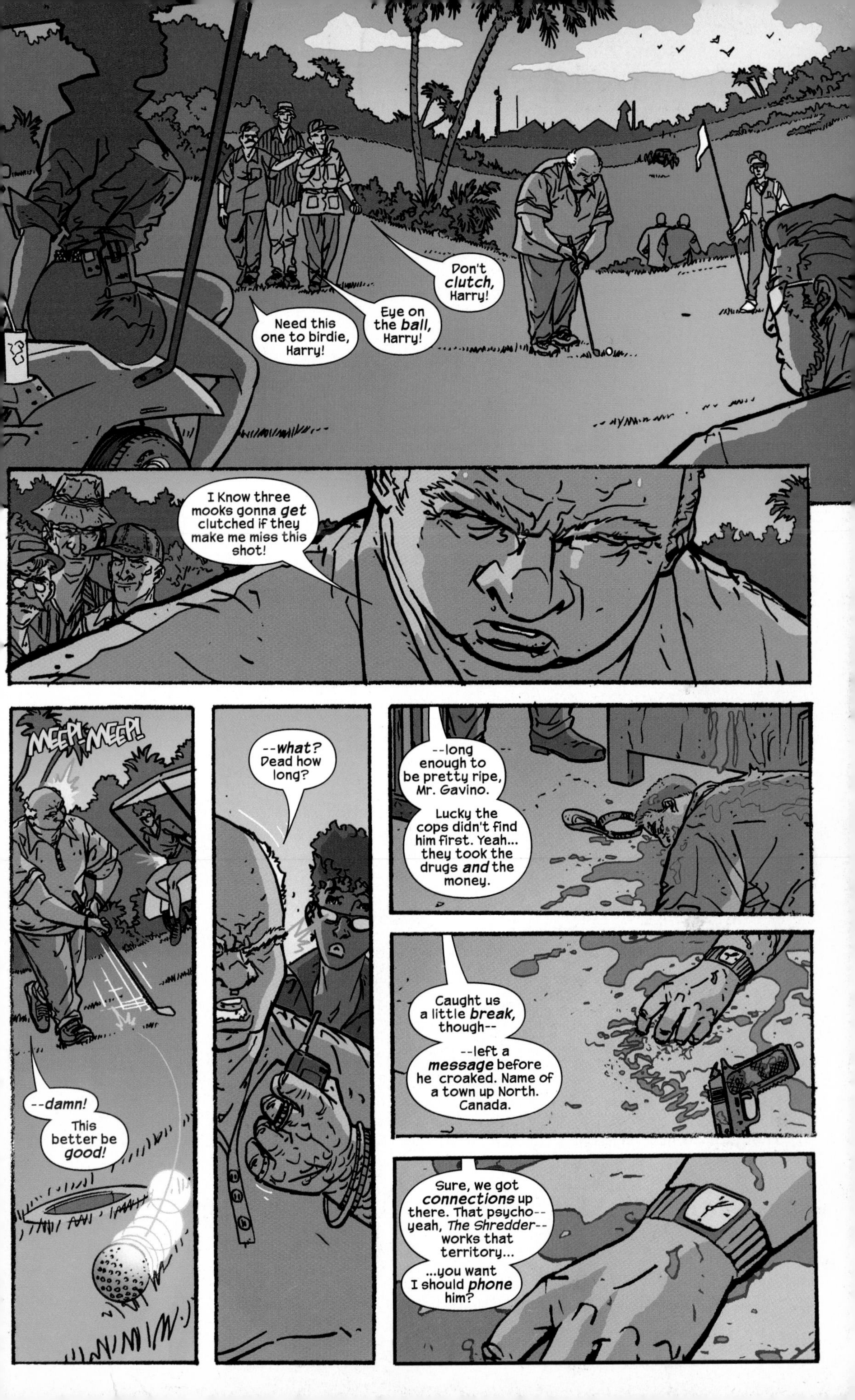
Need this one to birdie, Harry!
Eye on the *ball,* Harry!
Don't *clutch,* Harry!
I Know three mooks gonna *get* clutched if they make me miss this shot!
MEEP! MEEP!
--*damn!* This better be *good!*
--*what?* Dead how long?
--long enough to be pretty ripe, Mr. Gavino. Lucky the cops didn't find him first. Yeah... they took the drugs *and* the money.
Caught us a little *break,* though--
--left a *message* before he croaked. Name of a town up North. Canada.
Sure, we got *connections* up there. That psycho--yeah, *The Shredder*--works that territory... ...you want I should *phone* him?

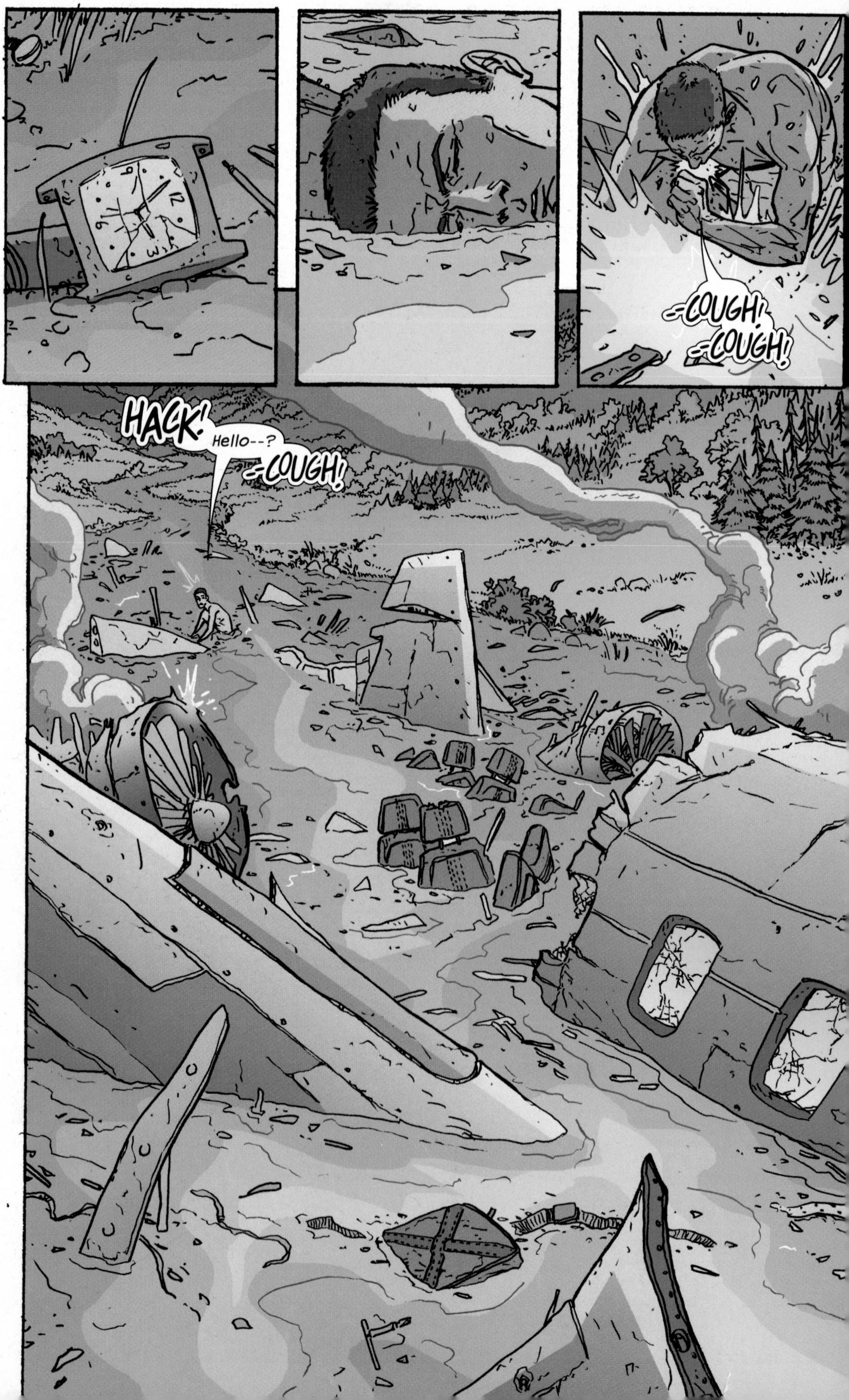
-COUGH!
-COUGH!
HACK!
Hello--?
-COUGH!

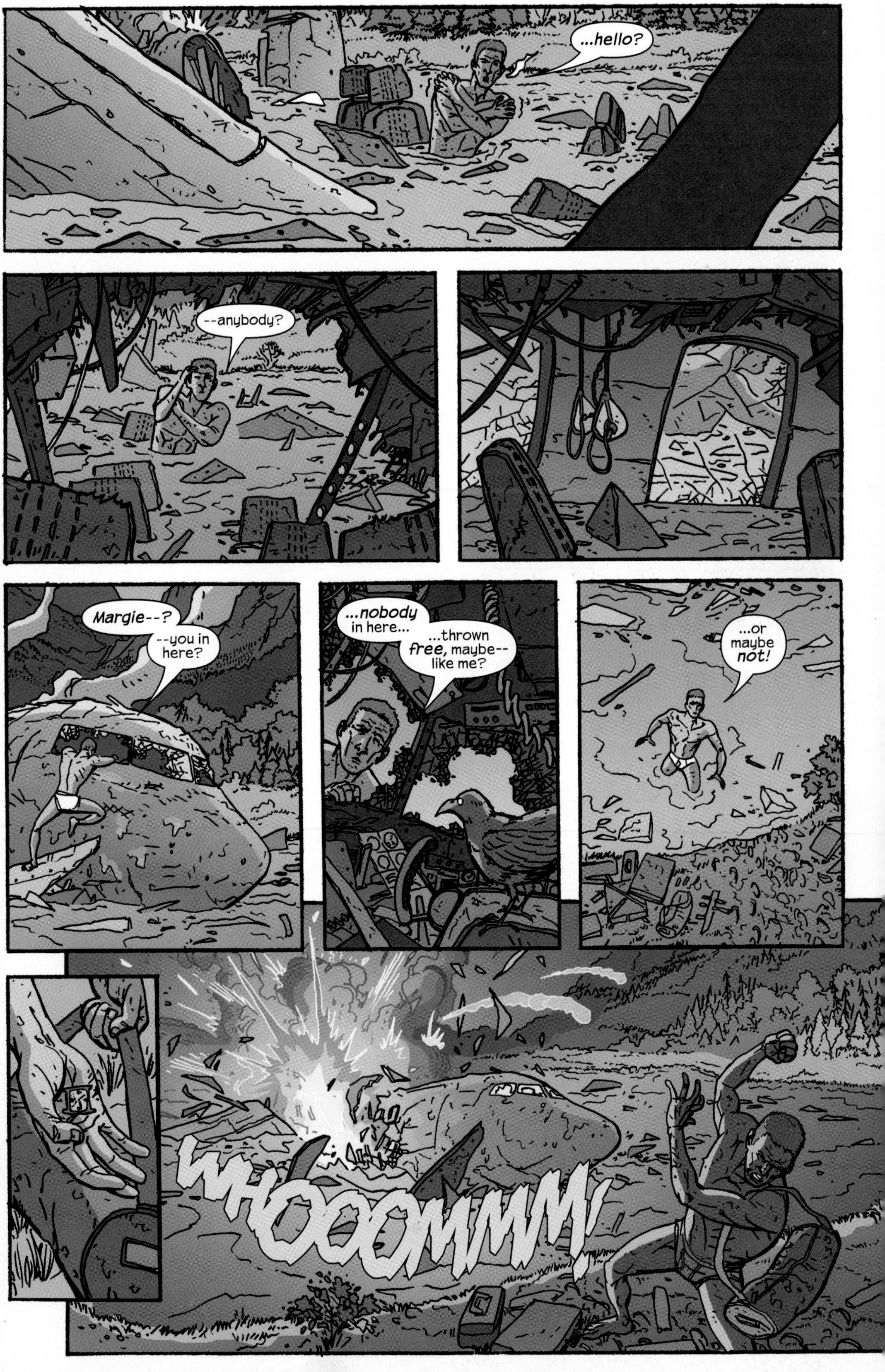
...hello?
--anybody?
Margie--?
--you in here?
...nobody in here...
...thrown free, maybe--like me?
...or maybe not!
WHOOOMMM!

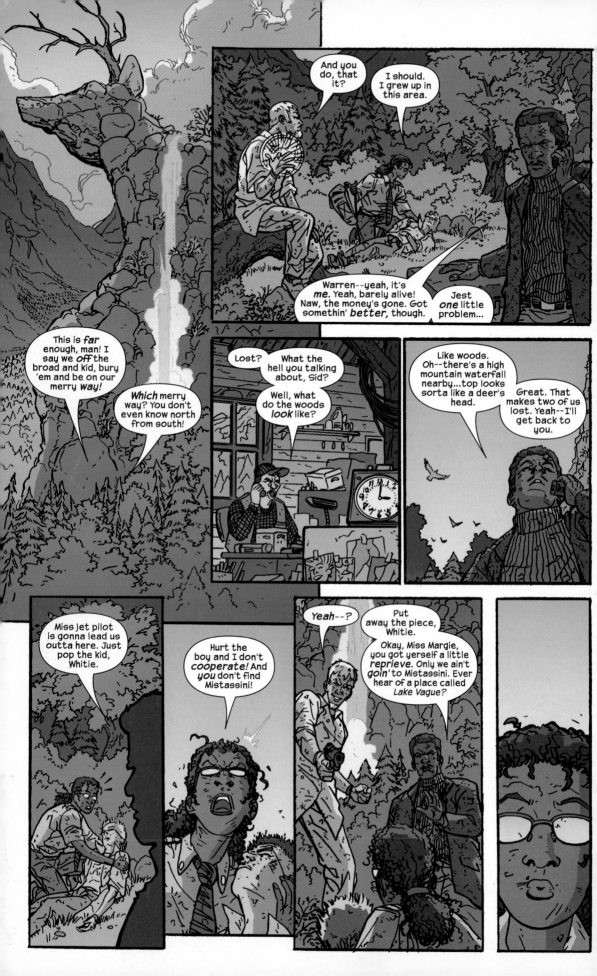

And you do, that it?

I should. I grew up in this area.

Warren--yeah, it's *me*. Yeah, barely alive! Naw, the money's gone. *Got* somethin' *better*, though.

Jest *one* little problem...

This is *far* enough, man! I say we *off* the broad and kid, bury 'em and be on our merry *way*!

Which merry way? You don't even know north from south!

Lost?

What the hell you talking about, Sid?

Well, what do the woods *look* like?

Like woods. Oh--there's a high mountain waterfall nearby...top looks sorta like a deer's head.

Great. That makes two of us lost. Yeah--I'll get back to you.

Miss jet pilot is gonna lead us outta here. Just pop the kid, Whitie.

Hurt the boy and I don't *cooperate*! And *you* don't find Mistassini!

Yeah--?

Put away the piece, Whitie. Okay, Miss Margie, you got yerself a little *reprieve*. Only we ain't *goin'* to Mistassini. Ever hear of a place called *Lake Vague*?

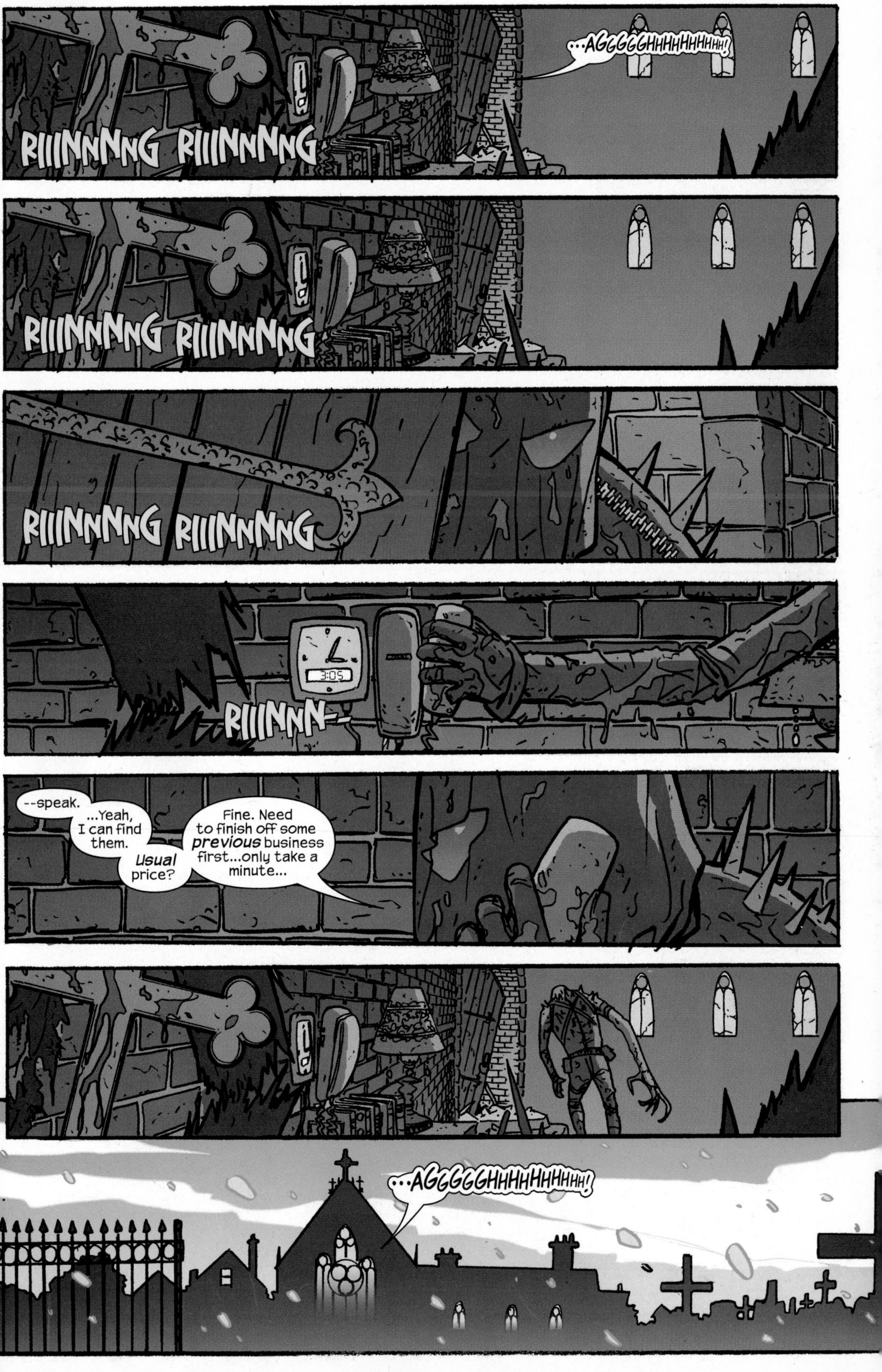
...AGGGGGHHHHHHHHHH!
RIIINNNNG RIIINNNNG
RIIINNNNG RIIINNNNG
RIIINNNNG RIIINNNNG
3:05
RIIINNN--
--speak.
...Yeah, I can find them.
Usual price?
Fine. Need to finish off some previous business first...only take a minute...
...AGGGGGHHHHHHHHHH!

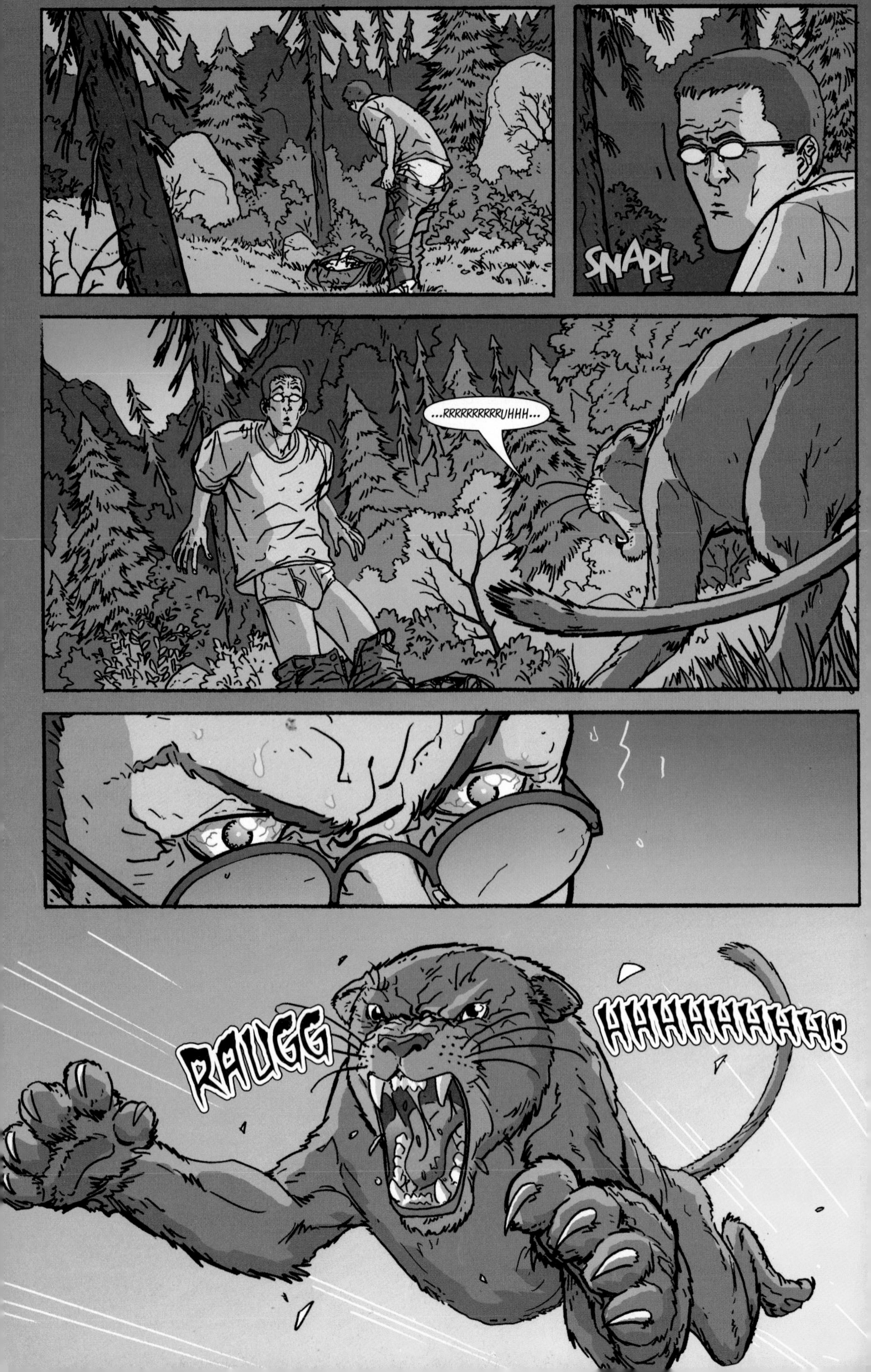
SNAP!
...RRRRRRRRRRUHHH...
RAUGG
HHHHHHHHH!

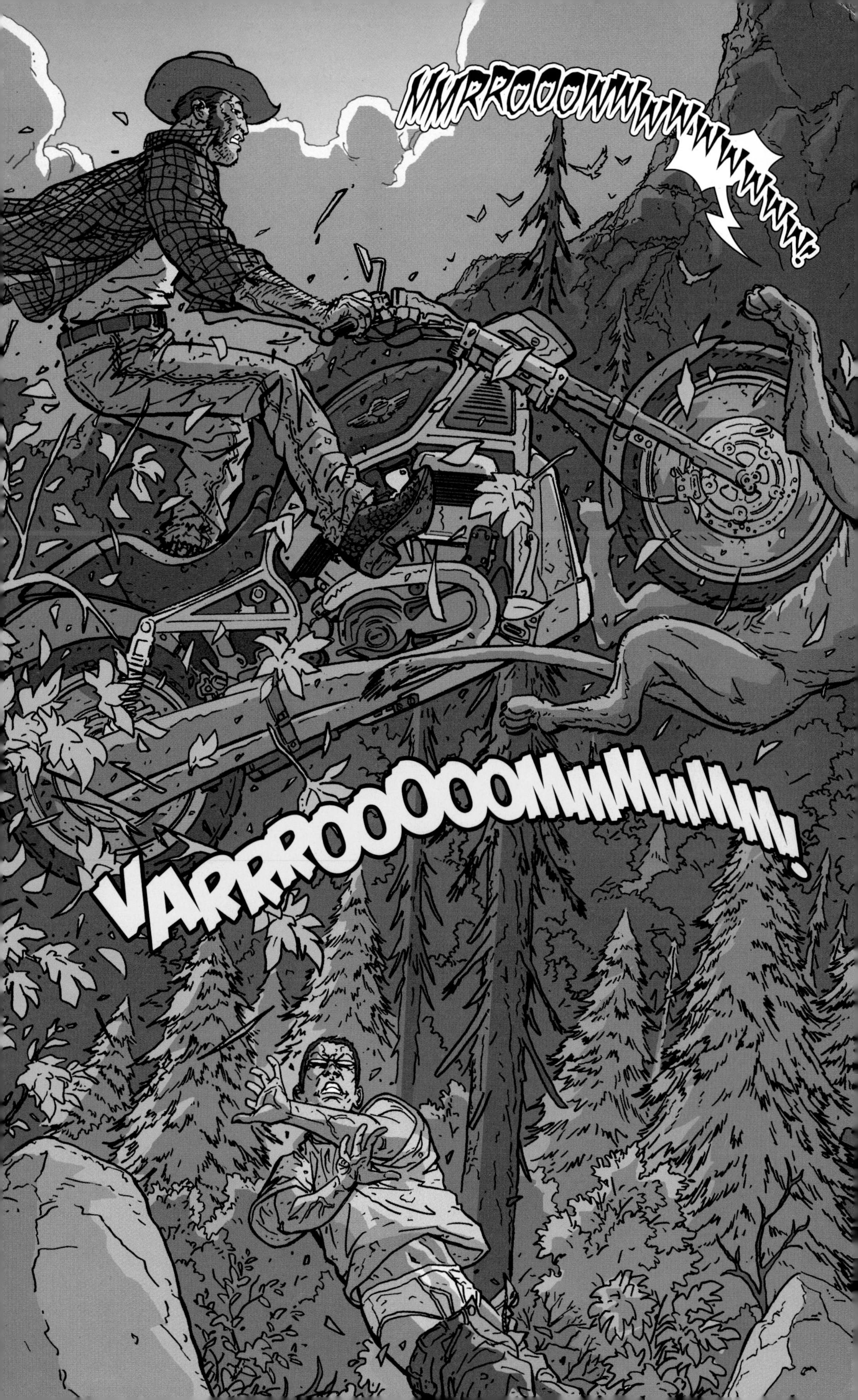
MNRROOOOWWWWWWWWWW!
VARRROOOOOOMMMMMMM!

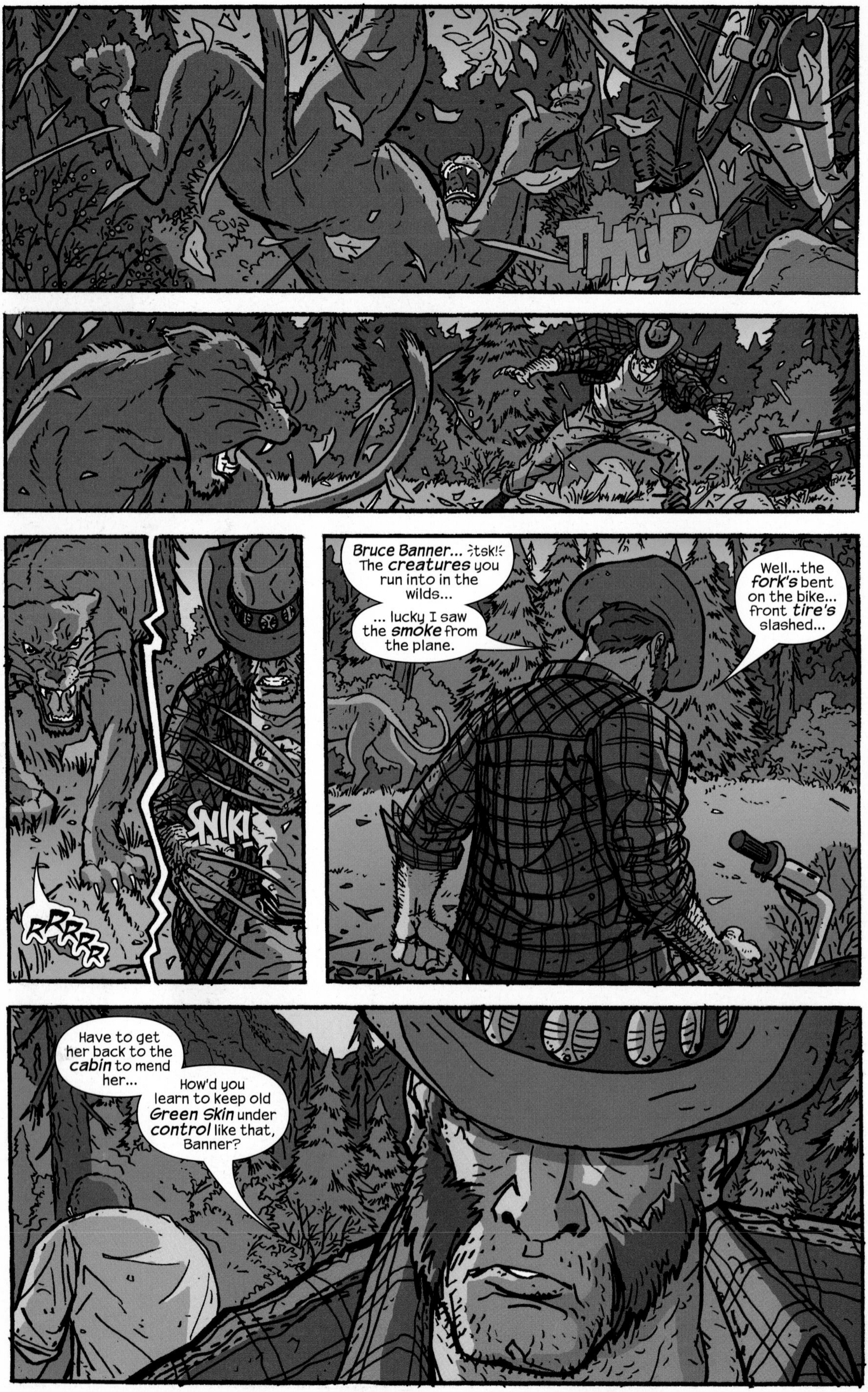
THUD!
SNIKT!
RRRRR
Bruce Banner... -tsk!- The creatures you run into in the wilds...
... lucky I saw the smoke from the plane.
Well...the fork's bent on the bike... front tire's slashed...
Have to get her back to the cabin to mend her...
How'd you learn to keep old Green Skin under control like that, Banner?

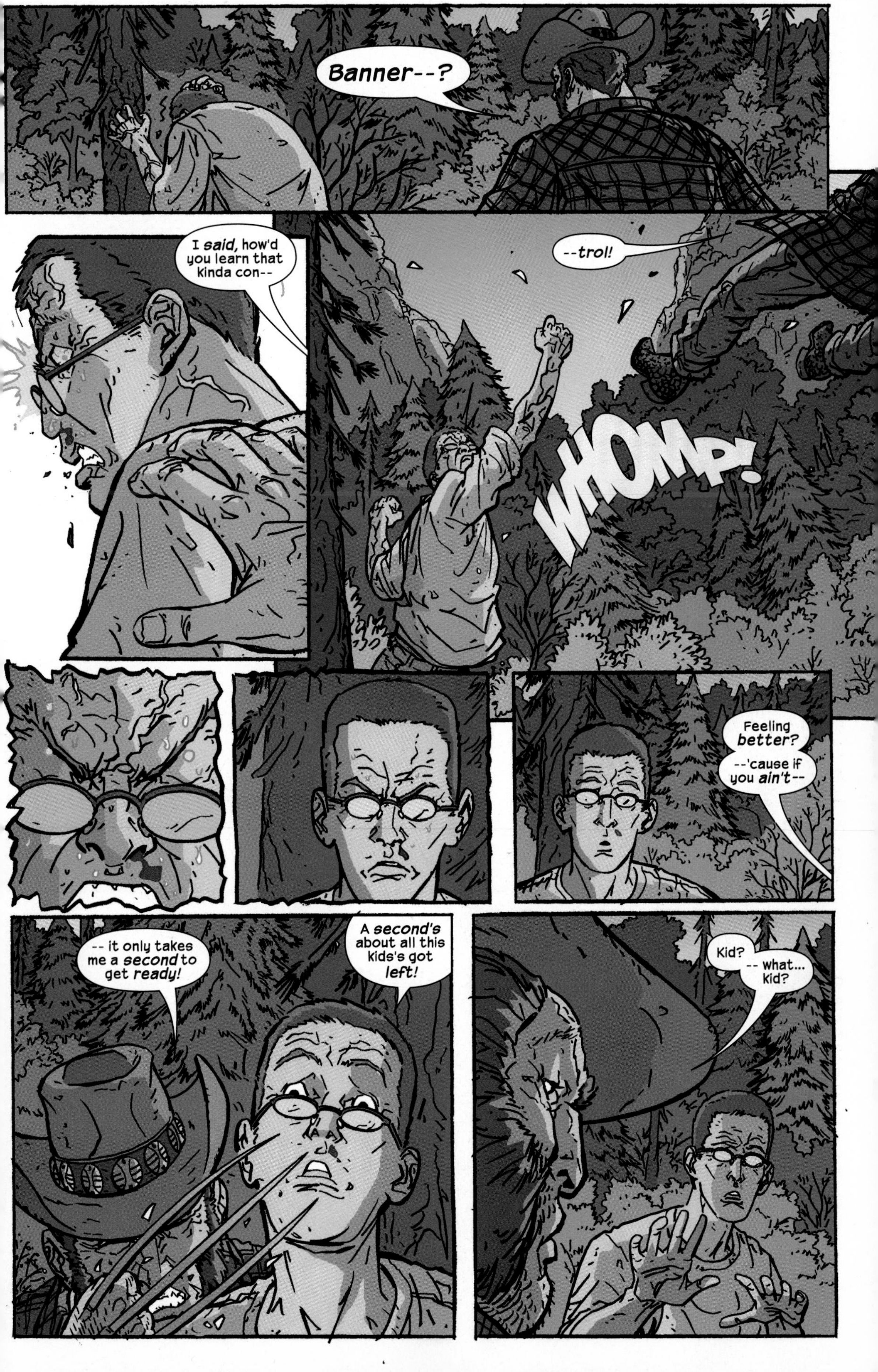
Banner--?
I said, how'd you learn that kinda con--
--trol!
WHOMP!
Feeling better?
--'cause if you ain't--
-- it only takes me a second to get ready!
A second's about all this kids's got left!
Kid?
-- what... kid?

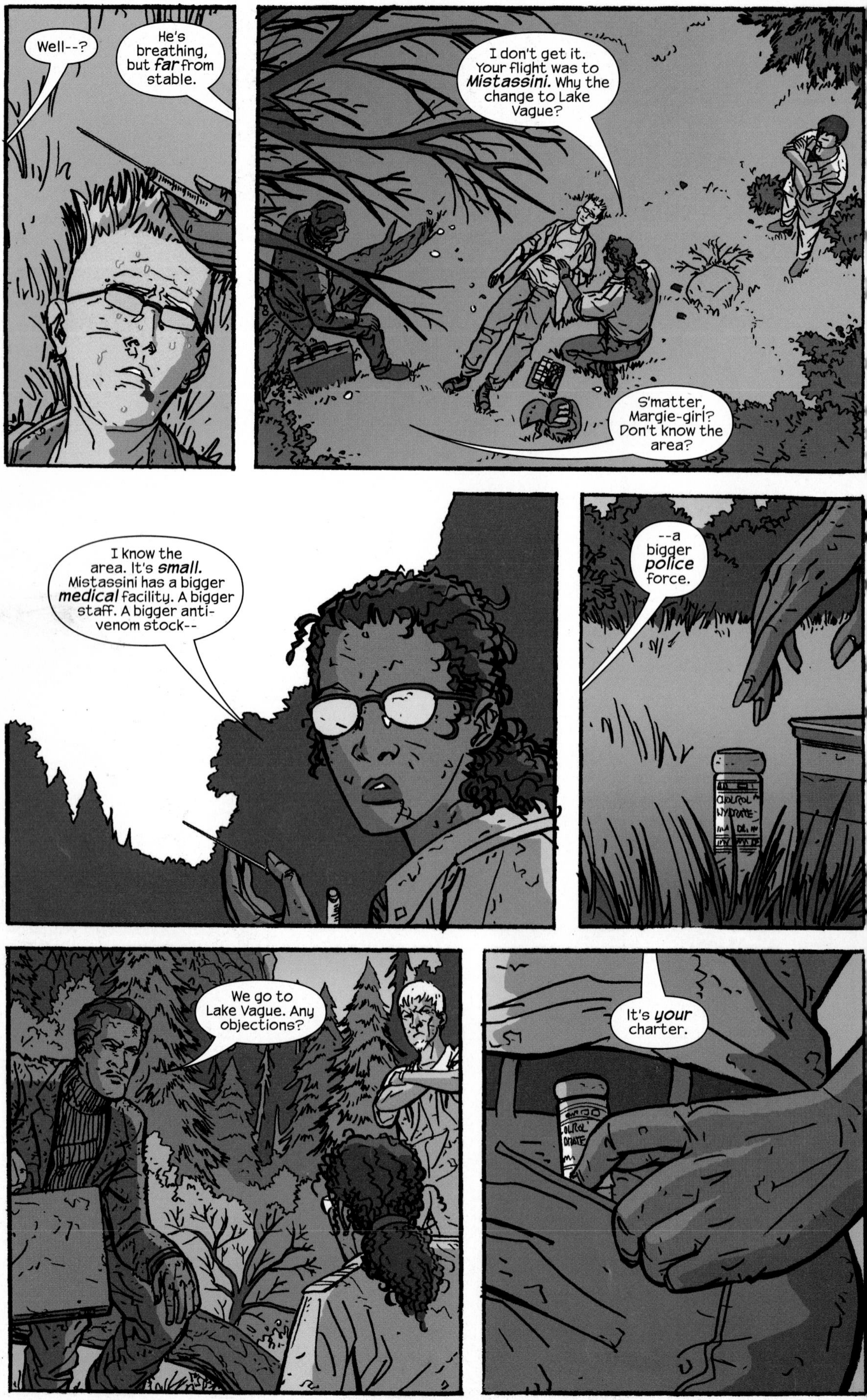
Well--?
He's breathing, but far from stable.
I don't get it. Your flight was to Mistassini. Why the change to Lake Vague?
S'matter, Margie-girl? Don't know the area?
I know the area. It's small. Mistassini has a bigger medical facility. A bigger staff. A bigger anti-venom stock--
--a bigger police force.
We go to Lake Vague. Any objections?
It's your charter.

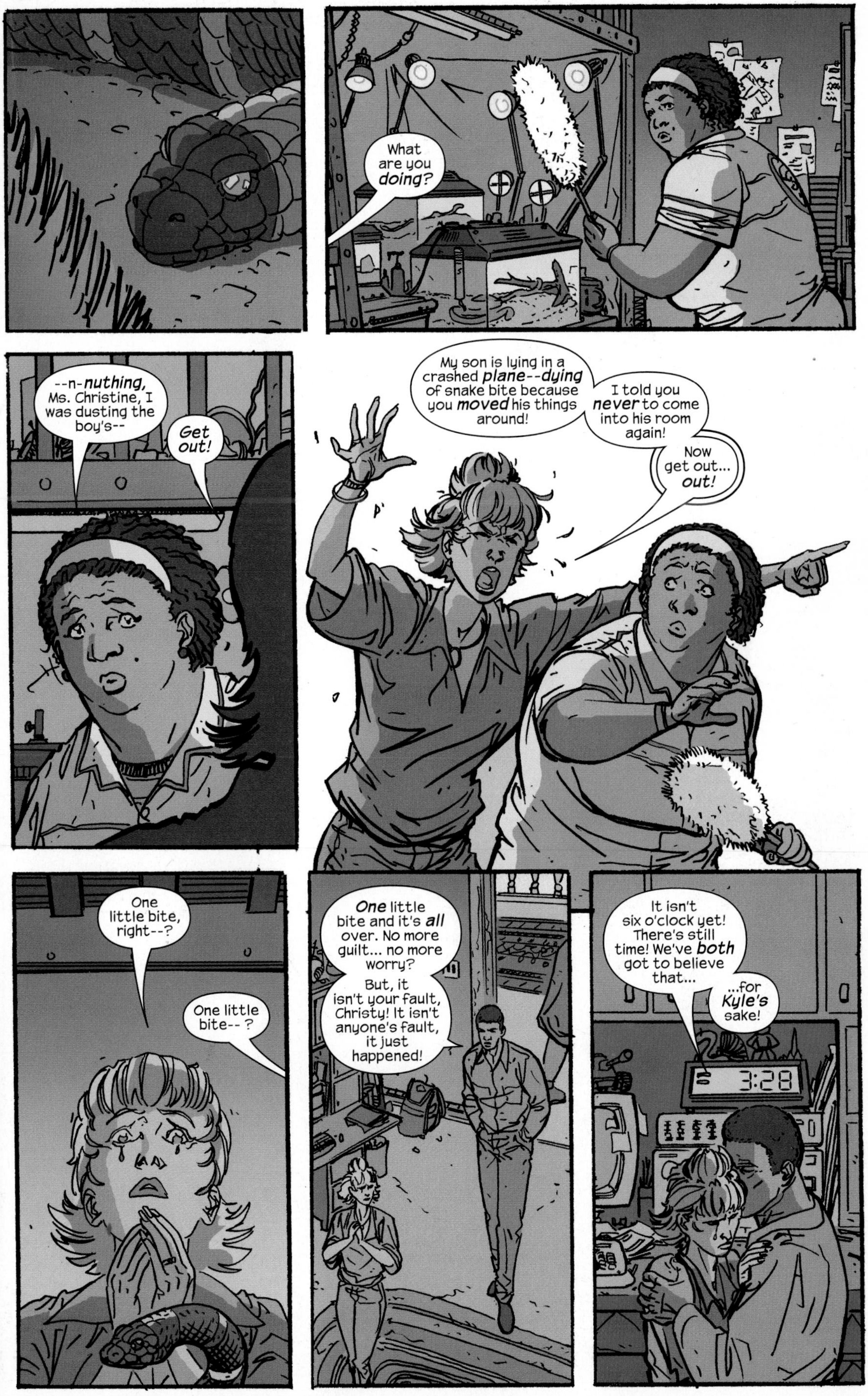

What are you *doing?*
--n-*nuthing,* Ms. Christine, I was dusting the boy's--
Get out!
My son is lying in a crashed *plane--dying* of snake bite because you *moved* his things around!
I told you *never* to come into his room again!
Now get out... *out!*
One little bite, right--?
One little bite-- ?
One little bite and it's *all* over. No more guilt... no more worry?
But, it isn't your fault, Christy! It isn't anyone's fault, it just happened!
It isn't six o'clock yet! There's still time! We've *both* got to believe that...
...for *Kyle's* sake!
3:28

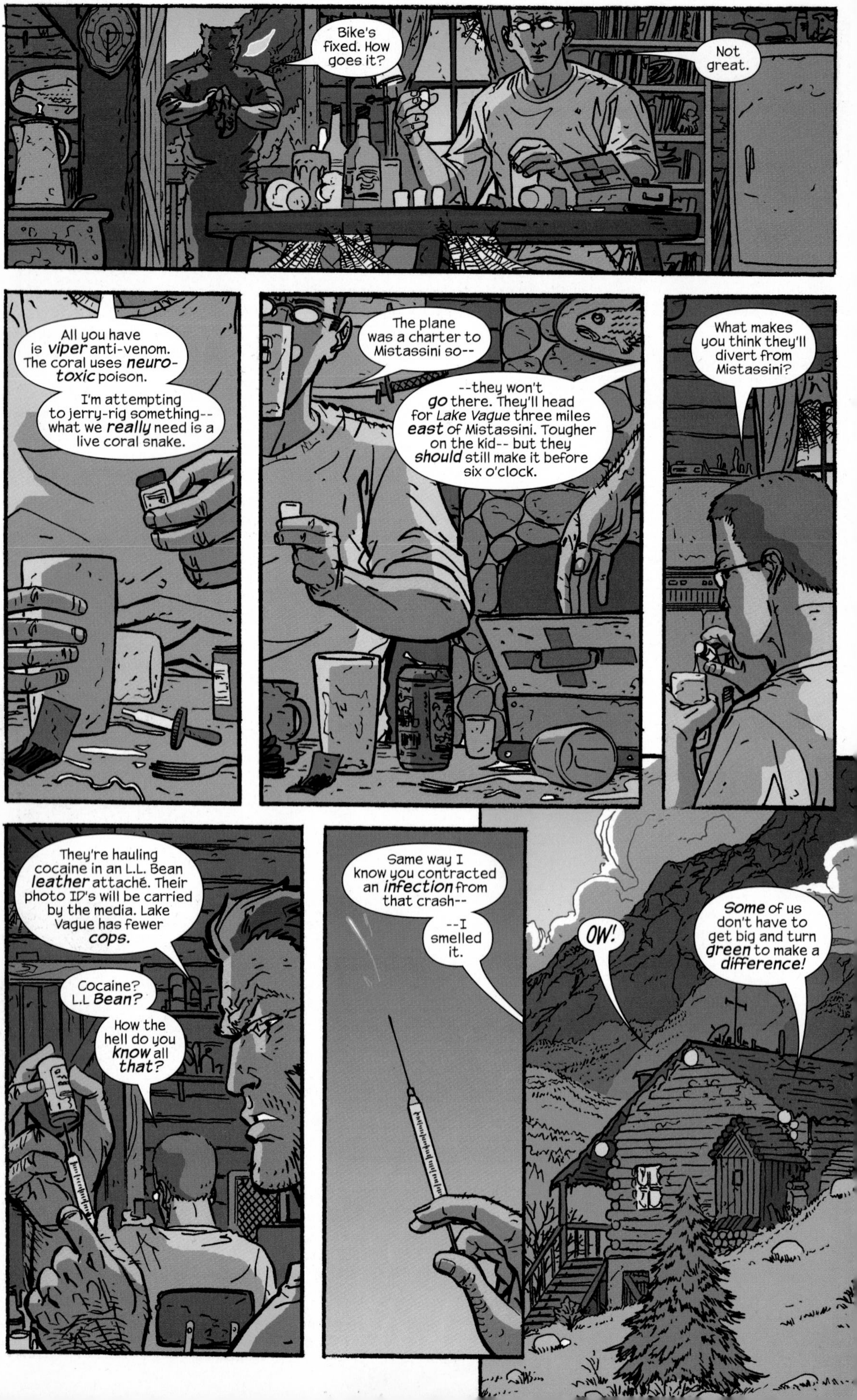
Bike's fixed. How goes it?
Not great.
All you have is viper anti-venom. The coral uses neuro-toxic poison.
I'm attempting to jerry-rig something-- what we really need is a live coral snake.
The plane was a charter to Mistassini so--
--they won't go there. They'll head for Lake Vague three miles east of Mistassini. Tougher on the kid-- but they should still make it before six o'clock.
What makes you think they'll divert from Mistassini?
They're hauling cocaine in an L.L. Bean leather attaché. Their photo ID's will be carried by the media. Lake Vague has fewer cops.
Cocaine? L.L Bean?
How the hell do you know all that?
Same way I know you contracted an infection from that crash--
--I smelled it.
OW!
Some of us don't have to get big and turn green to make a difference!

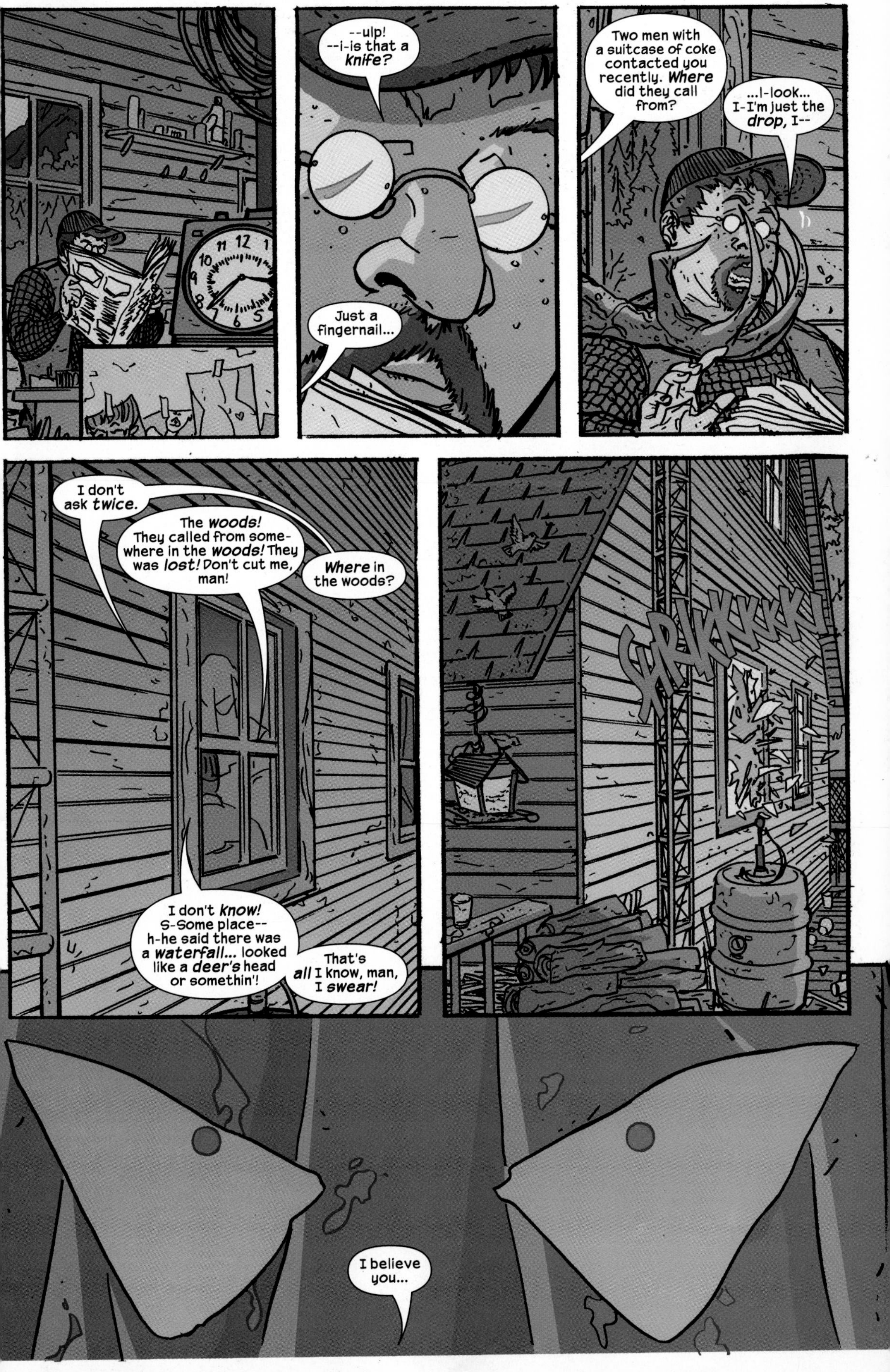
--ulp!
--i-is that a knife?
Just a fingernail...
Two men with a suitcase of coke contacted you recently. Where did they call from?
...I-look... I-I'm just the drop, I--
I don't ask twice.
The woods! They called from somewhere in the woods! They was lost! Don't cut me, man!
Where in the woods?
I don't know! S-Some place-- h-he said there was a waterfall... looked like a deer's head or somethin'!
That's all I know, man, I swear!
I believe you...

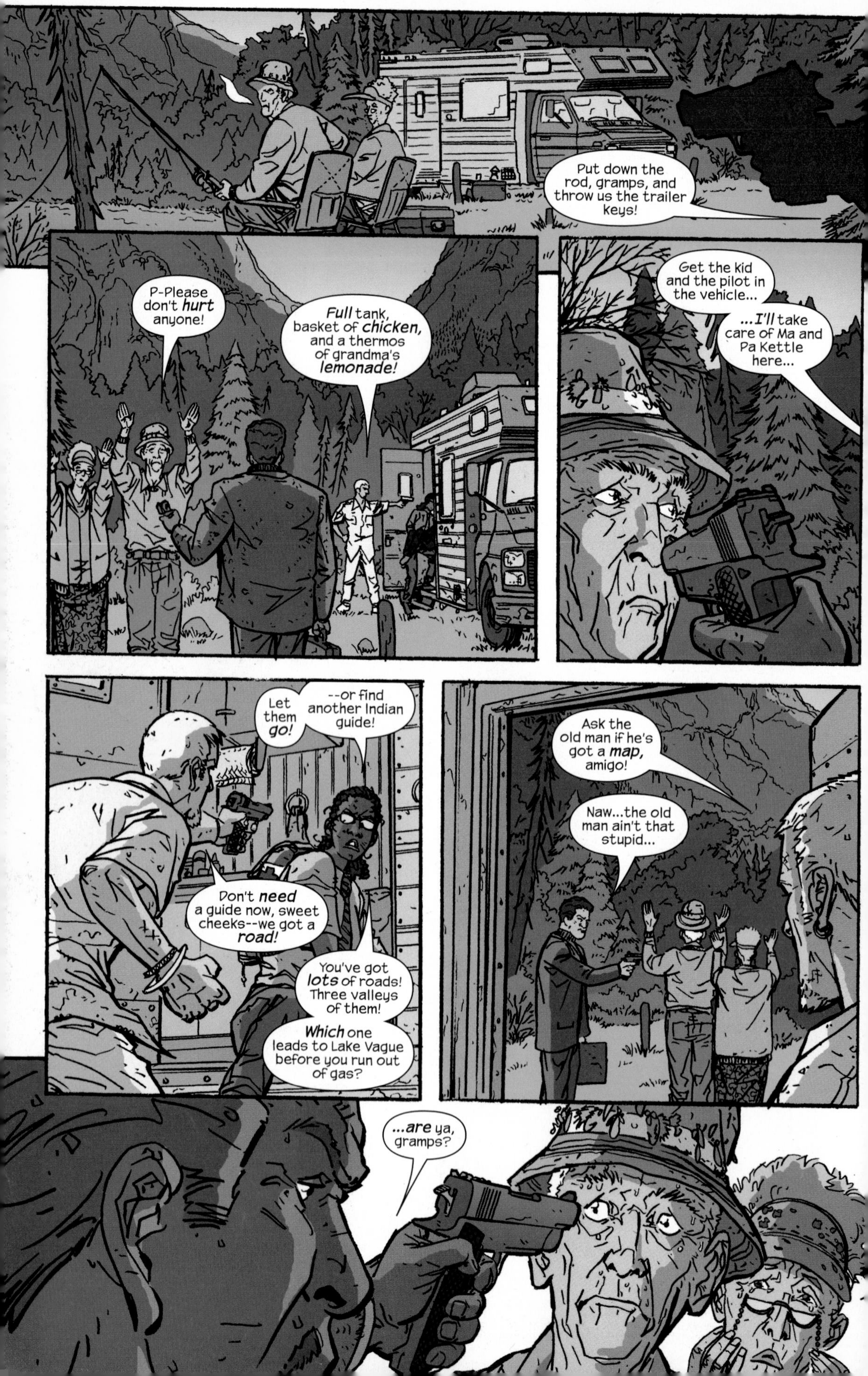
Put down the rod, gramps, and throw us the trailer keys!
P-Please don't hurt anyone!
Full tank, basket of chicken, and a thermos of grandma's lemonade!
Get the kid and the pilot in the vehicle...
...I'll take care of Ma and Pa Kettle here...
Let them go!
--or find another Indian guide!
Don't need a guide now, sweet cheeks--we got a road!
You've got lots of roads! Three valleys of them!
Which one leads to Lake Vague before you run out of gas?
Ask the old man if he's got a map, amigo!
Naw...the old man ain't that stupid...
...are ya, gramps?

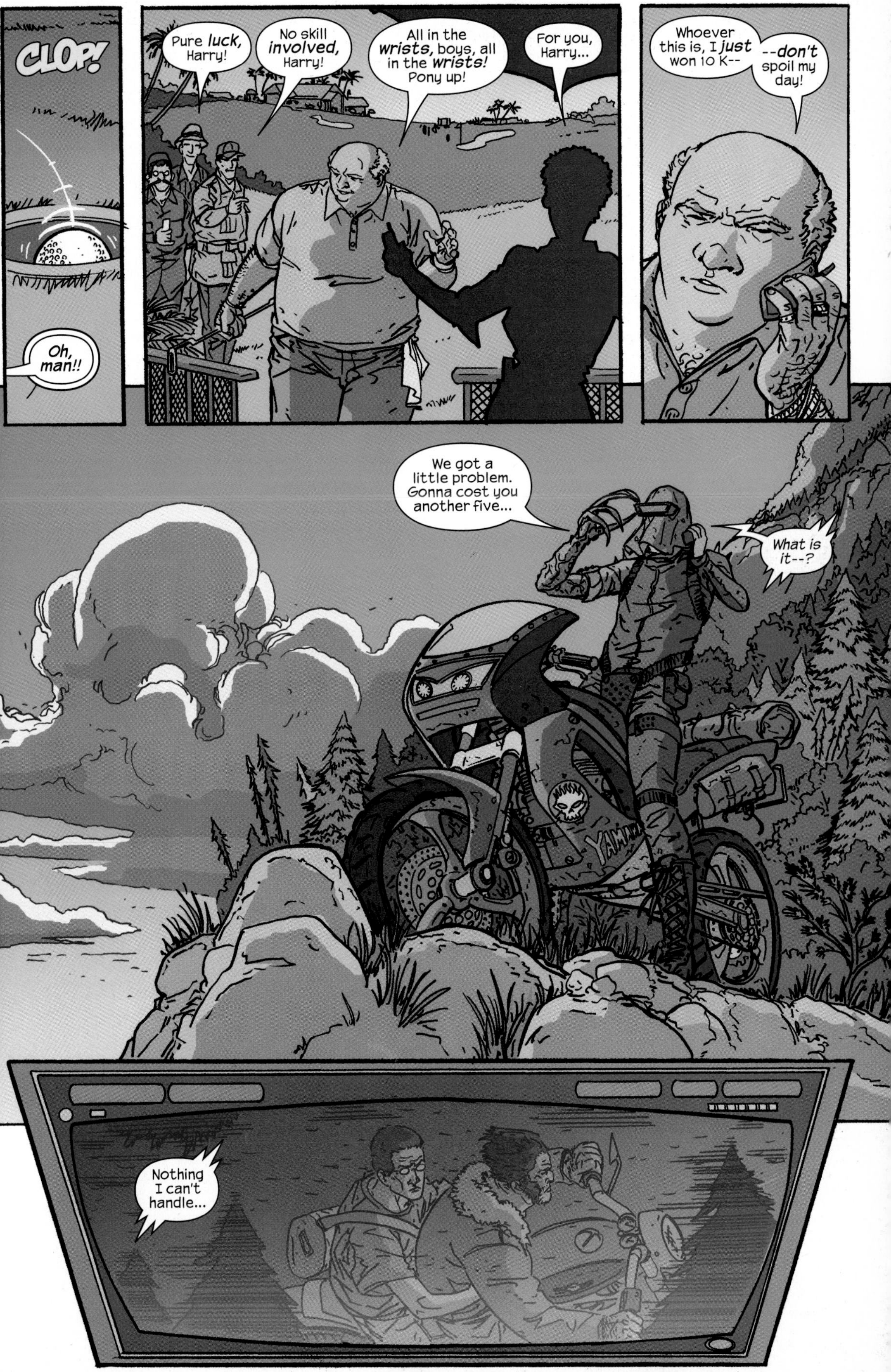
CLOP!
Oh, man!!
Pure luck, Harry!
No skill involved, Harry!
All in the wrists, boys, all in the wrists! Pony up!
For you, Harry...
Whoever this is, I just won 10 K--
--don't spoil my day!
We got a little problem. Gonna cost you another five...
What is it--?
Nothing I can't handle...

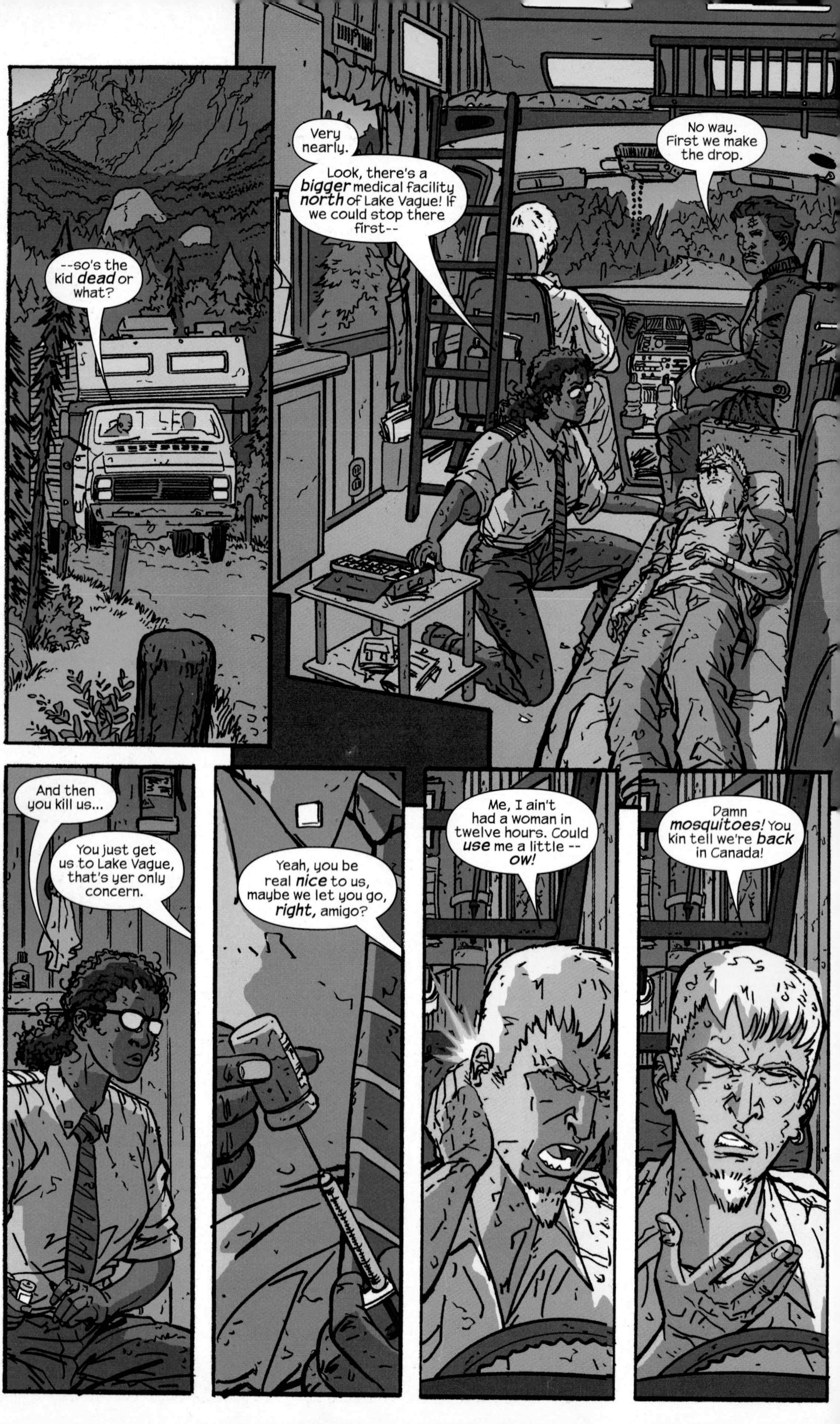
--so's the kid dead or what?
Very nearly.
Look, there's a bigger medical facility north of Lake Vague! If we could stop there first--
No way. First we make the drop.
And then you kill us...
You just get us to Lake Vague, that's yer only concern.
Yeah, you be real nice to us, maybe we let you go, right, amigo?
Me, I ain't had a woman in twelve hours. Could use me a little -- ow!
Damn mosquitoes! You kin tell we're back in Canada!

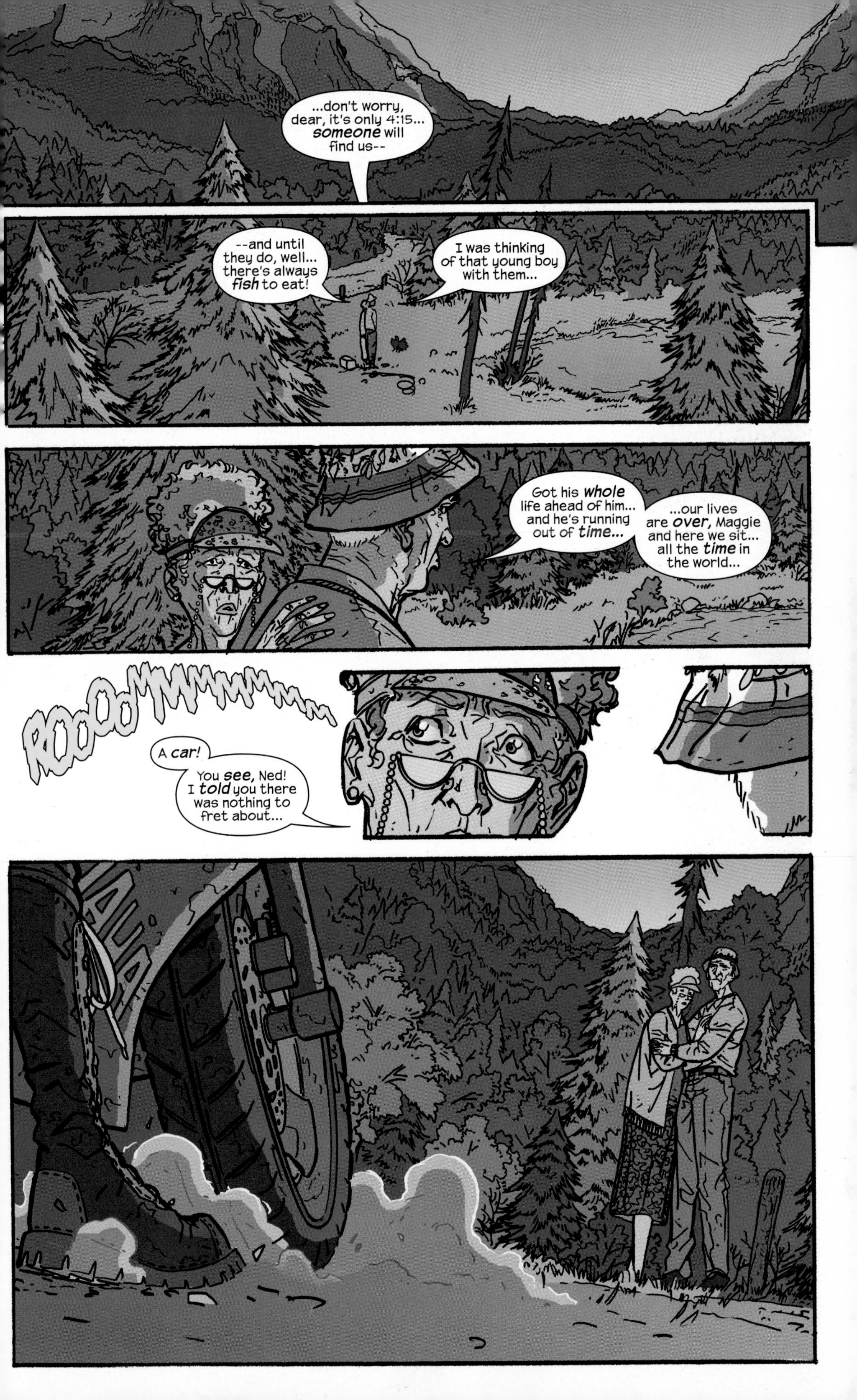
...don't worry, dear, it's only 4:15... *someone* will find us--
--and until they do, well... there's always *fish* to eat!
I was thinking of that young boy with them...
Got his *whole* life ahead of him... and he's running out of *time*...
...our lives are *over,* Maggie and here we sit... all the *time* in the world...
ROOOOMMMMMMM
A *car!*
You *see,* Ned! I *told* you there was nothing to fret about...

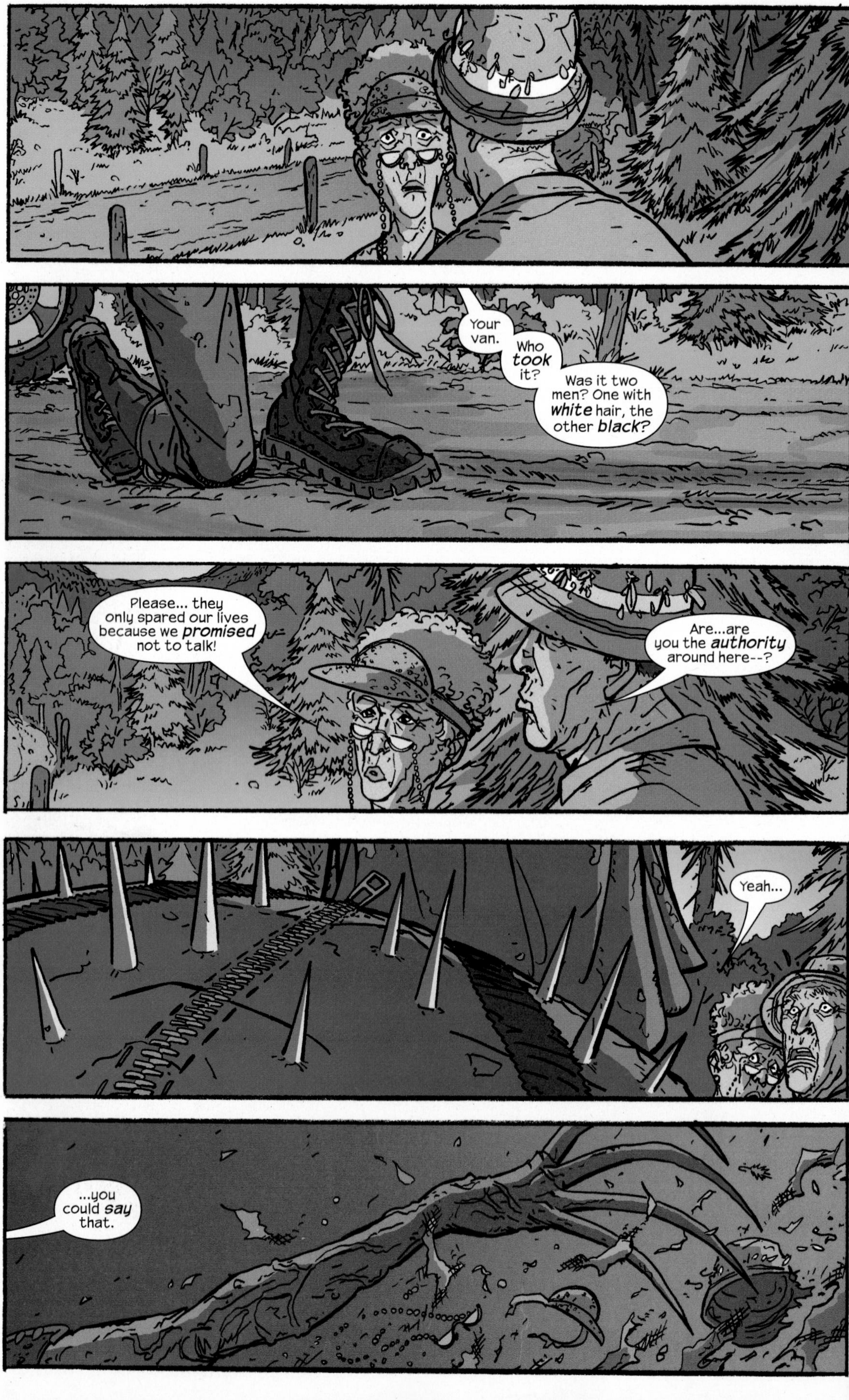

Your van.
Who took it?
Was it two men? One with white hair, the other black?
Please... they only spared our lives because we promised not to talk!
Are...are you the authority around here--?
Yeah...
...you could say that.

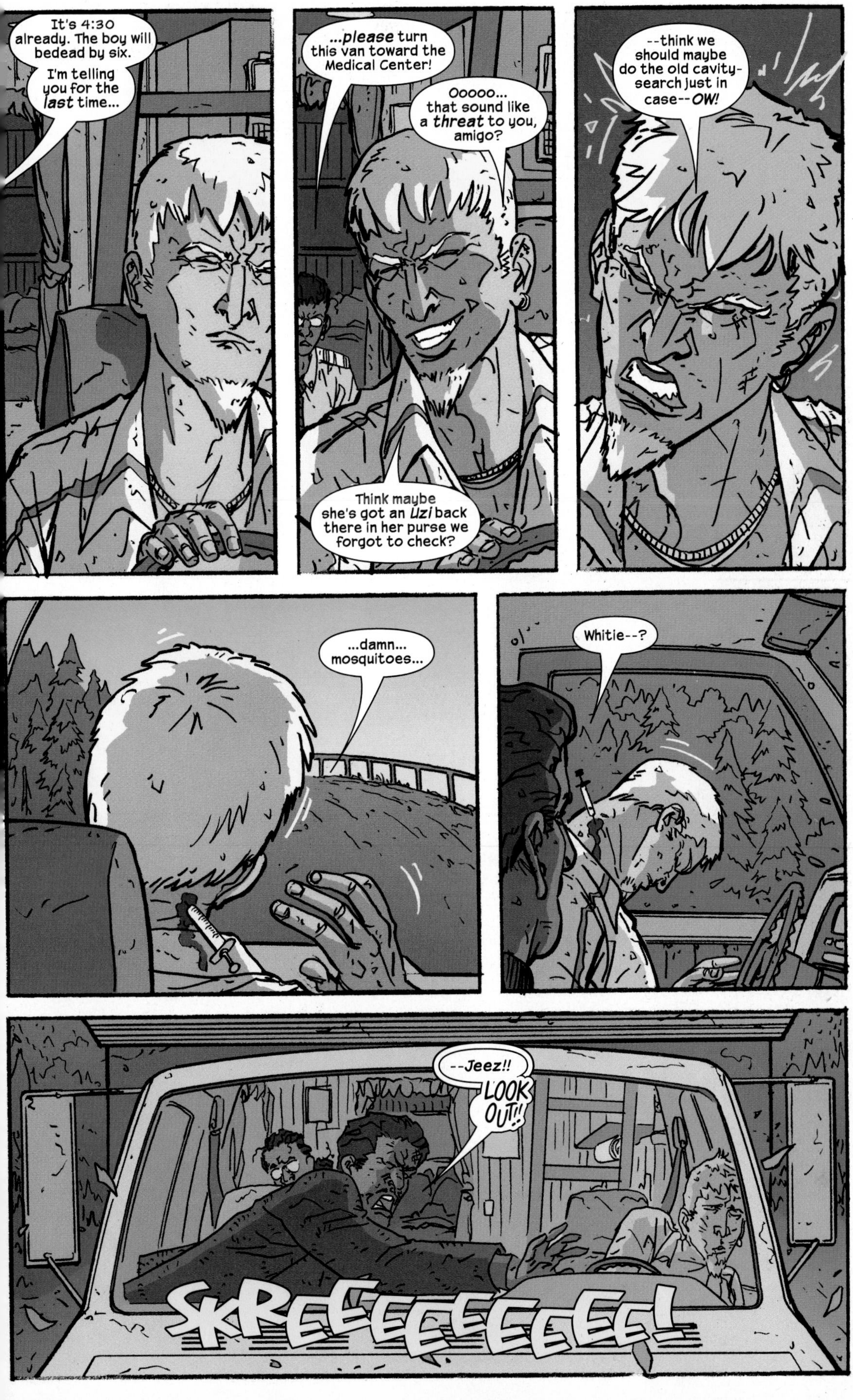
It's 4:30 already. The boy will bedead by six.
I'm telling you for the last time...
...please turn this van toward the Medical Center!
Ooooo... that sound like a threat to you, amigo?
Think maybe she's got an Uzi back there in her purse we forgot to check?
--think we should maybe do the old cavity-search just in case--OW!
...damn... mosquitoes...
Whitie--?
--Jeez!!
LOOK OUT!!
SKREEEEEEEEEEE!

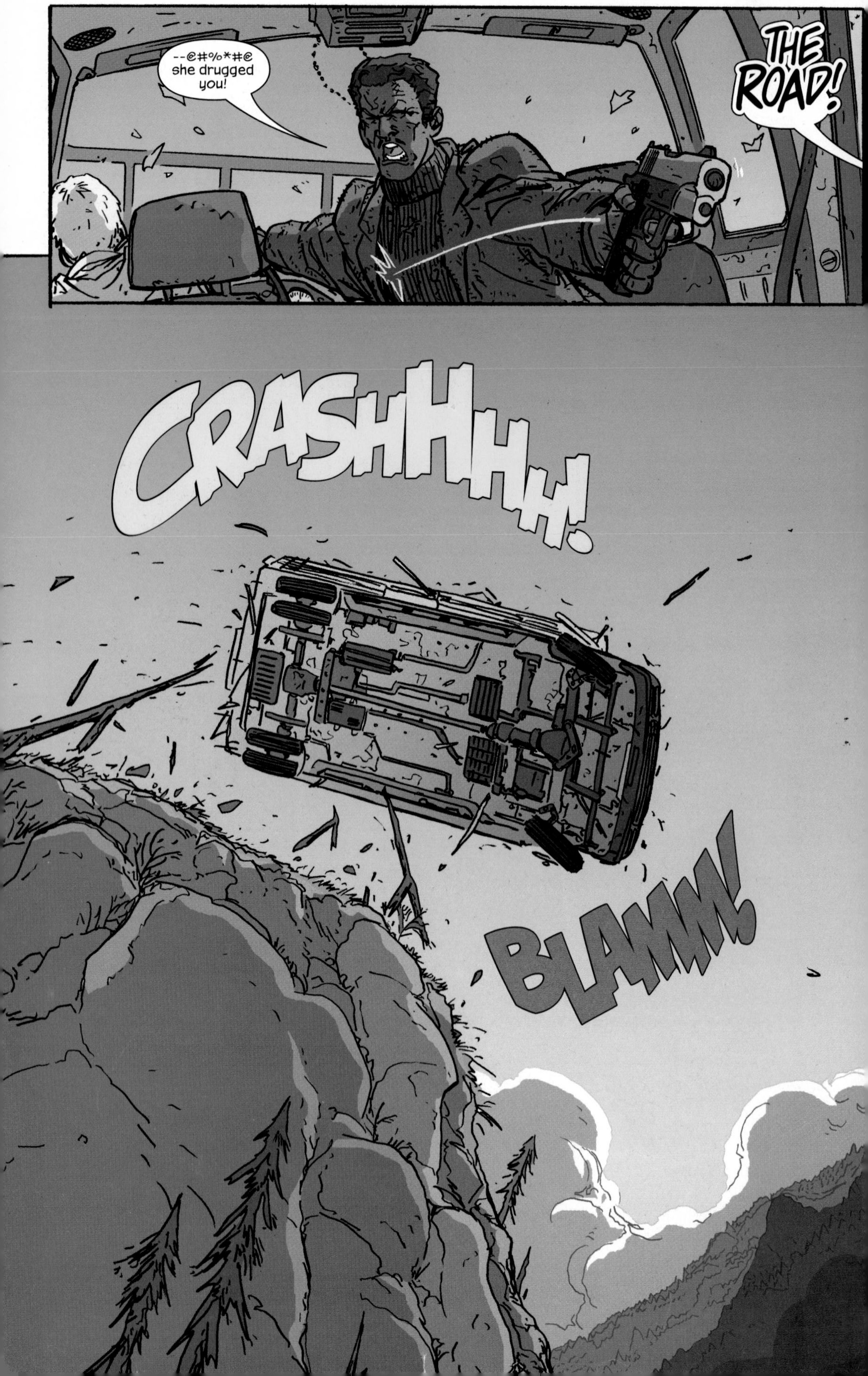
--@#%*#@ she drugged you!
THE ROAD!
CRASHHHH!
BLAMM!

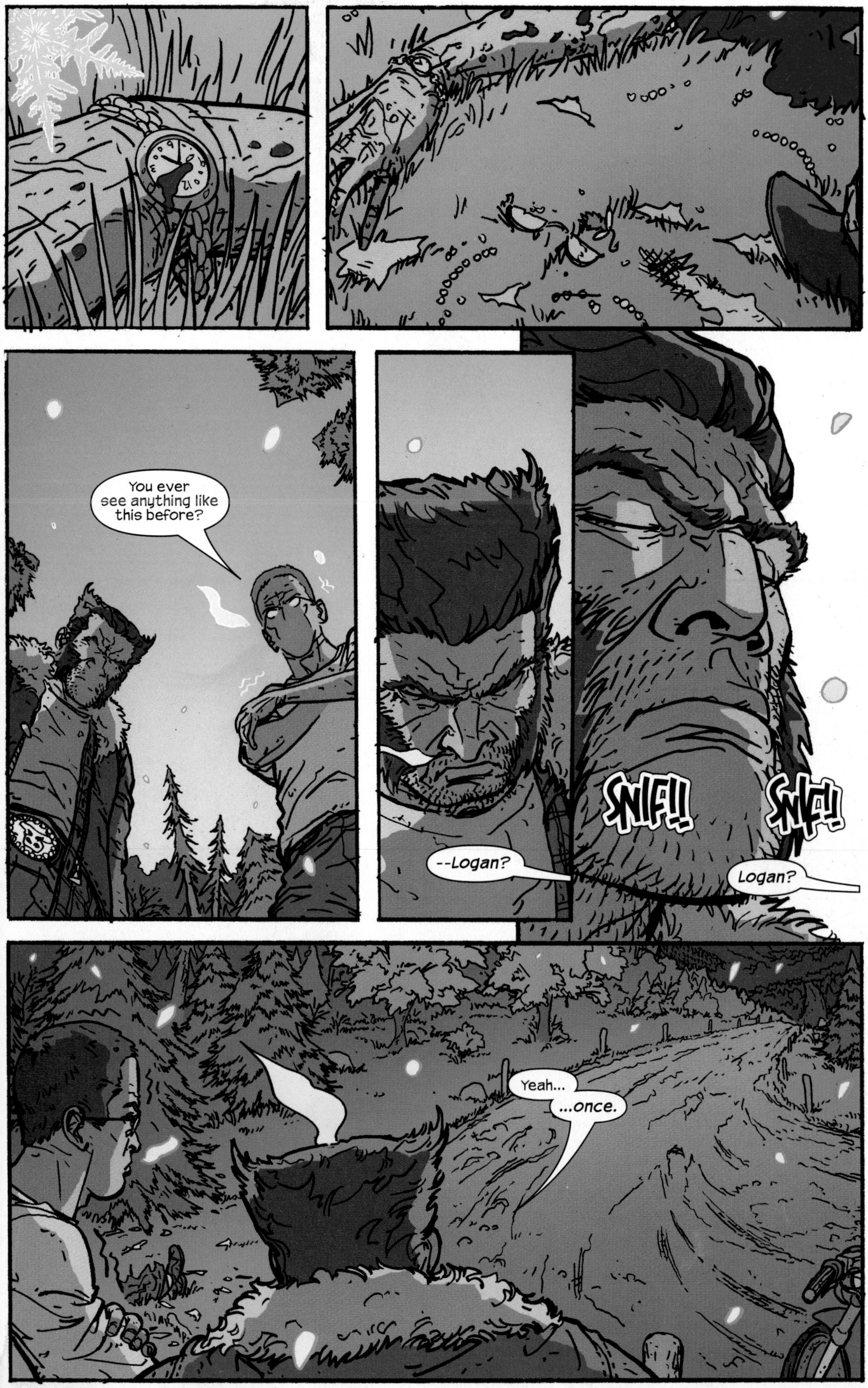
You ever see anything like this before?
--Logan?
SNIF!!
SNIF!!
Logan?
Yeah...
...once.

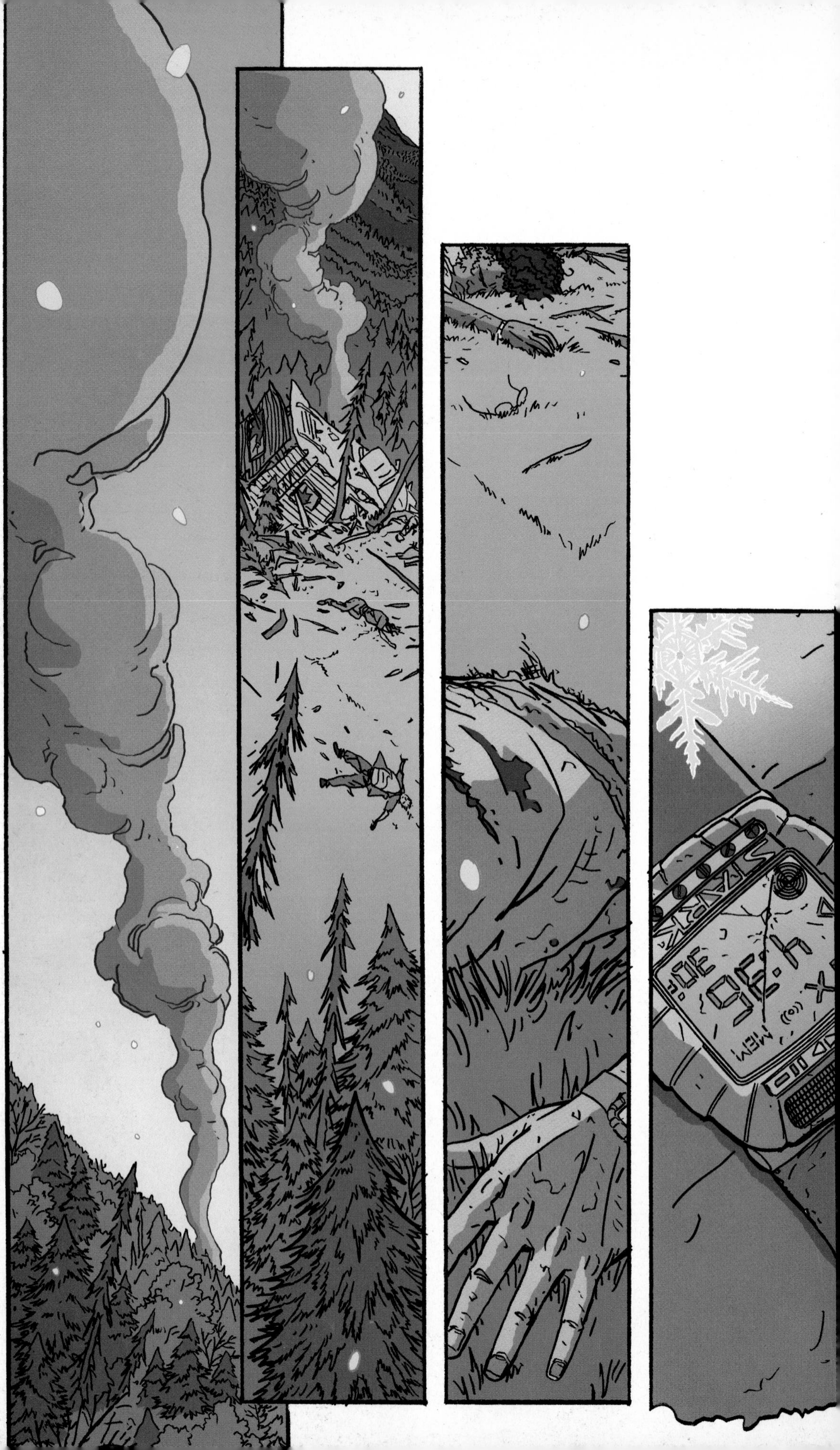

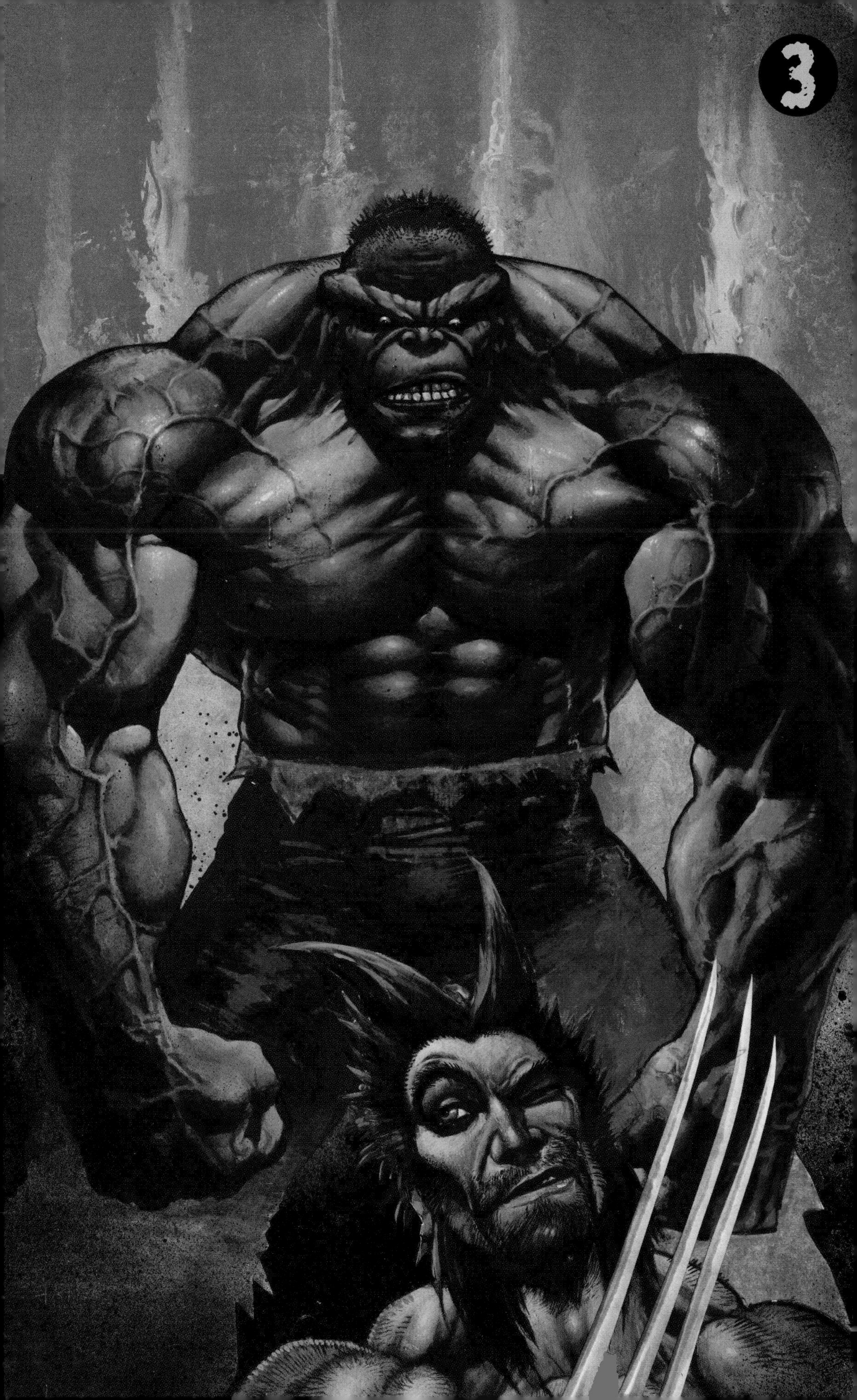
3

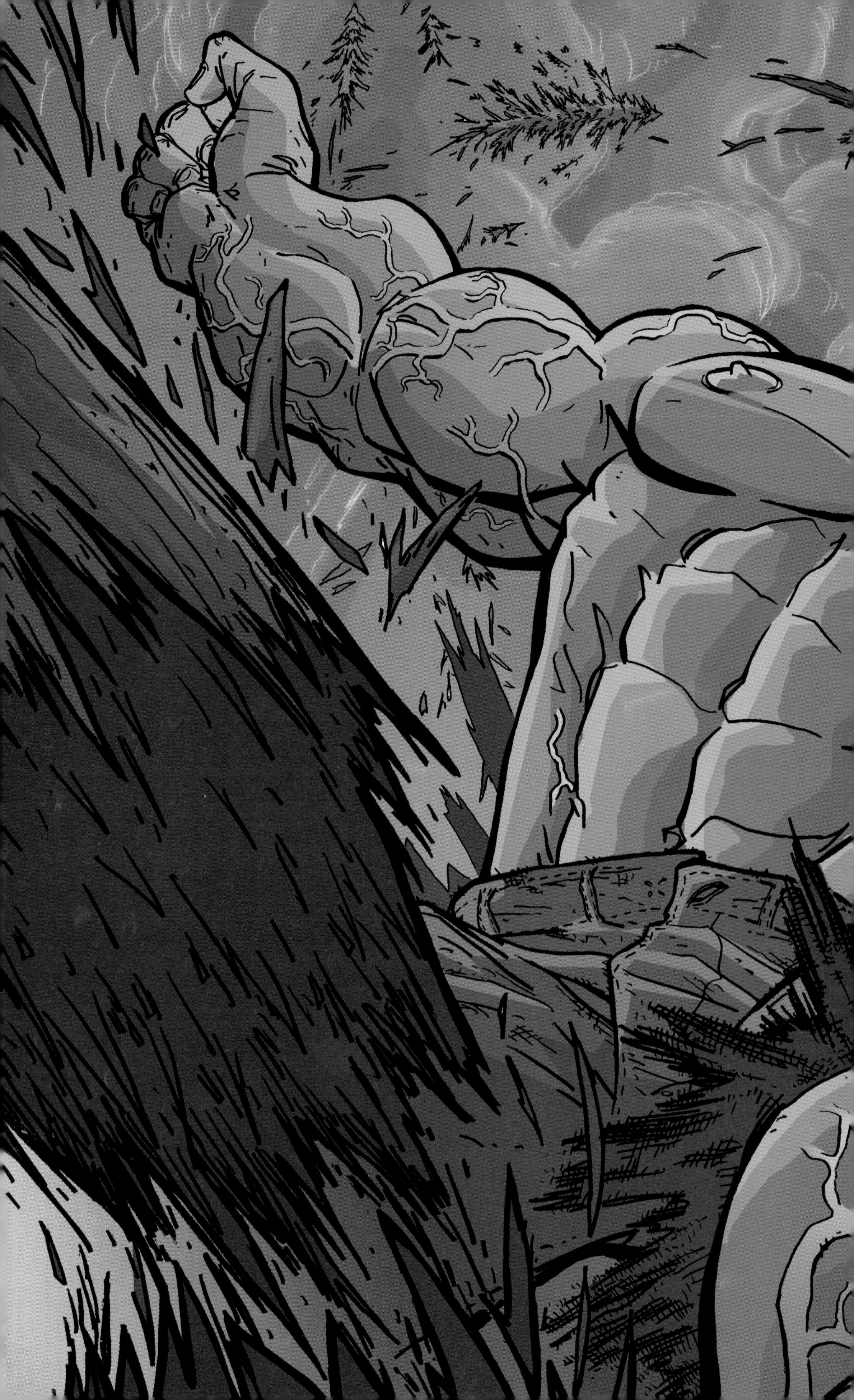

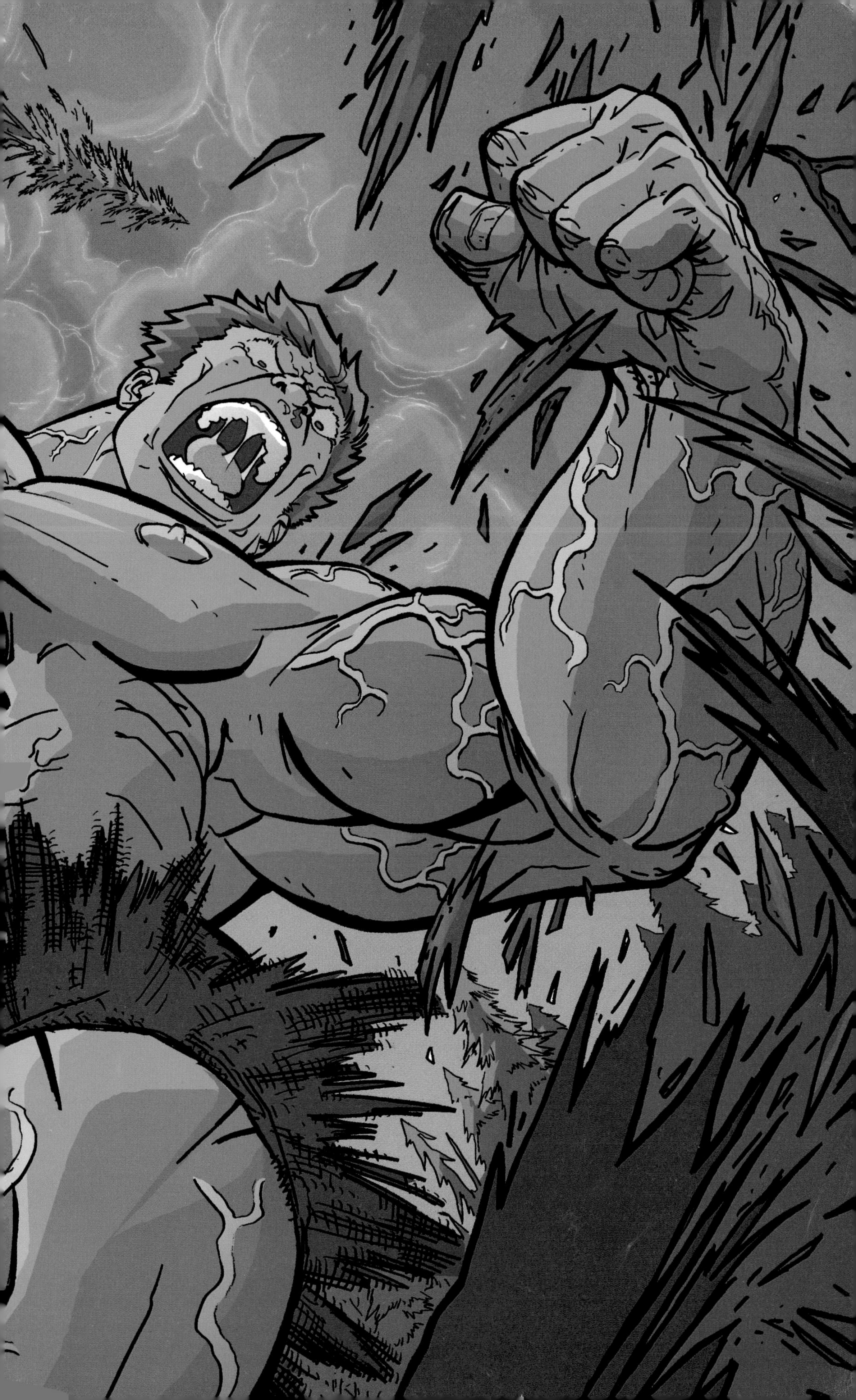

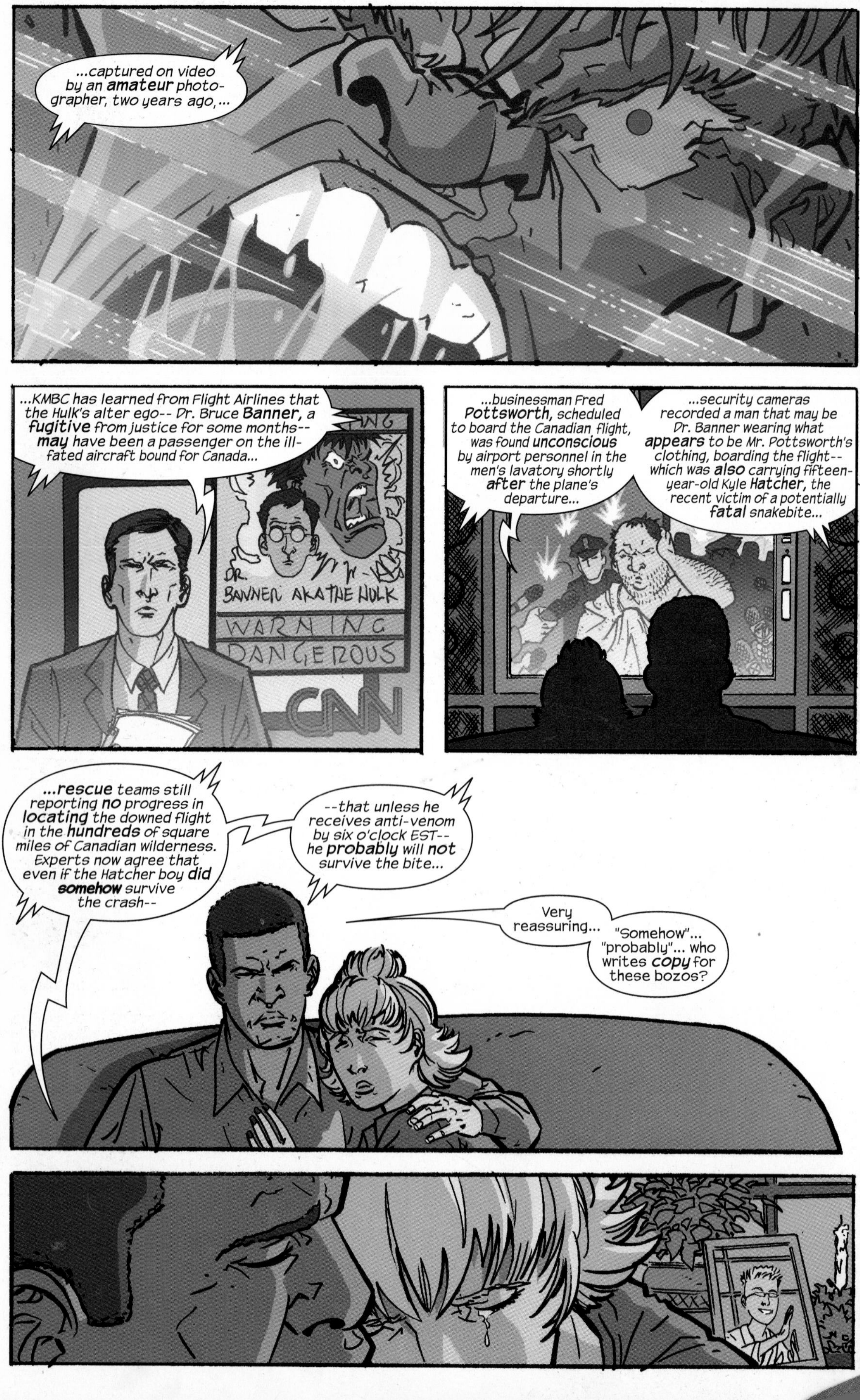
...captured on video by an amateur photo-grapher, two years ago,...
...KMBC has learned from Flight Airlines that the Hulk's alter ego-- Dr. Bruce Banner, a fugitive from justice for some months-- may have been a passenger on the ill-fated aircraft bound for Canada...
DR. BANNER AKA THE HULK
WARNING
DANGEROUS
CNN
...businessman Fred Pottsworth, scheduled to board the Canadian flight, was found unconscious by airport personnel in the men's lavatory shortly after the plane's departure...
...security cameras recorded a man that may be Dr. Banner wearing what appears to be Mr. Pottsworth's clothing, boarding the flight-- which was also carrying fifteen-year-old Kyle Hatcher, the recent victim of a potentially fatal snakebite...
...rescue teams still reporting no progress in locating the downed flight in the hundreds of square miles of Canadian wilderness. Experts now agree that even if the Hatcher boy did somehow survive the crash--
--that unless he receives anti-venom by six o'clock EST-- he probably will not survive the bite...
Very reassuring...
"Somehow"... "probably"... who writes copy for these bozos?

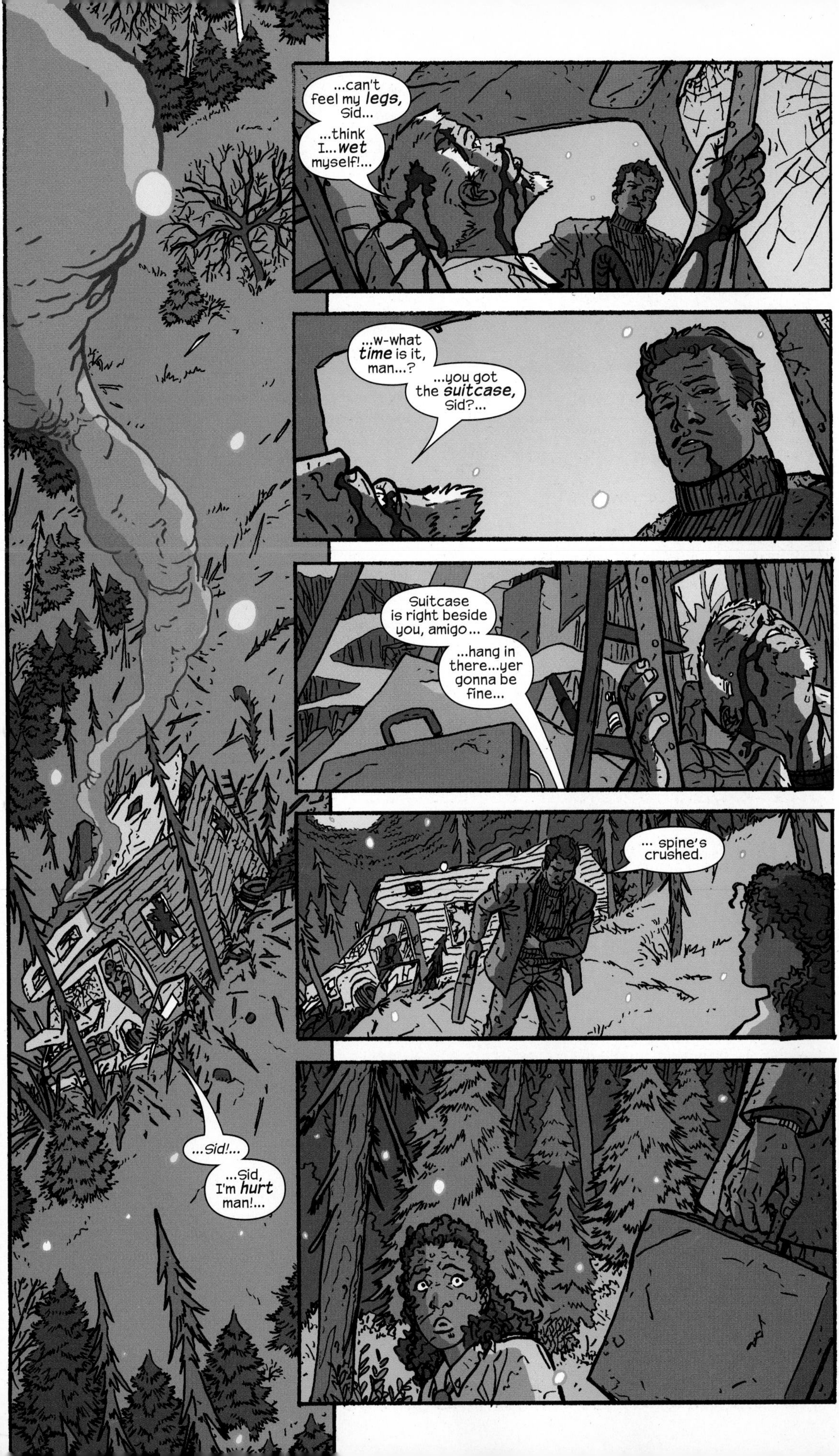
...Sid!...
...Sid, I'm hurt man!...
...can't feel my legs, Sid...
...think I...wet myself!...
...w-what time is it, man...?
...you got the suitcase, Sid?...
Suitcase is right beside you, amigo...
...hang in there...yer gonna be fine...
... spine's crushed.

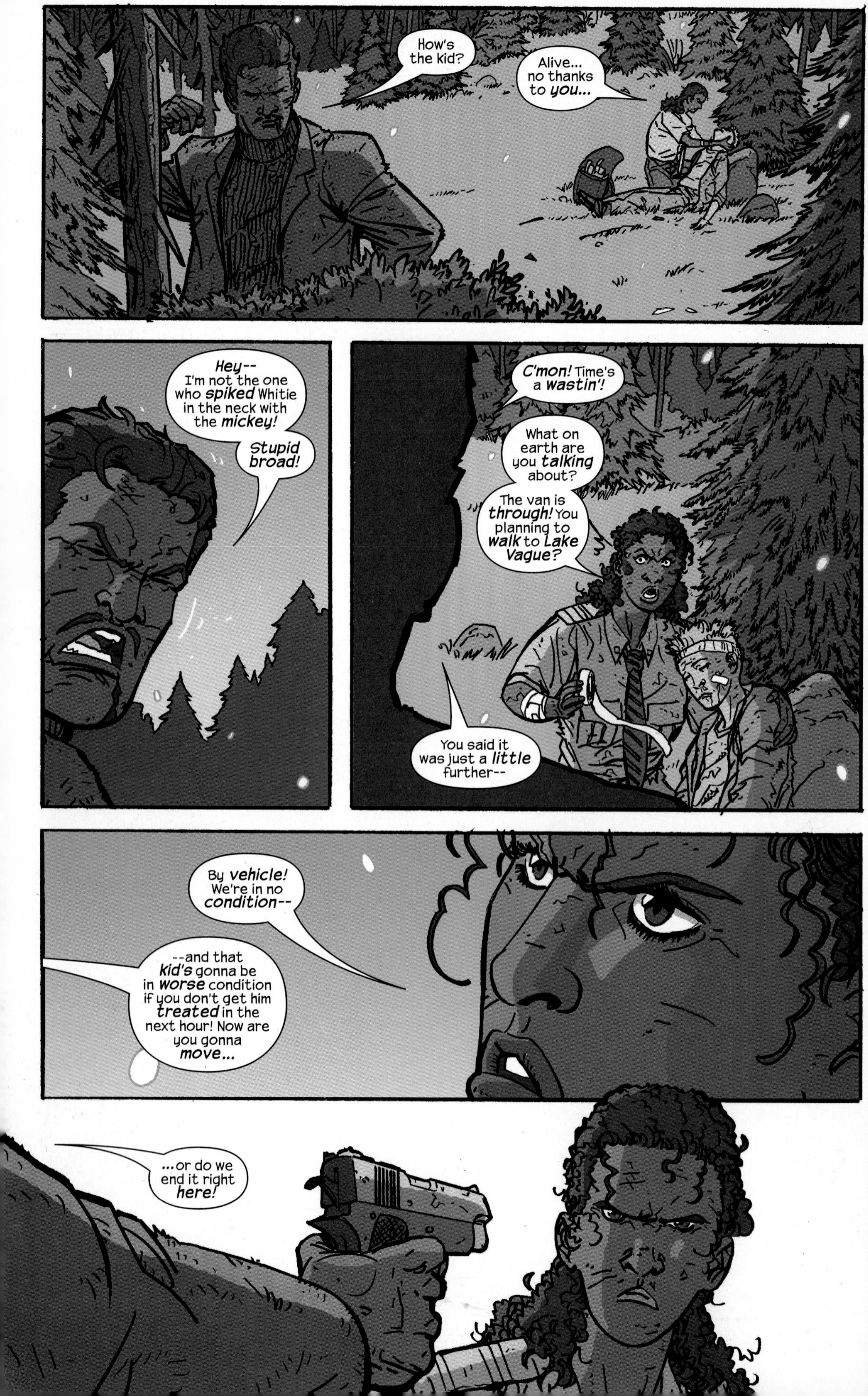
How's the kid?
Alive... no thanks to you...
Hey-- I'm not the one who spiked Whitie in the neck with the mickey!
Stupid broad!
C'mon! Time's a wastin'!
What on earth are you talking about?
The van is through! You planning to walk to Lake Vague?
You said it was just a little further--
By vehicle! We're in no condition--
--and that kid's gonna be in worse condition if you don't get him treated in the next hour! Now are you gonna move...
...or do we end it right here!

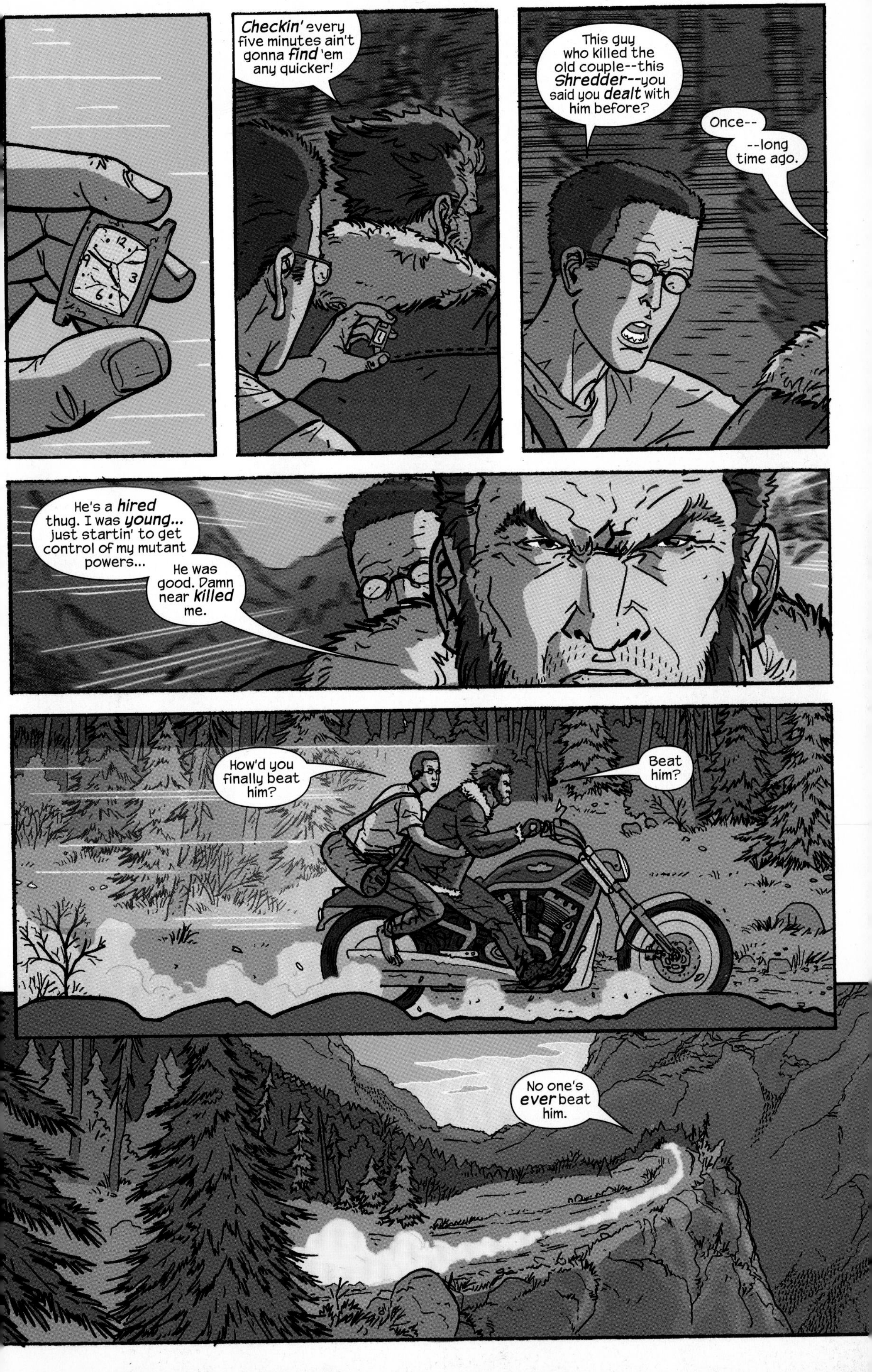
Checkin' every five minutes ain't gonna find 'em any quicker!
This guy who killed the old couple--this Shredder--you said you dealt with him before?
Once--
--long time ago.
He's a hired thug. I was young... just startin' to get control of my mutant powers...
He was good. Damn near killed me.
How'd you finally beat him?
Beat him?
No one's ever beat him.

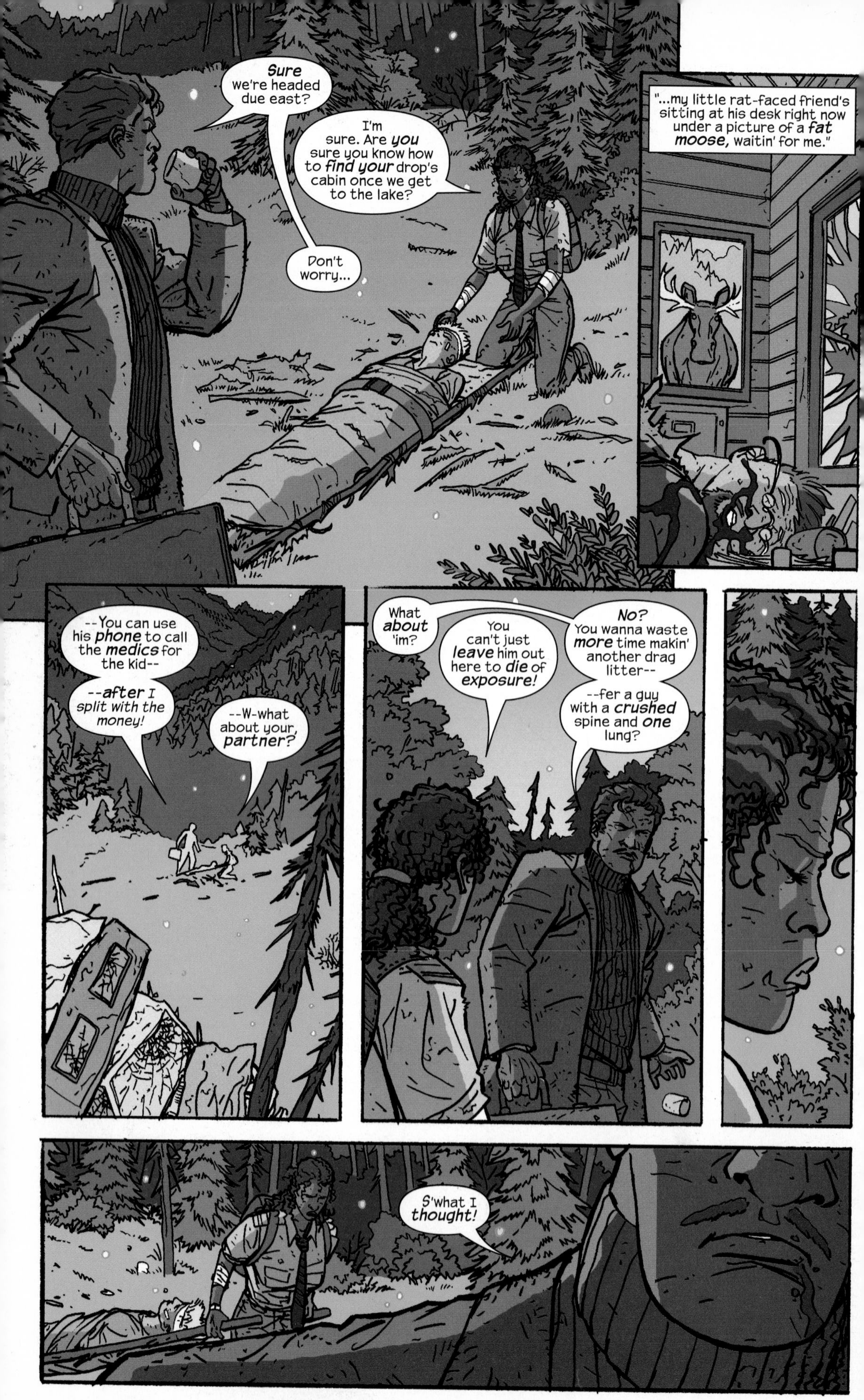
Sure we're headed due east?
I'm sure. Are you sure you know how to find your drop's cabin once we get to the lake?
Don't worry...
"...my little rat-faced friend's sitting at his desk right now under a picture of a fat moose, waitin' for me."
--You can use his phone to call the medics for the kid--
--after I split with the money!
--W-what about your, partner?
What about 'im?
You can't just leave him out here to die of exposure!
No? You wanna waste more time makin' another drag litter--
--fer a guy with a crushed spine and one lung?
S'what I thought!

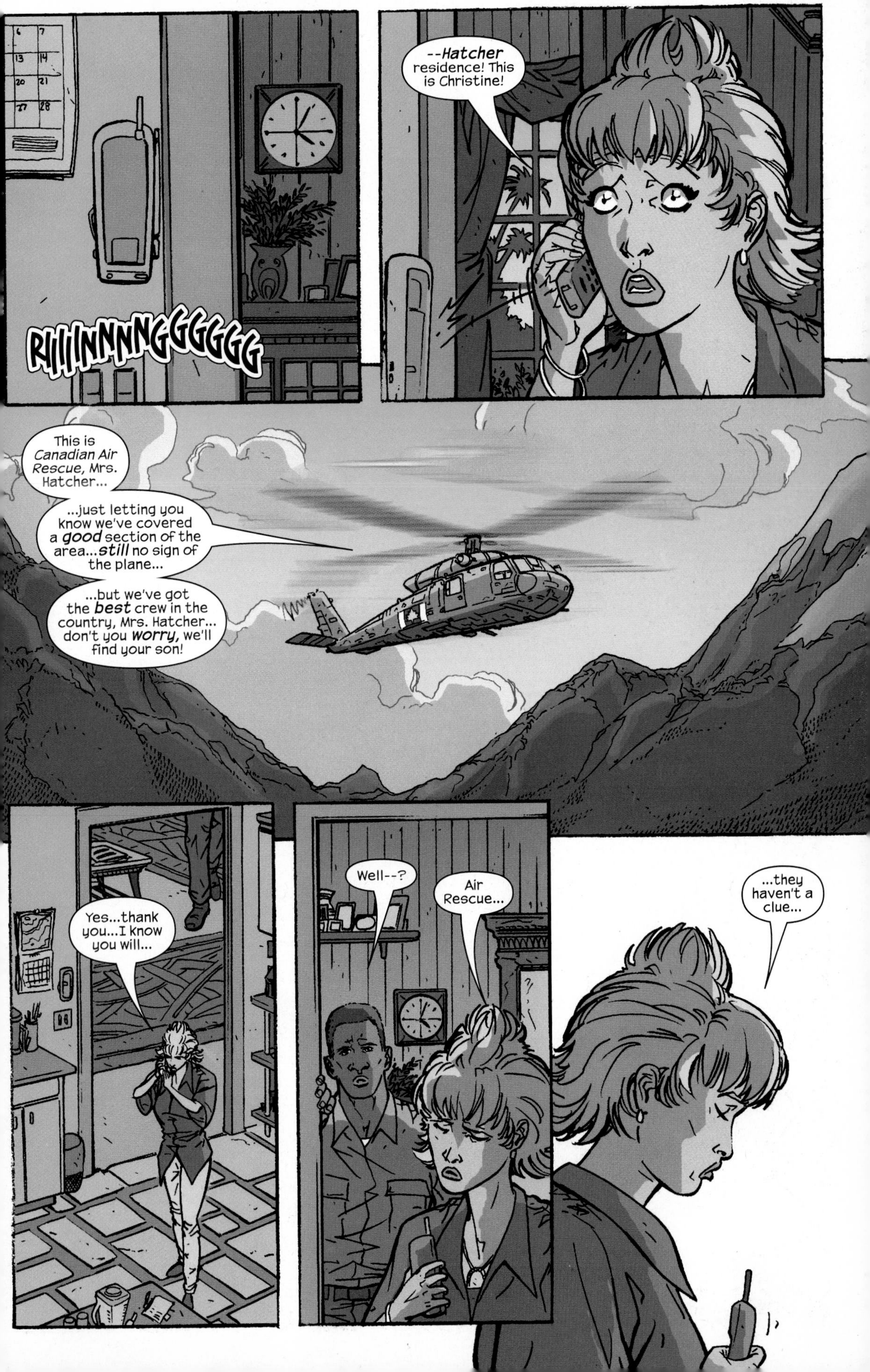
RIIIINNNNGGGGGG
--Hatcher residence! This is Christine!
This is Canadian Air Rescue, Mrs. Hatcher...
...just letting you know we've covered a good section of the area...still no sign of the plane...
...but we've got the best crew in the country, Mrs. Hatcher... don't you worry, we'll find your son!
Yes...thank you...I know you will...
Well--?
Air Rescue...
...they haven't a clue...

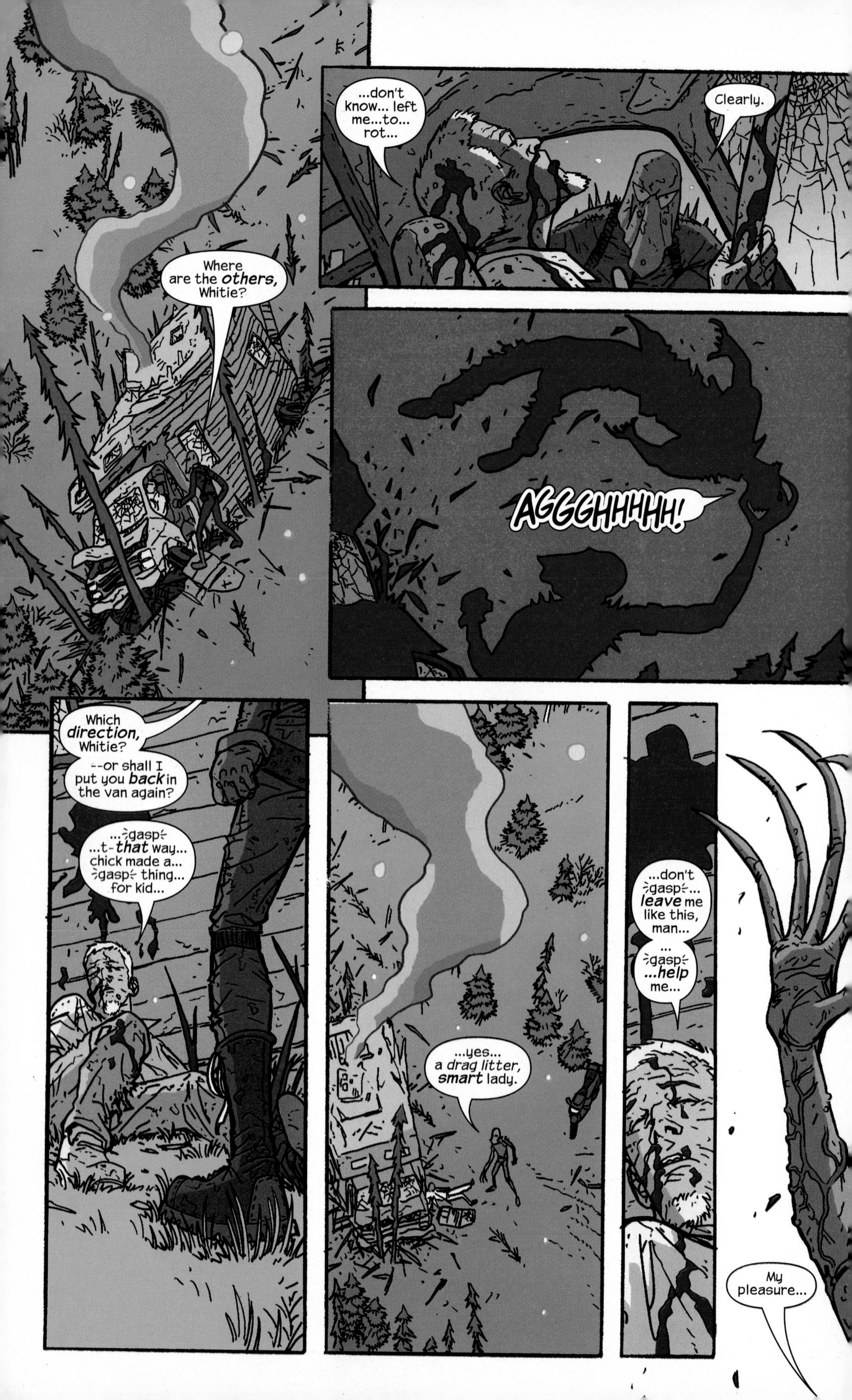
Where are the others, Whitie?
...don't know... left me...to... rot...
Clearly.
AGGGHHHHH!
Which direction, Whitie?
--or shall I put you back in the van again?
...gasp ...t-that way... chick made a... gasp thing... for kid...
...yes... a drag litter, smart lady.
...don't gasp... leave me like this, man...
... gasp ...help me...
My pleasure...

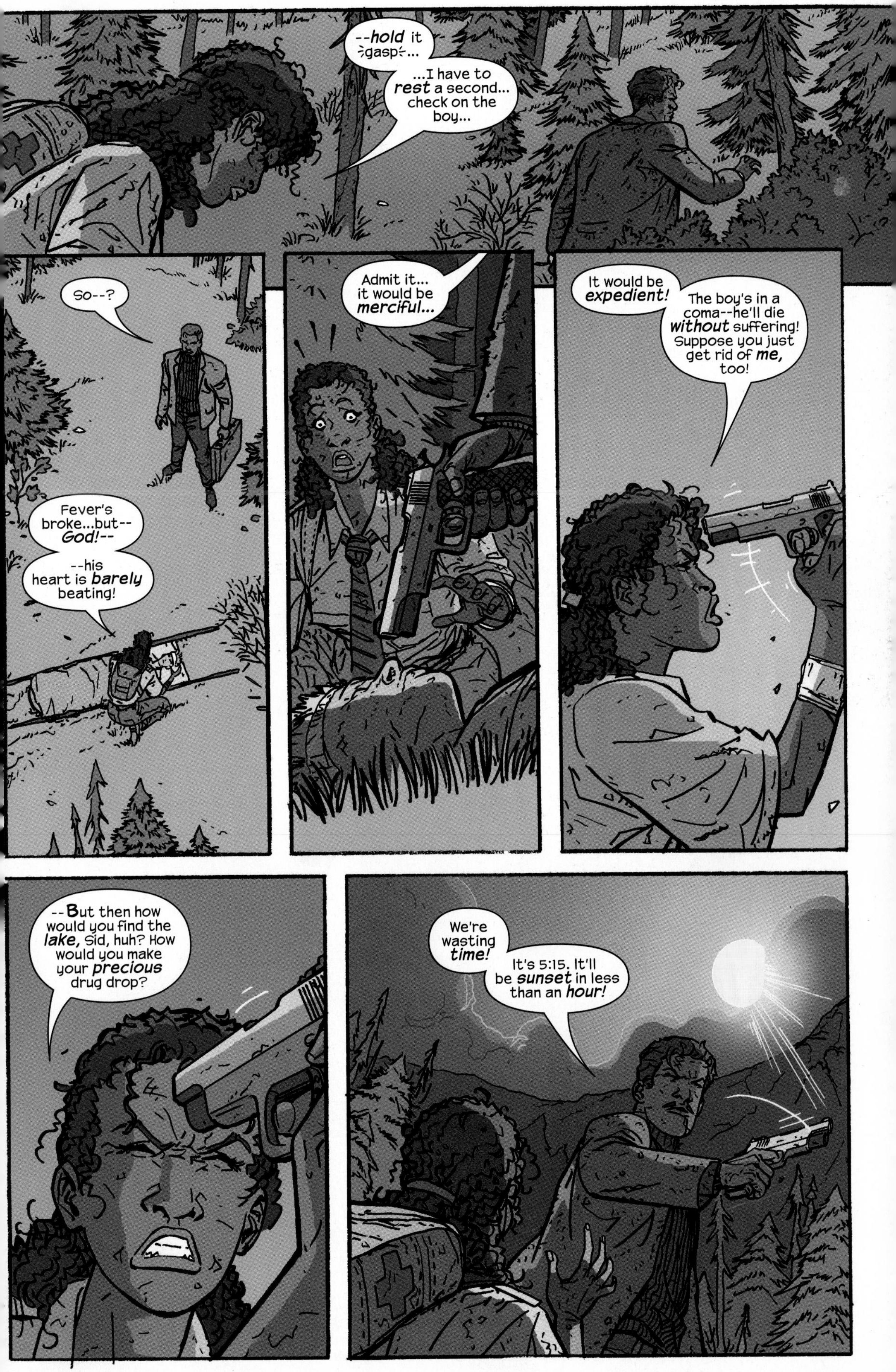
--hold it
⸗gasp⸗...
...I have to rest a second... check on the boy...
So--?
Fever's broke...but-- God!--
--his heart is barely beating!
Admit it... it would be merciful...
It would be expedient!
The boy's in a coma--he'll die without suffering! Suppose you just get rid of me, too!
--But then how would you find the lake, Sid, huh? How would you make your precious drug drop?
We're wasting time!
It's 5:15. It'll be sunset in less than an hour!

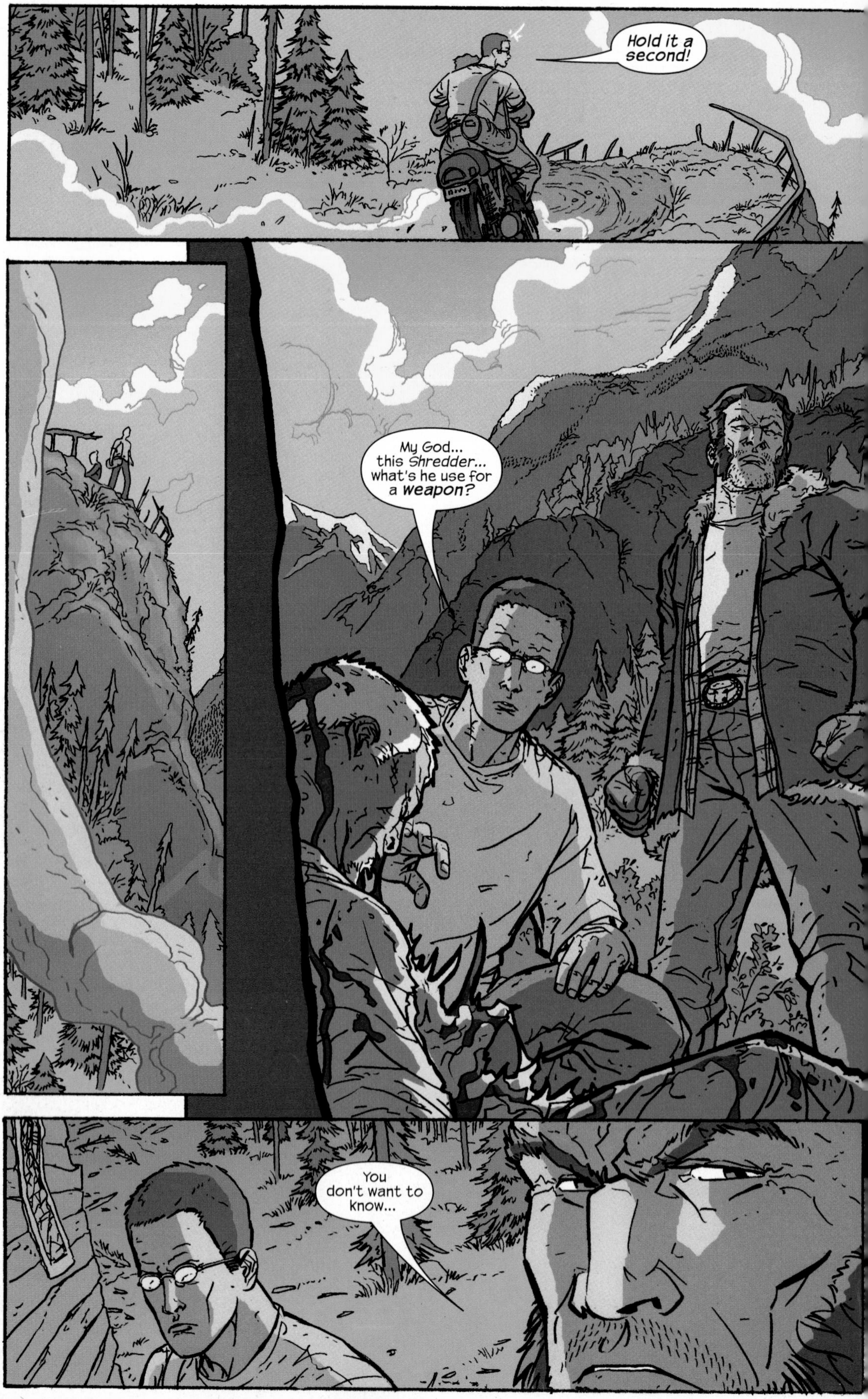
Hold it a second!
My God... this Shredder... what's he use for a weapon?
You don't want to know...

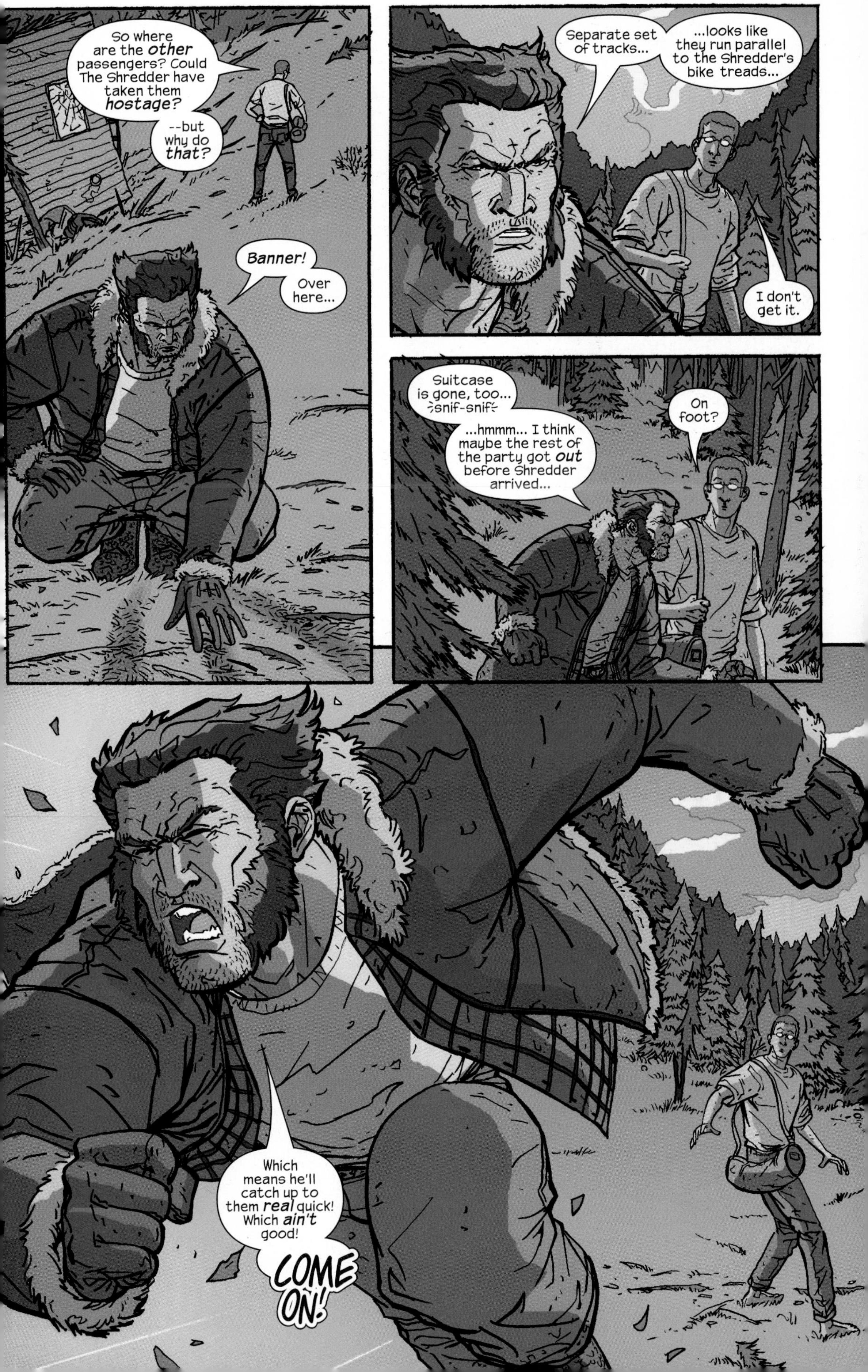
So where are the *other* passengers? Could The Shredder have taken them *hostage*?
--but why do *that*?
Banner!
Over here...
Separate set of tracks...
...looks like they run parallel to the Shredder's bike treads...
I don't get it.
Suitcase is gone, too... *snif-snif*
...hmmm... I think maybe the rest of the party got *out* before Shredder arrived...
On foot?
Which means he'll catch up to them *real* quick! Which *ain't* good!
COME ON!

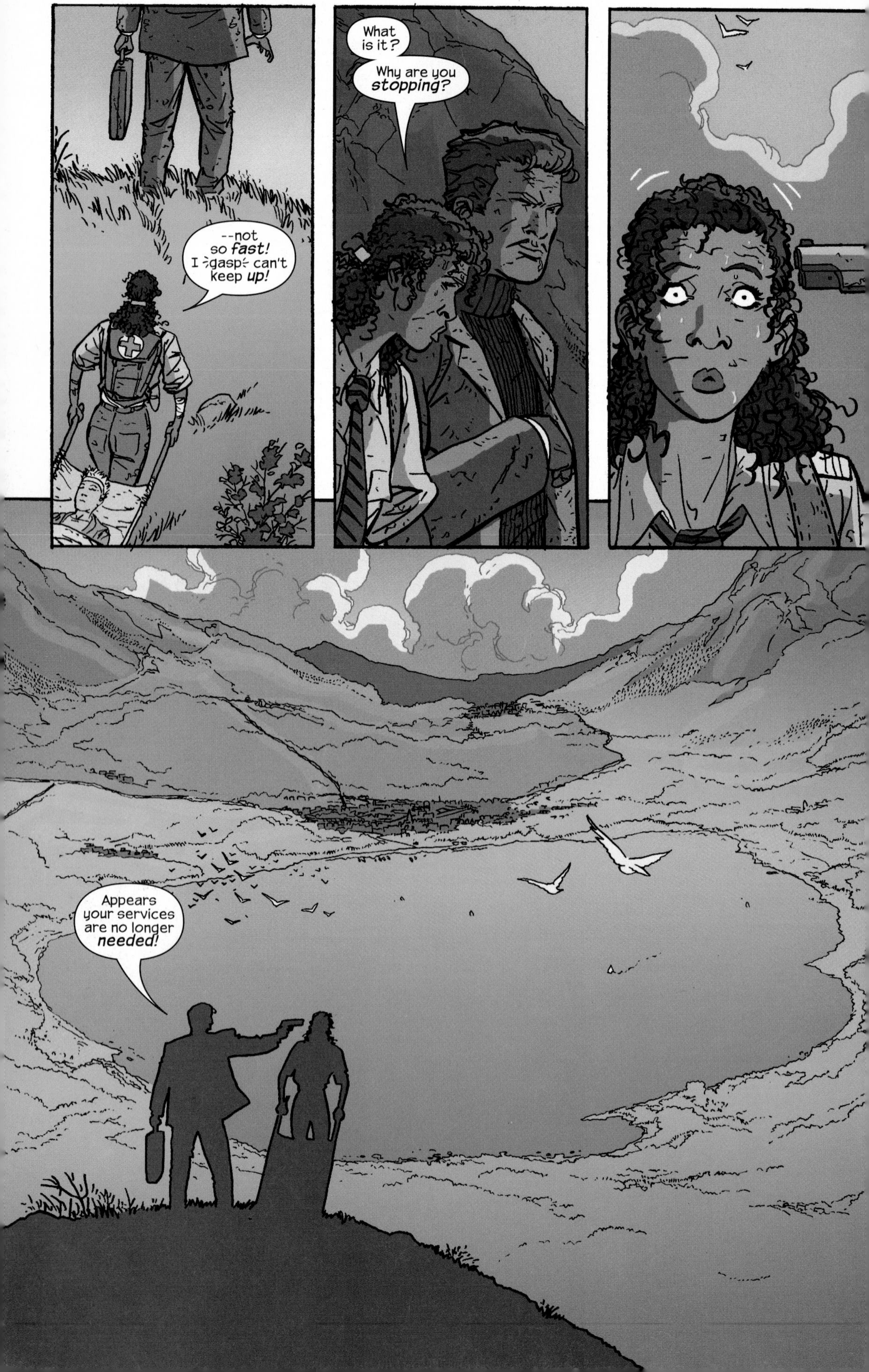
--not so *fast!* I ~gasp~ can't keep *up!*
What is it?
Why are you *stopping?*
Appears your services are no longer *needed!*

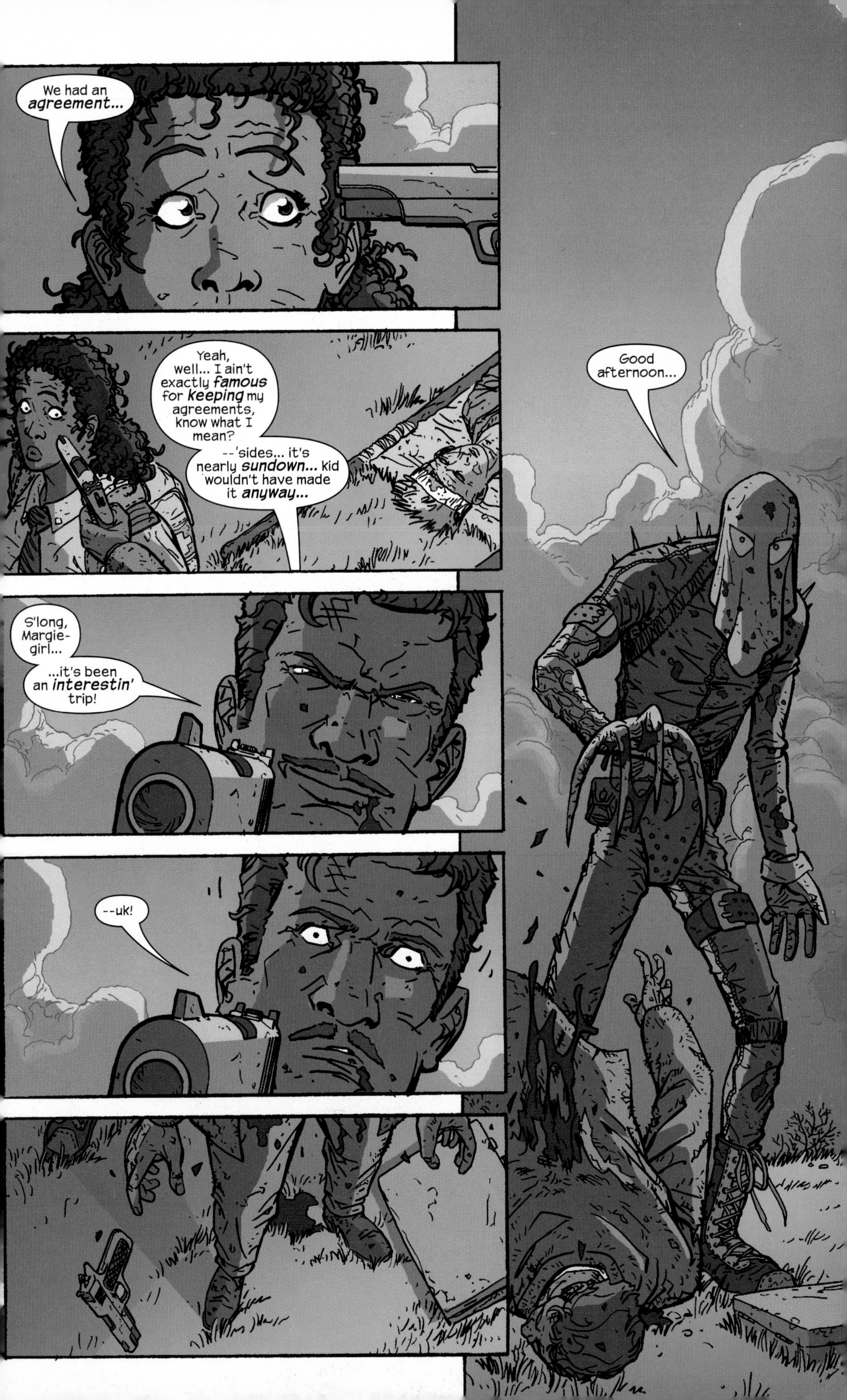
We had an *agreement...*
Yeah, well... I ain't exactly *famous* for *keeping* my agreements, know what I mean?
--'sides... it's nearly *sundown...* kid wouldn't have made it *anyway...*
S'long, Margie-girl...
...it's been an *interestin'* trip!
--uk!
Good afternoon...

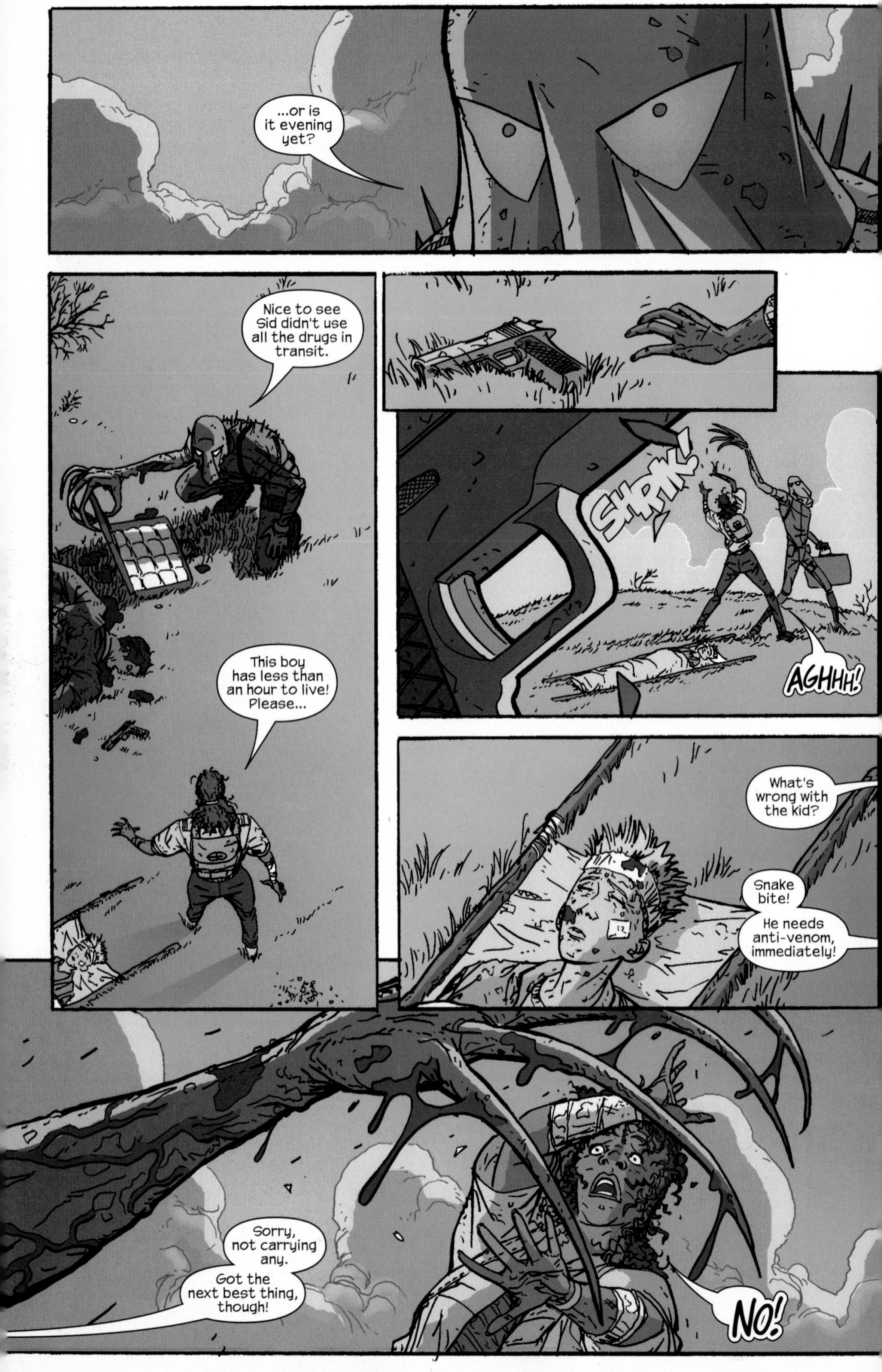

...or is it evening yet?
Nice to see Sid didn't use all the drugs in transit.
This boy has less than an hour to live! Please...
SHPTIK!
AGHHH!
What's wrong with the kid?
Snake bite!
He needs anti-venom, immediately!
Sorry, not carrying any.
Got the next best thing, though!
NO!

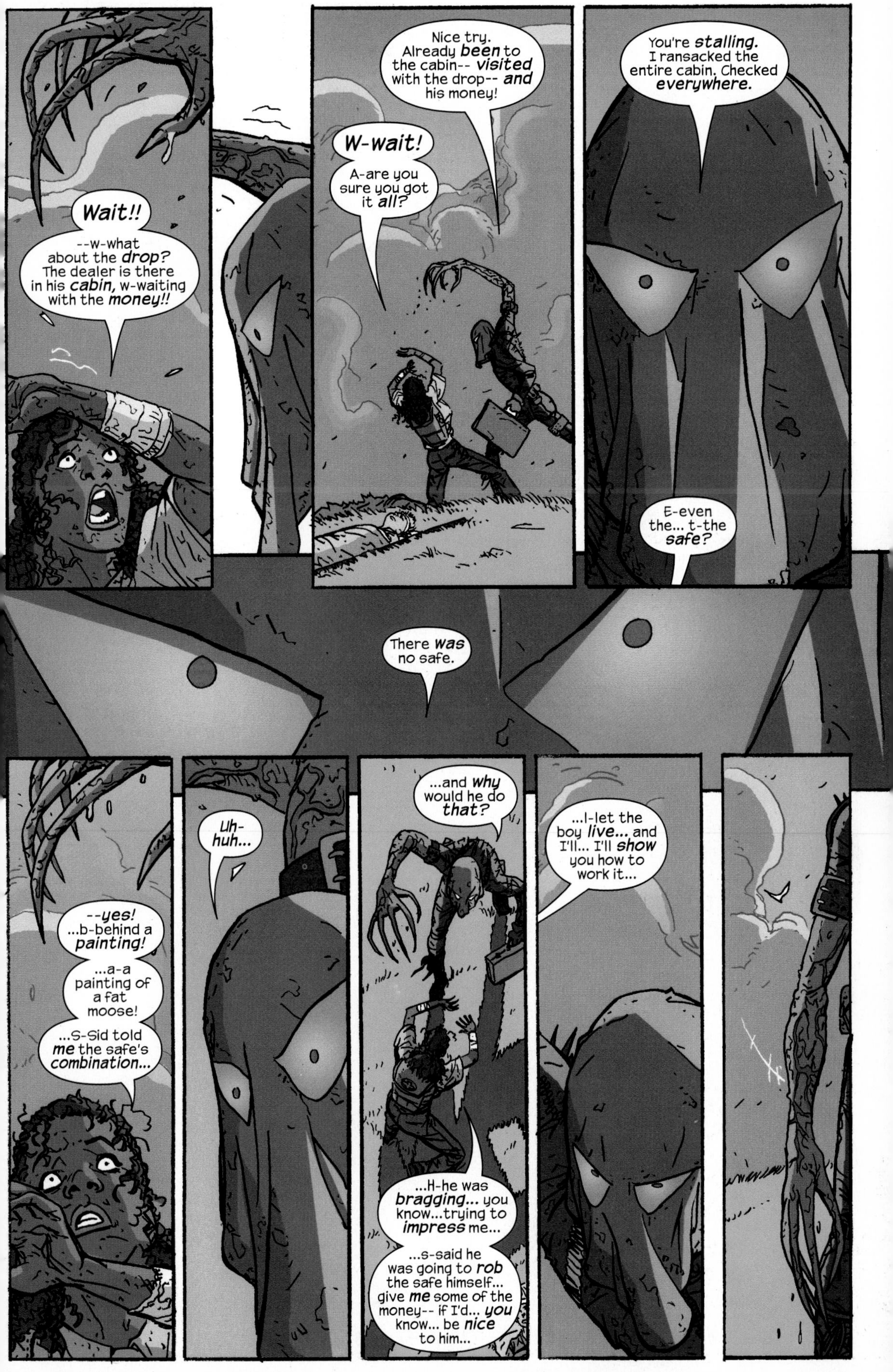
Wait!!
--w-what about the drop? The dealer is there in his cabin, w-waiting with the money!!
Nice try. Already been to the cabin-- visited with the drop-- and his money!
W-wait!
A-are you sure you got it all?
You're stalling. I ransacked the entire cabin. Checked everywhere.
E-even the... t-the safe?
There was no safe.
--yes! ...b-behind a painting!
...a-a painting of a fat moose!
...S-Sid told me the safe's combination...
Uh-huh...
...and why would he do that?
...H-he was bragging... you know...trying to impress me...
...s-said he was going to rob the safe himself... give me some of the money-- if I'd... you know... be nice to him...
...I-let the boy live... and I'll... I'll show you how to work it...

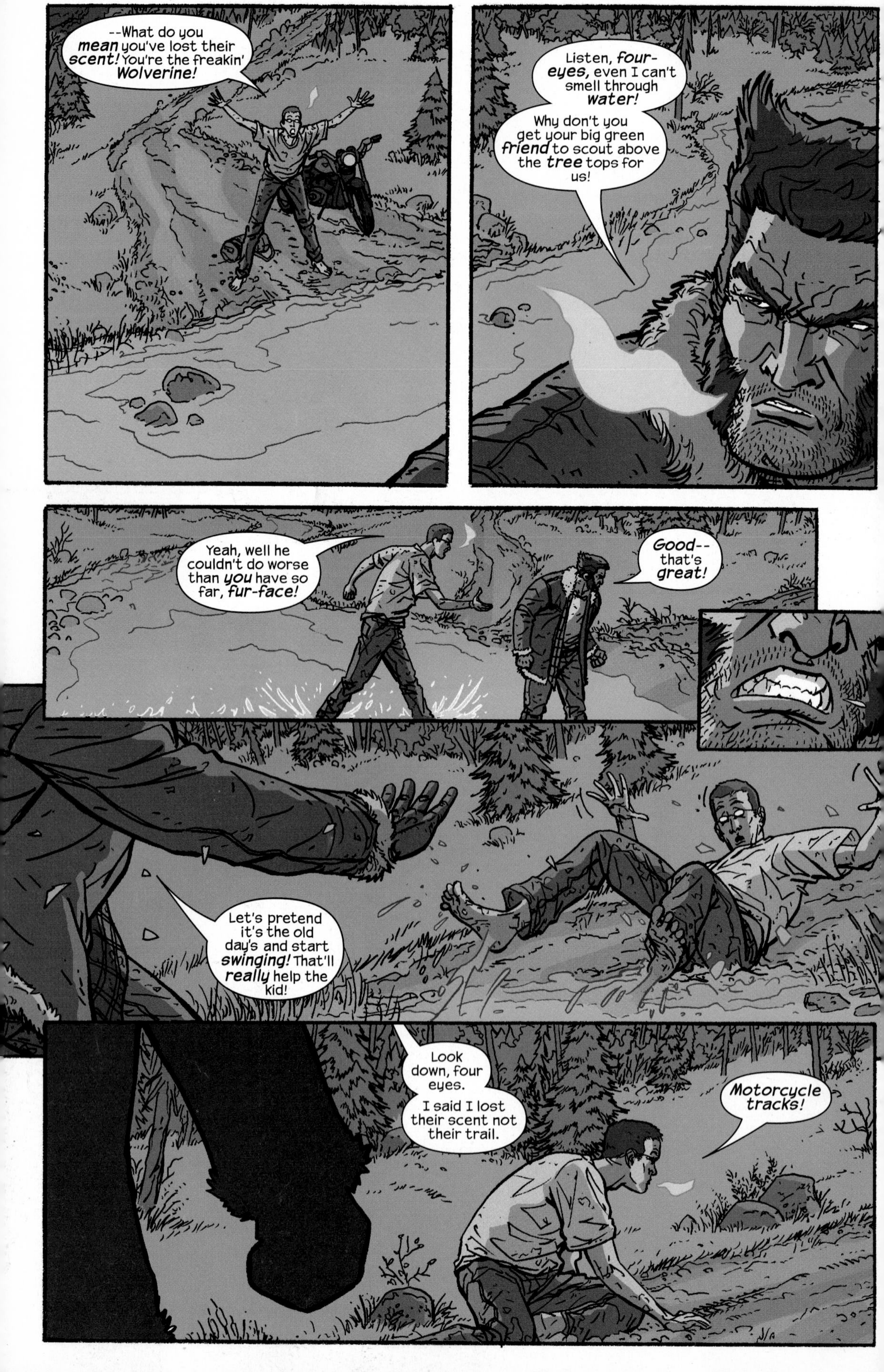
--What do you mean you've lost their scent! You're the freakin' Wolverine!
Listen, four-eyes, even I can't smell through water!
Why don't you get your big green friend to scout above the tree tops for us!
Yeah, well he couldn't do worse than you have so far, fur-face!
Good--that's great!
Let's pretend it's the old day's and start swinging! That'll really help the kid!
Look down, four eyes.
I said I lost their scent not their trail.
Motorcycle tracks!

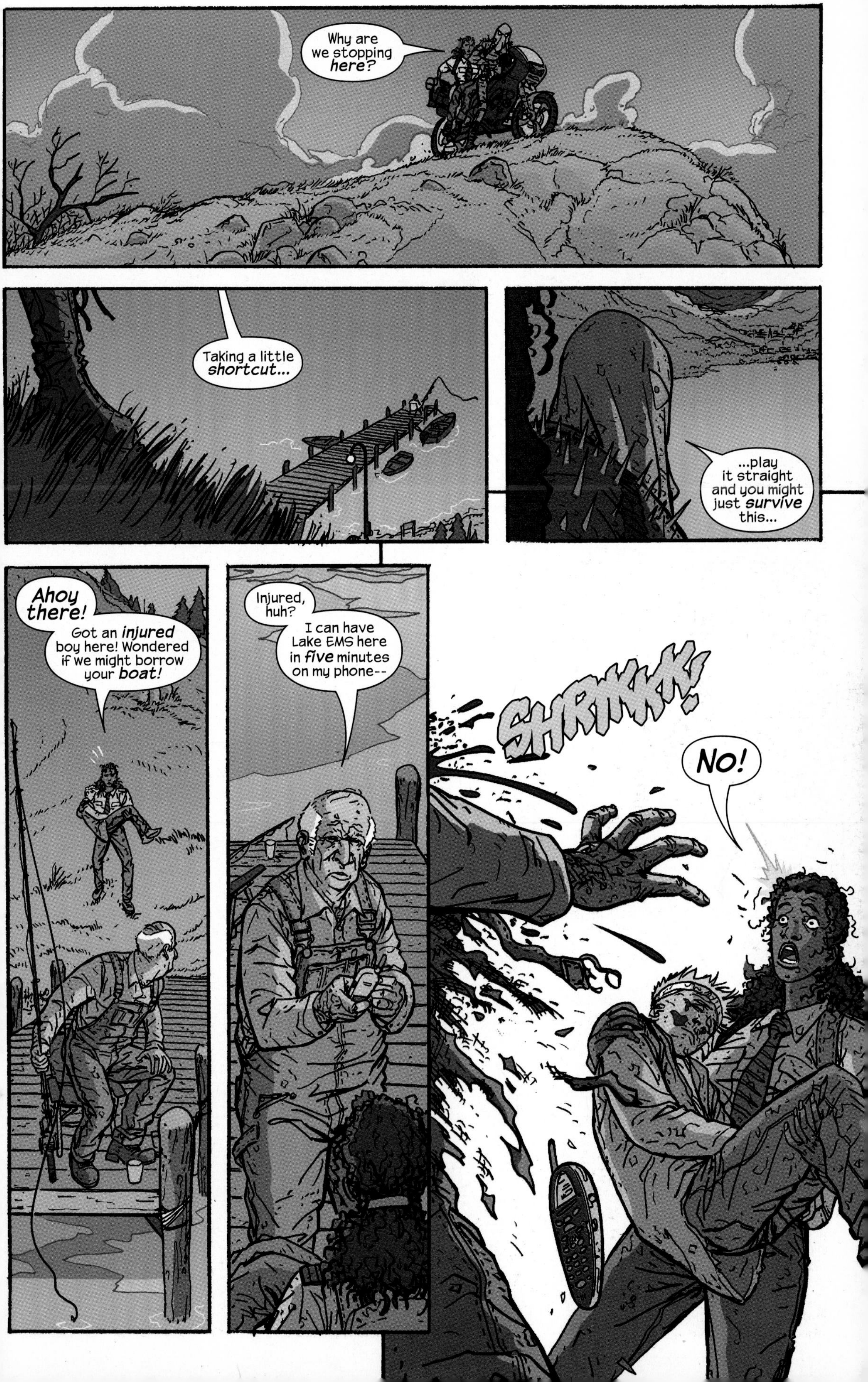
Why are we stopping here?
Taking a little shortcut...
...play it straight and you might just survive this...
Ahoy there!
Got an injured boy here! Wondered if we might borrow your boat!
Injured, huh?
I can have Lake EMS here in five minutes on my phone--
SHRIKKK!
NO!

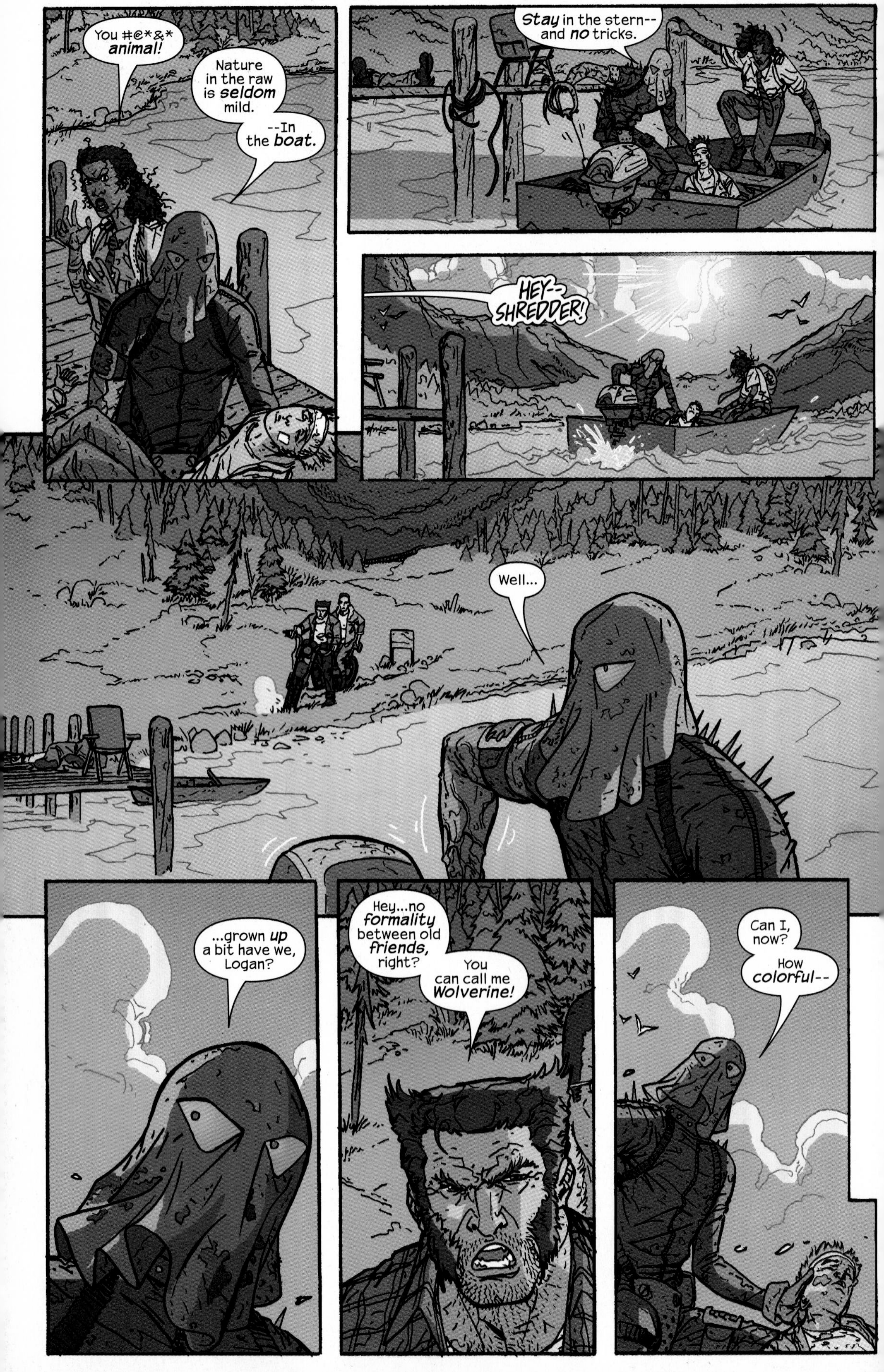
You #@*&* animal!
Nature in the raw is seldom mild.
--In the boat.
Stay in the stern-- and no tricks.
HEY-- SHREDDER!
Well...
...grown up a bit have we, Logan?
Hey...no formality between old friends, right?
You can call me Wolverine!
Can I, now?
How colorful--

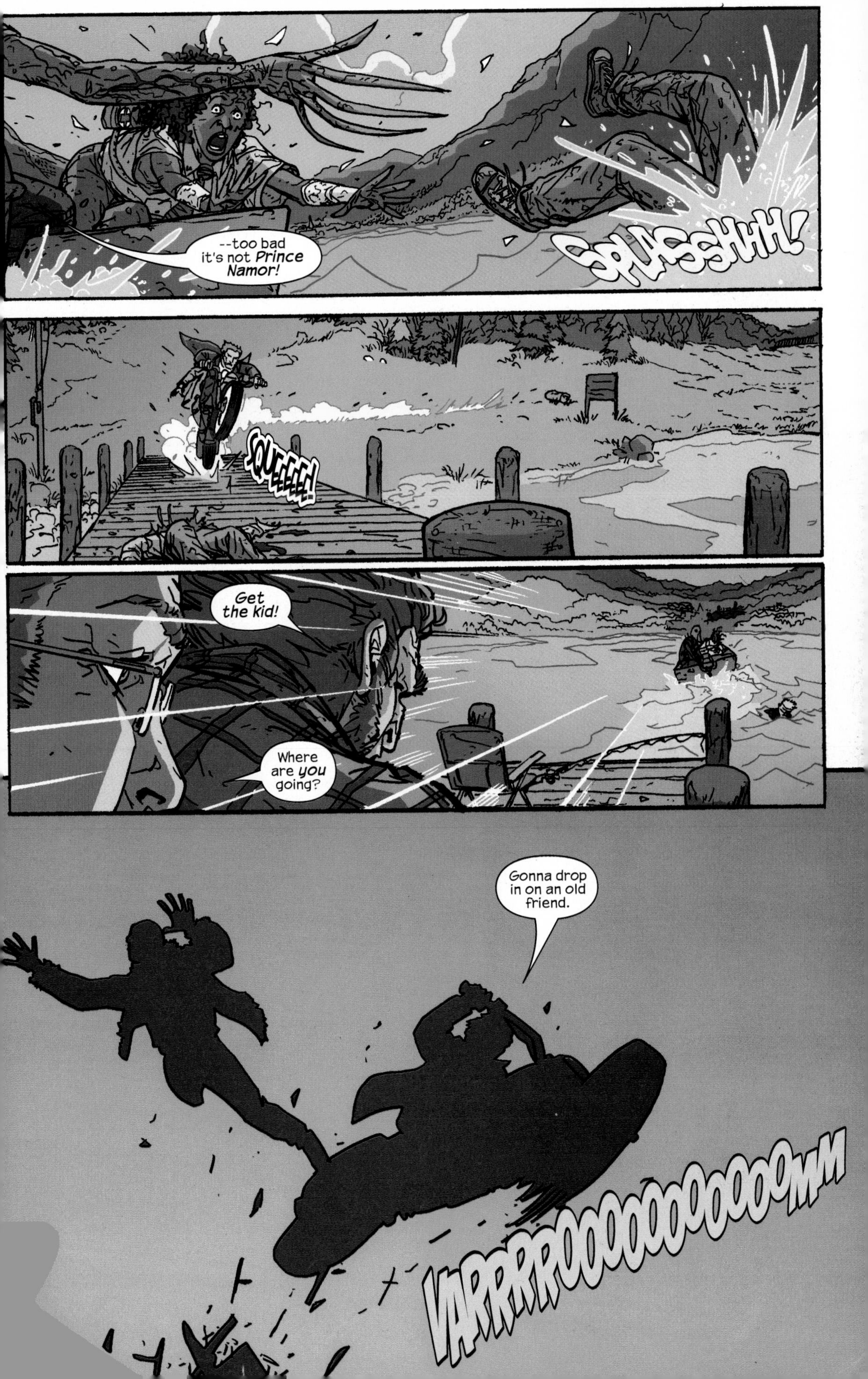
--too bad it's not *Prince Namor!*
SPLASSHHH!
SQUEEEEE!
Get the kid!
Where are *you* going?
Gonna drop in on an old friend.
VARRRROOOOOOOOOOOMM

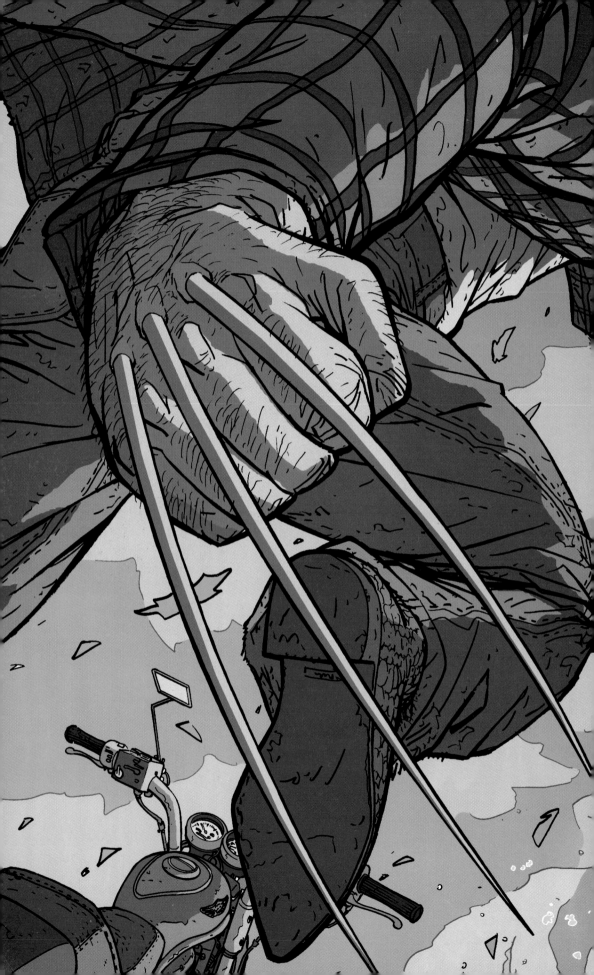

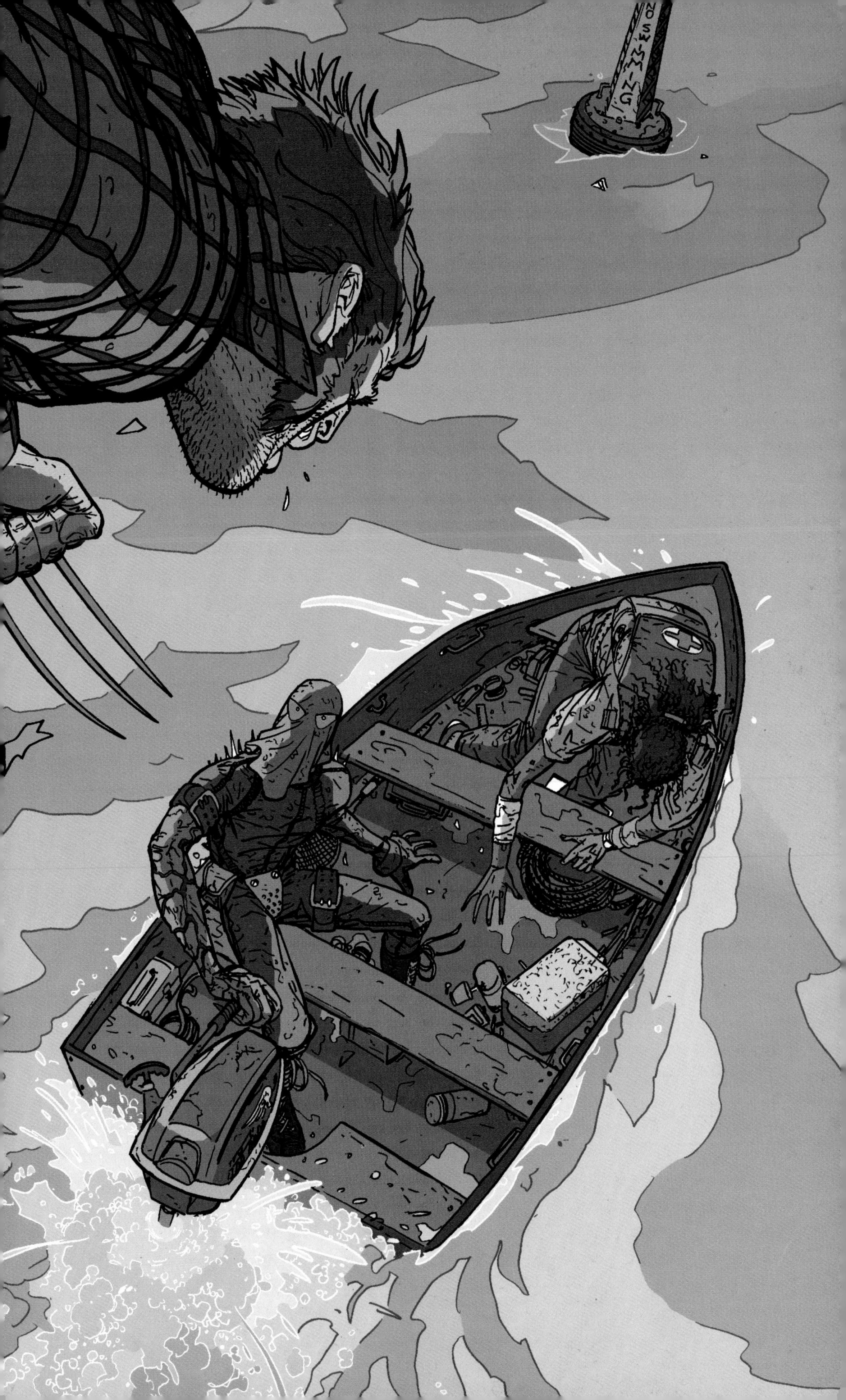
NO SWIMMING

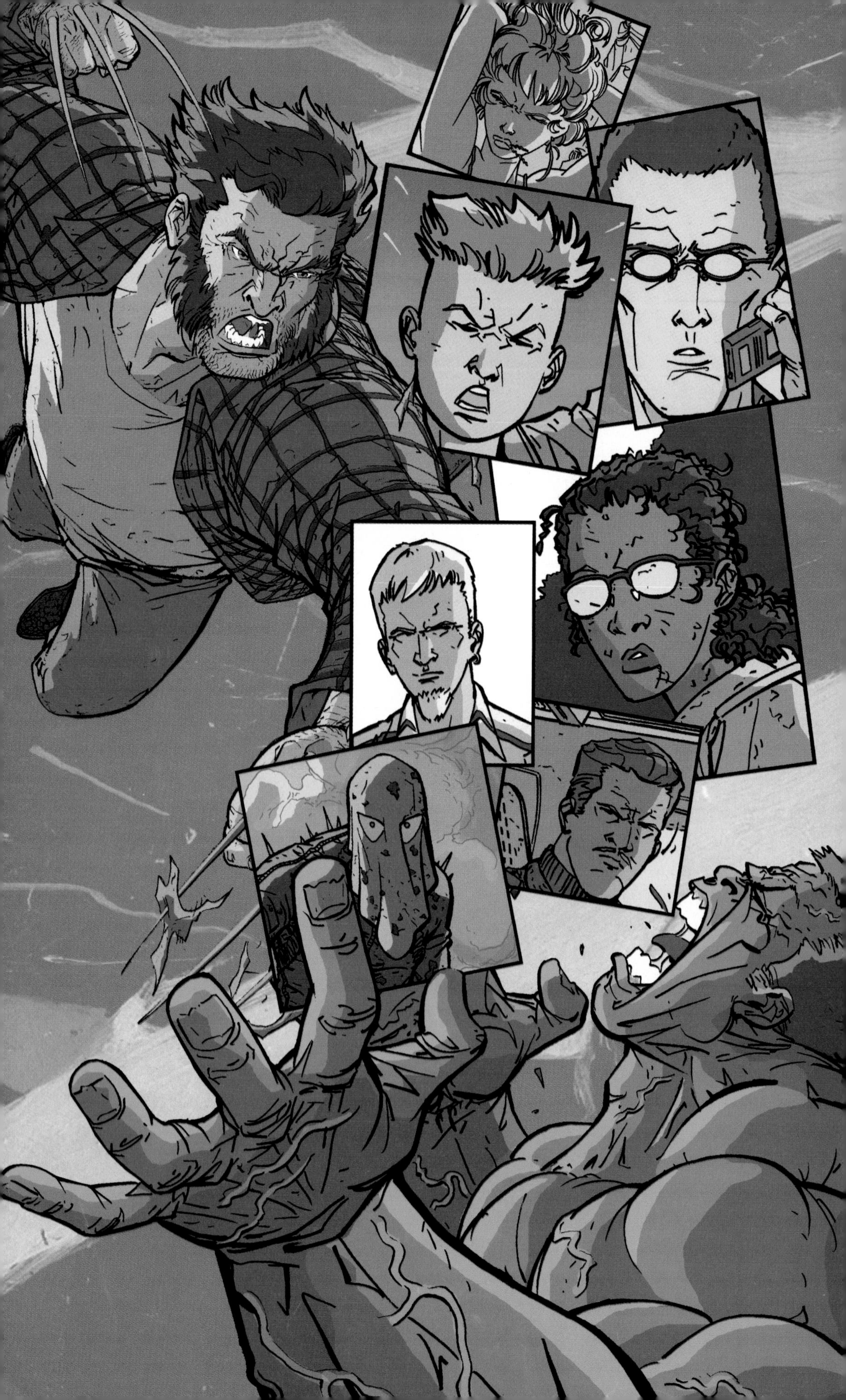

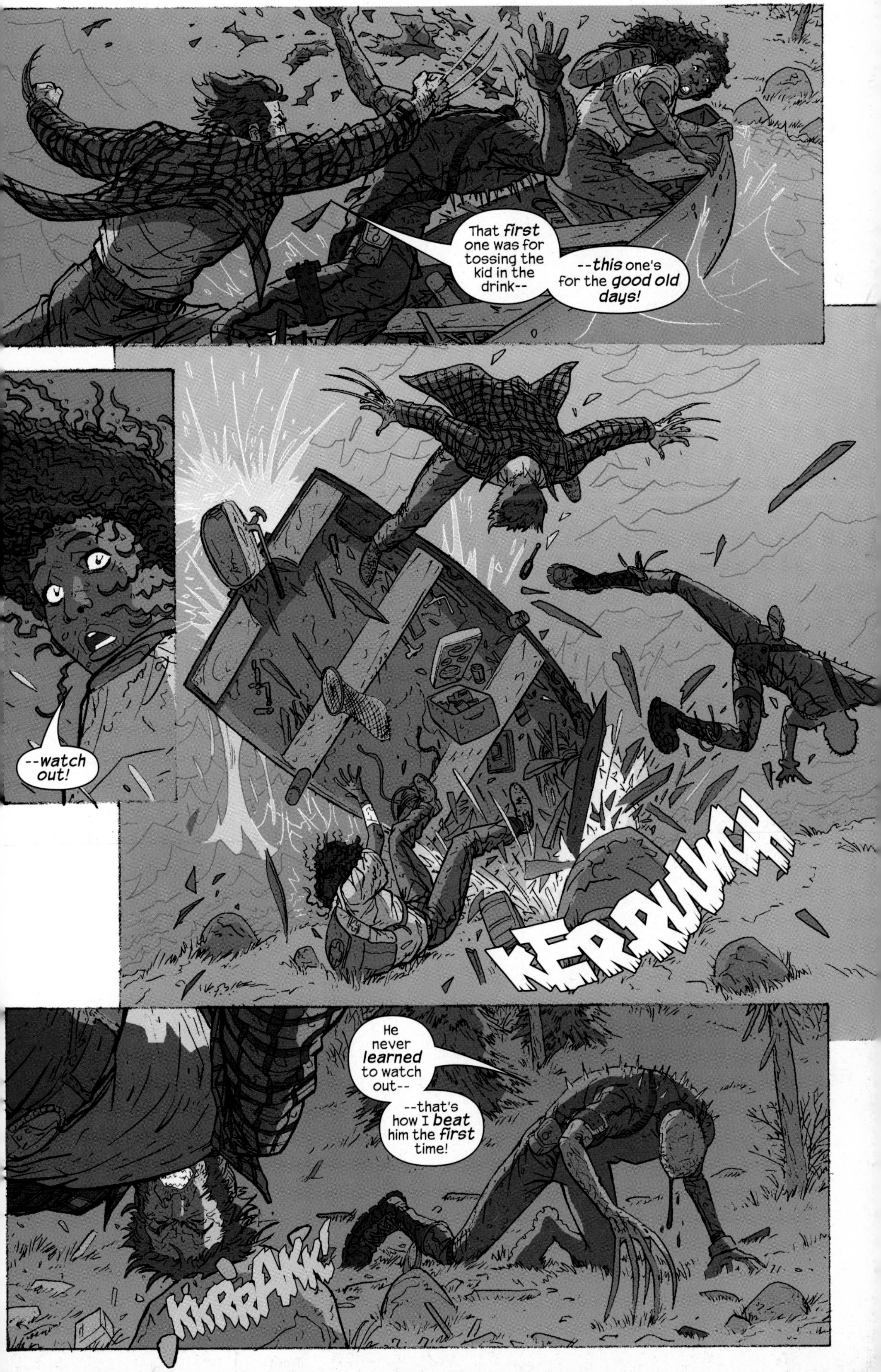
That first one was for tossing the kid in the drink--
--this one's for the good old days!
--watch out!
KERRUNCH
He never learned to watch out--
--that's how I beat him the first time!
KKRRAKK!

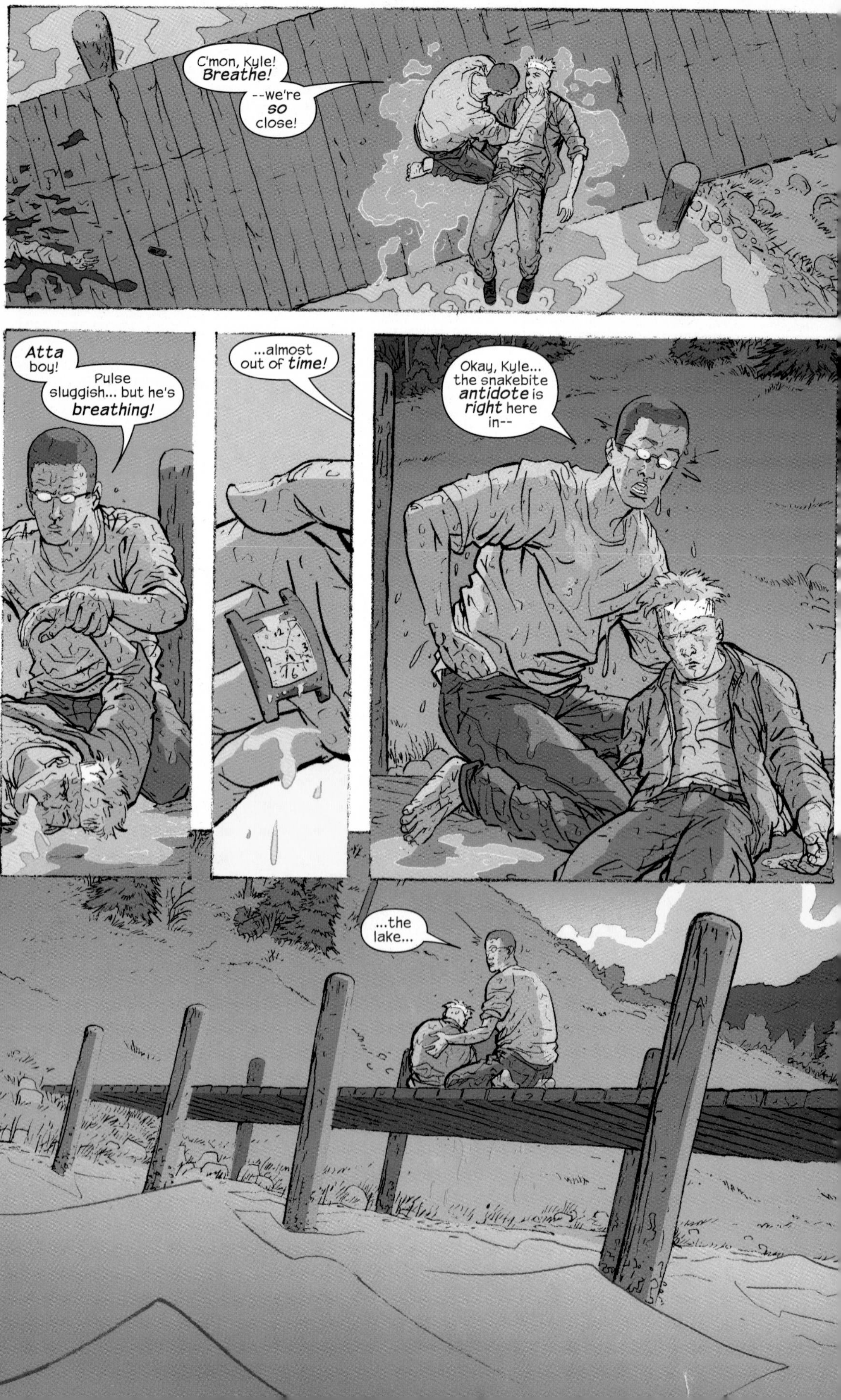
C'mon, Kyle! Breathe!
--we're so close!
Atta boy!
Pulse sluggish... but he's breathing!
...almost out of time!
Okay, Kyle... the snakebite antidote is right here in--
...the lake...

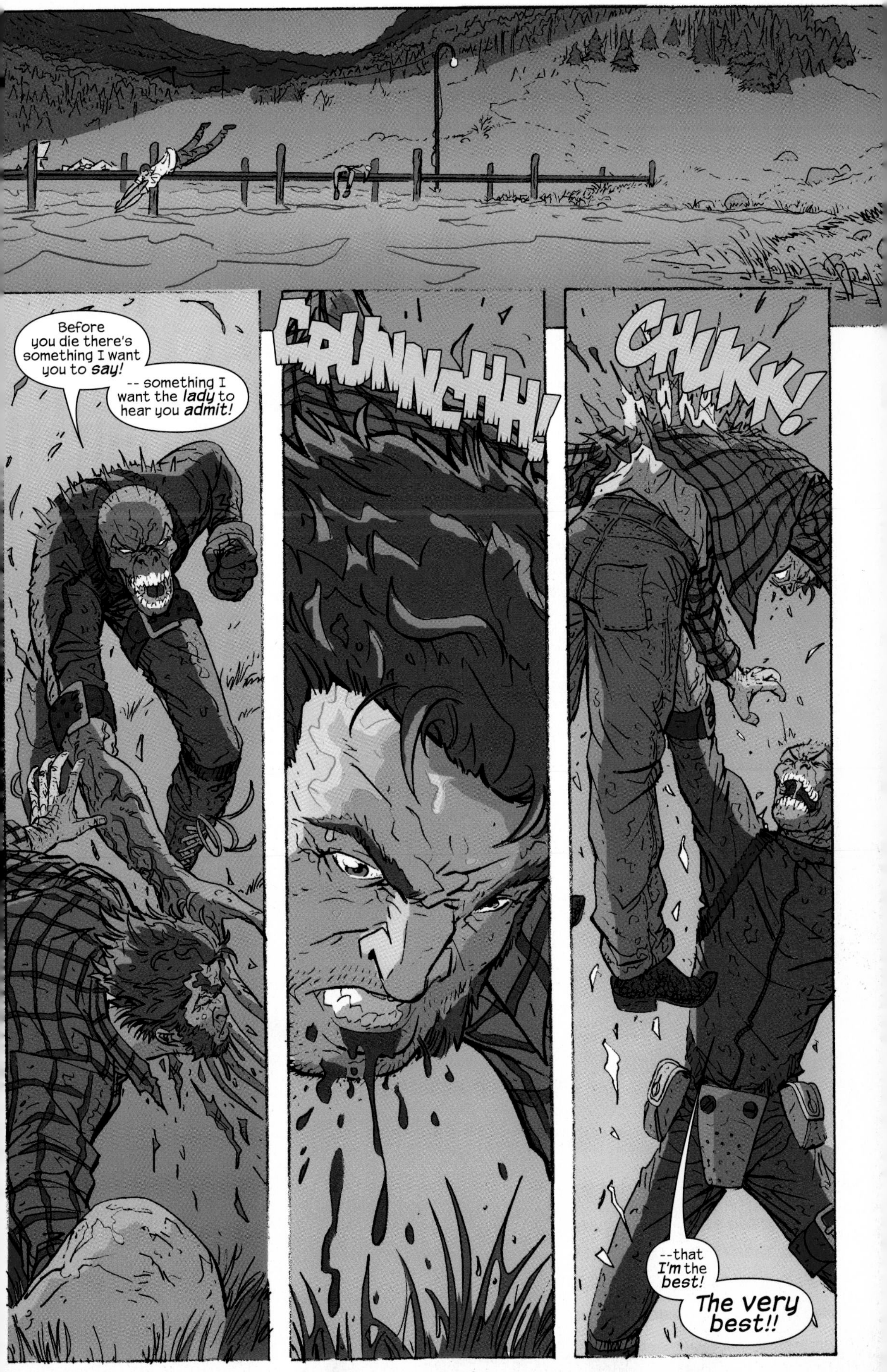
Before you die there's something I want you to say!
-- something I want the lady to hear you admit!
CRUNNCHHH!
CHUKK!
--that I'm the best!
The very best!!

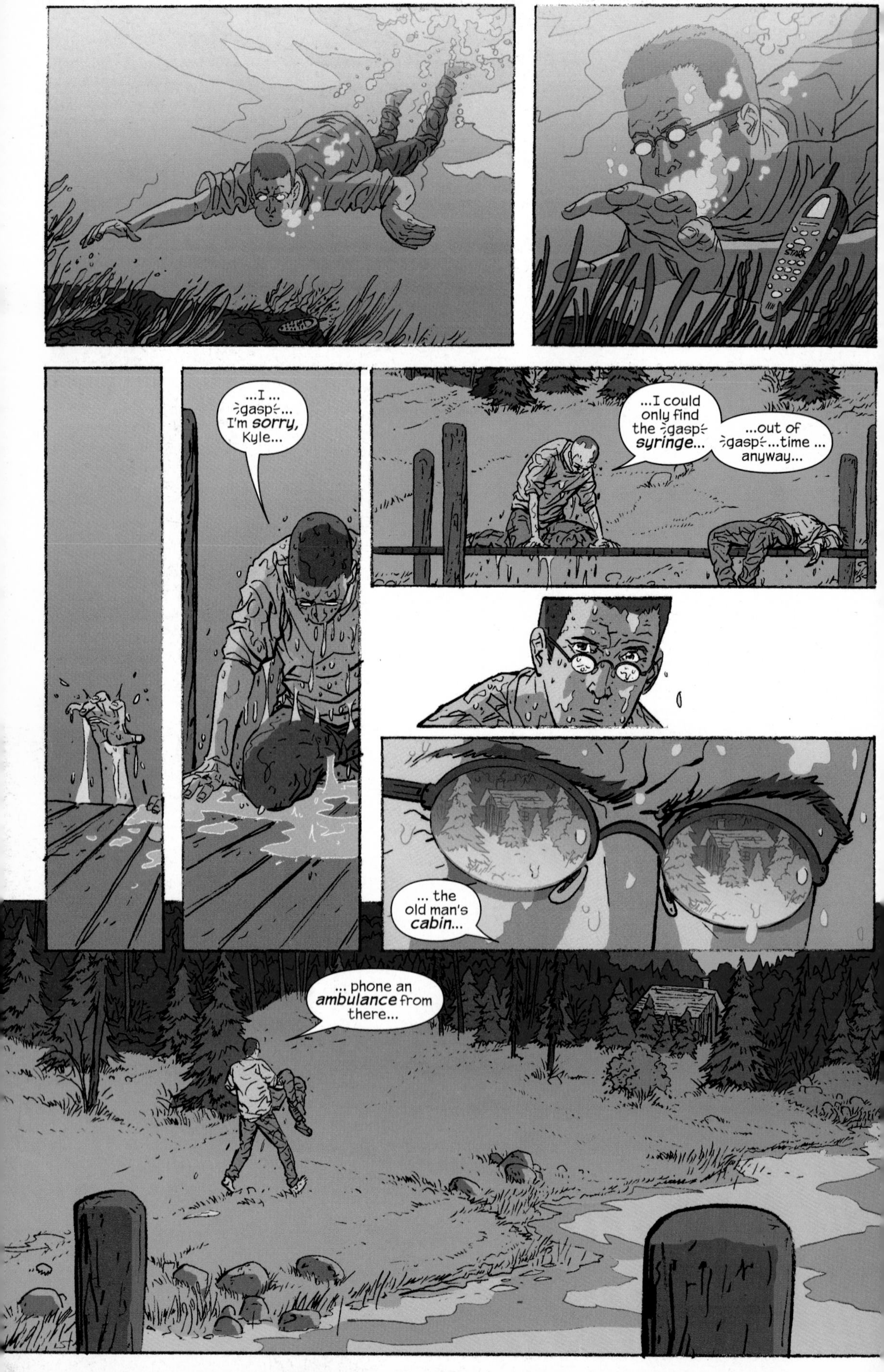
...I ... ⁓gasp⁓... I'm *sorry,* Kyle...
...I could only find the ⁓gasp⁓ *syringe*...
...out of ⁓gasp⁓...time ... anyway...
... the old man's *cabin*...
... phone an *ambulance* from there...

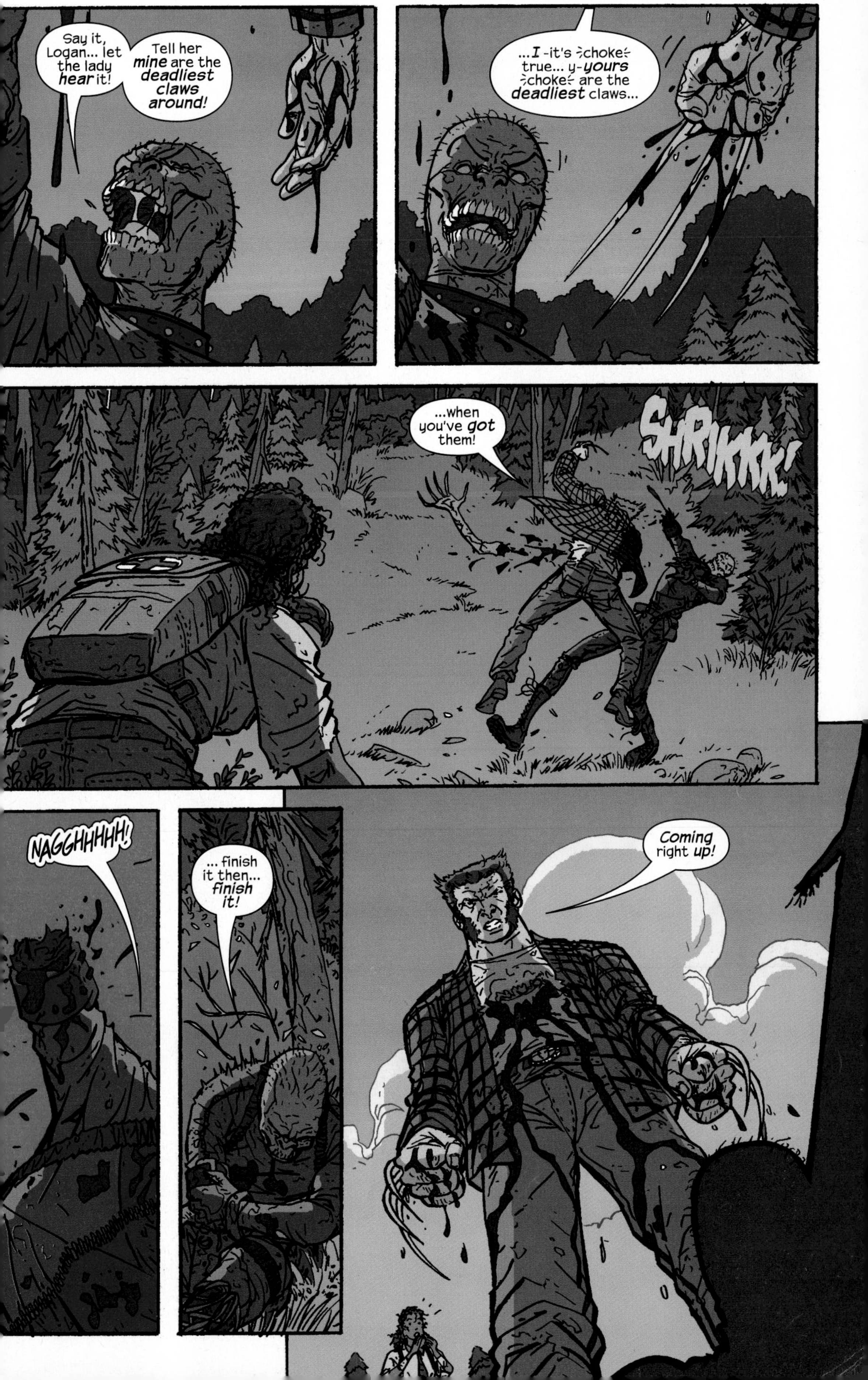
Say it, Logan... let the lady hear it!
Tell her mine are the deadliest claws around!
...I -it's ~choke~ true... y-yours ~choke~ are the deadliest claws...
...when you've got them!
SHRIKKK!
NAGGHHHHH!
... finish it then... finish it!
Coming right up!

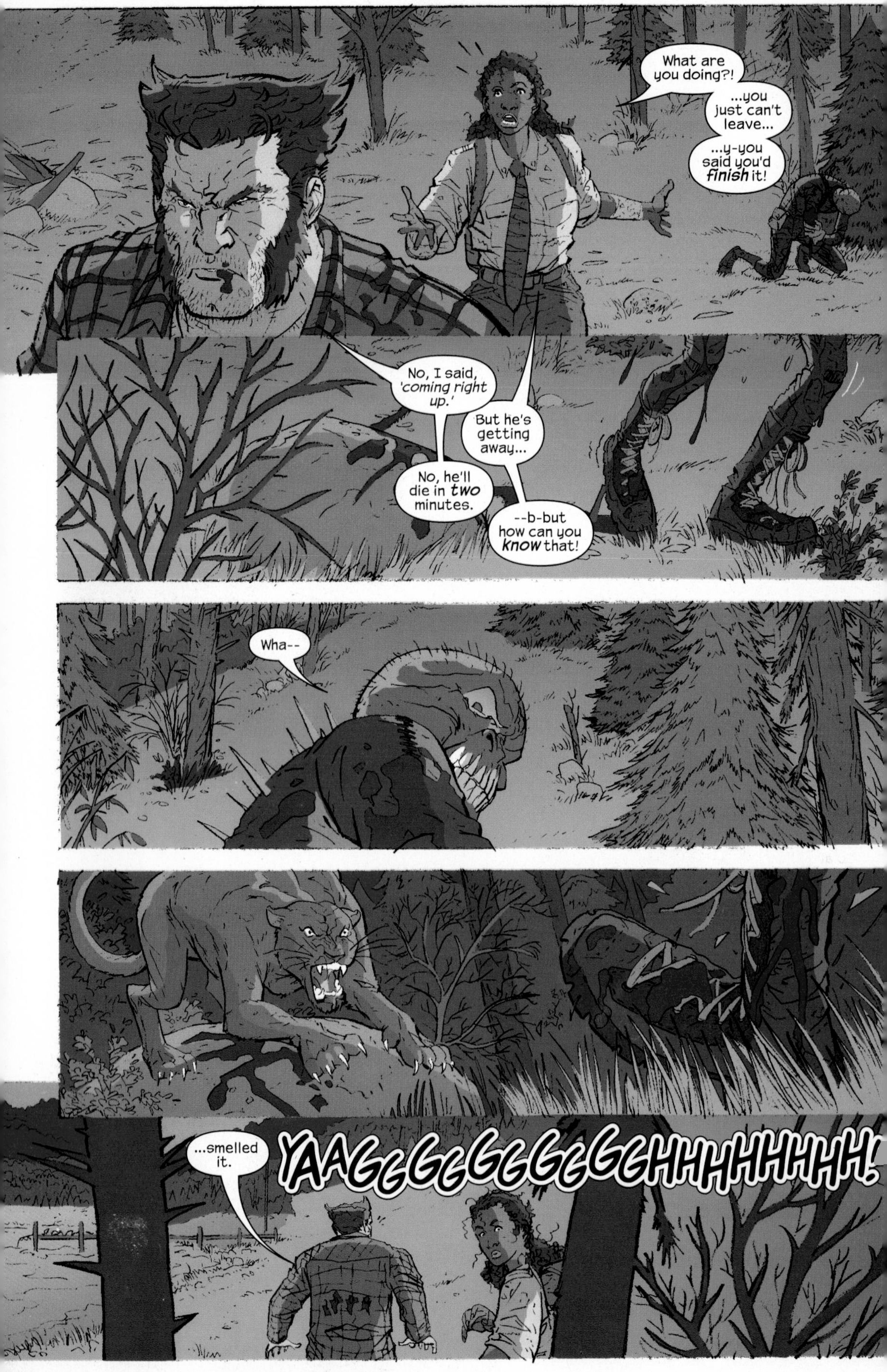
What are you doing?!
...you just can't leave...
...y-you said you'd finish it!
No, I said, 'coming right up.'
But he's getting away...
No, he'll die in two minutes.
--b-but how can you know that!
Wha--
...smelled it.
YAAGGGGGGGGGGHHHHHHHH!

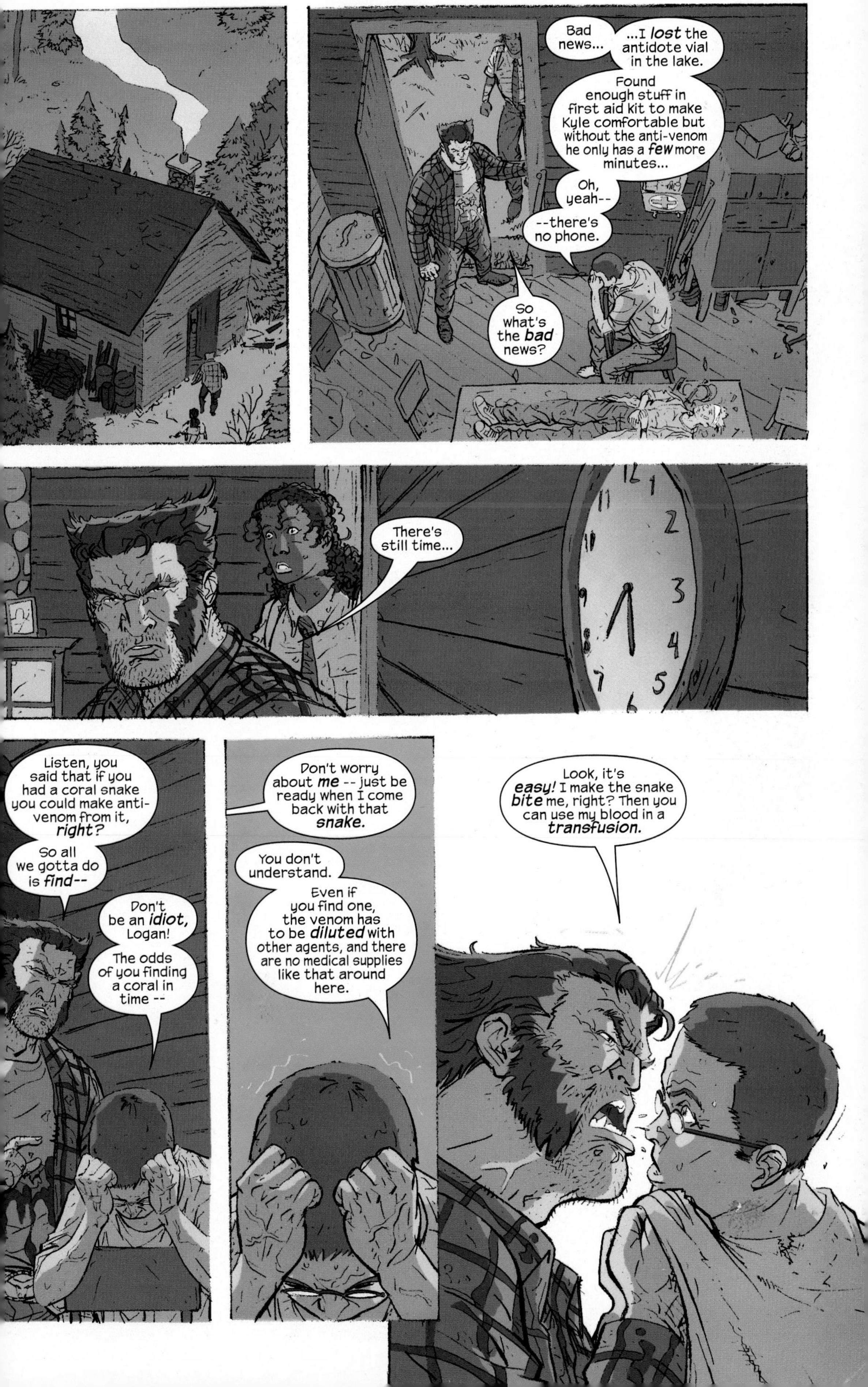
Bad news...
...I lost the antidote vial in the lake.
Found enough stuff in first aid kit to make Kyle comfortable but without the anti-venom he only has a few more minutes...
Oh, yeah--
--there's no phone.
So what's the bad news?
There's still time...
Listen, you said that if you had a coral snake you could make anti-venom from it, right?
So all we gotta do is find--
Don't be an idiot, Logan!
The odds of you finding a coral in time --
Don't worry about me -- just be ready when I come back with that snake.
You don't understand.
Even if you find one, the venom has to be diluted with other agents, and there are no medical supplies like that around here.
Look, it's easy! I make the snake bite me, right? Then you can use my blood in a transfusion.

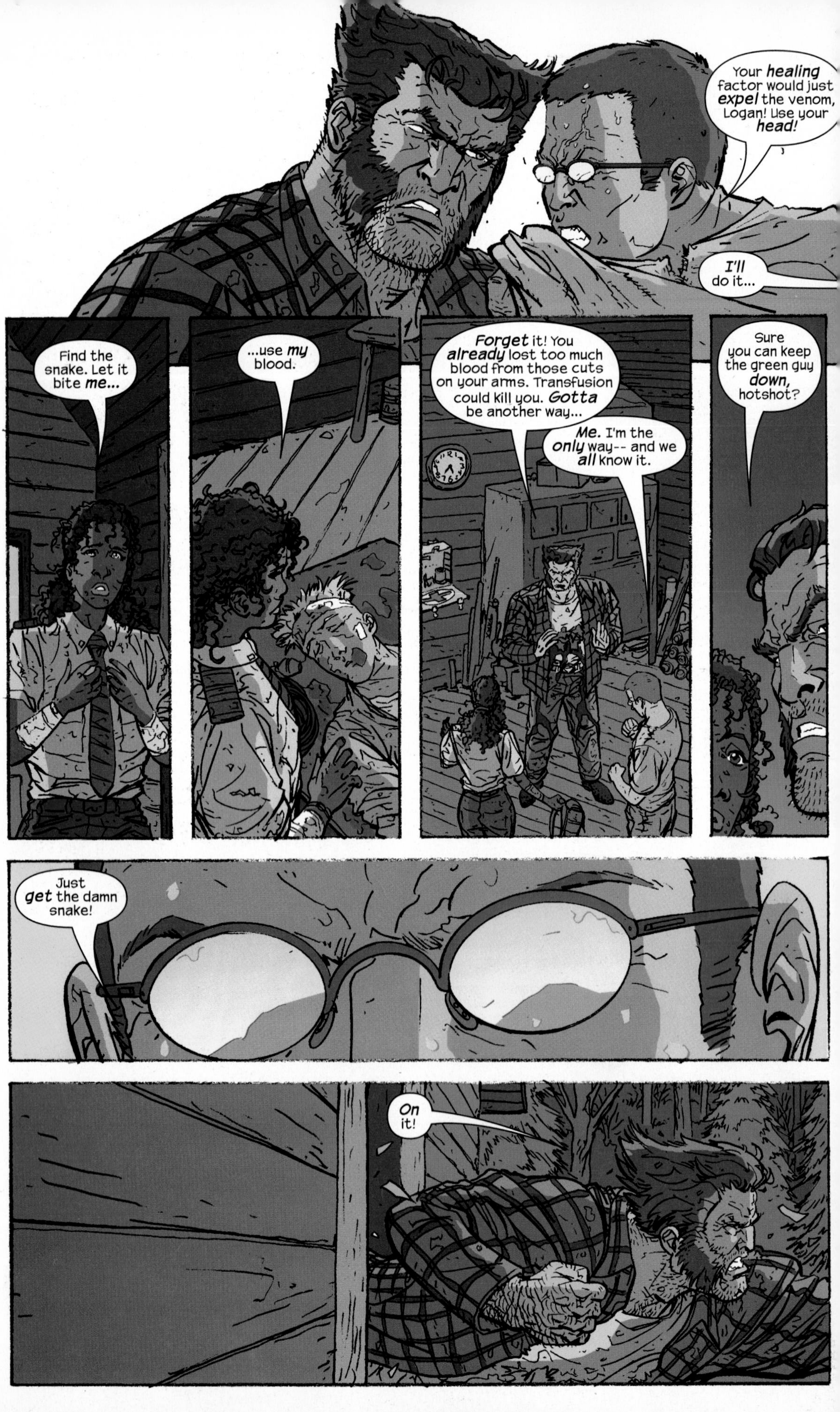
Your *healing* factor would just *expel* the venom, Logan! Use your *head!*
I'll do it...
Find the snake. Let it bite *me...*
...use *my* blood.
Forget it! You *already* lost too much blood from those cuts on your arms. Transfusion could kill you. *Gotta* be another way...
Me. I'm the *only* way-- and we *all* know it.
Sure you can keep the green guy *down,* hotshot?
Just *get* the damn snake!
On it!

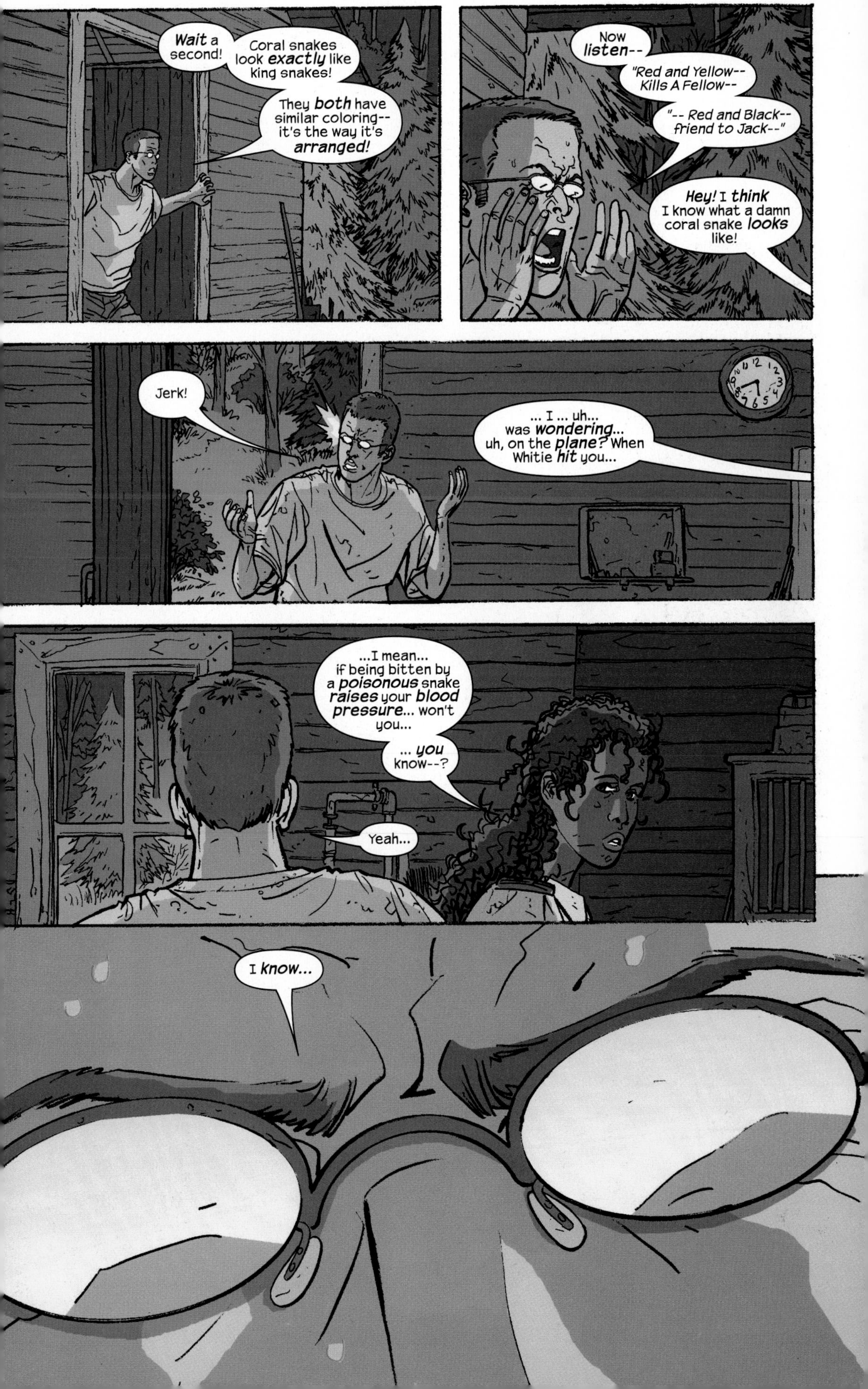
Wait a second!
Coral snakes look exactly like king snakes!
They both have similar coloring-- it's the way it's arranged!
Now listen--
"Red and Yellow-- Kills A Fellow--
"-- Red and Black-- friend to Jack--"
Hey! I think I know what a damn coral snake looks like!
Jerk!
... I ... uh... was wondering... uh, on the plane? When Whitie hit you...
...I mean... if being bitten by a poisonous snake raises your blood pressure... won't you...
... you know--?
Yeah...
I know...

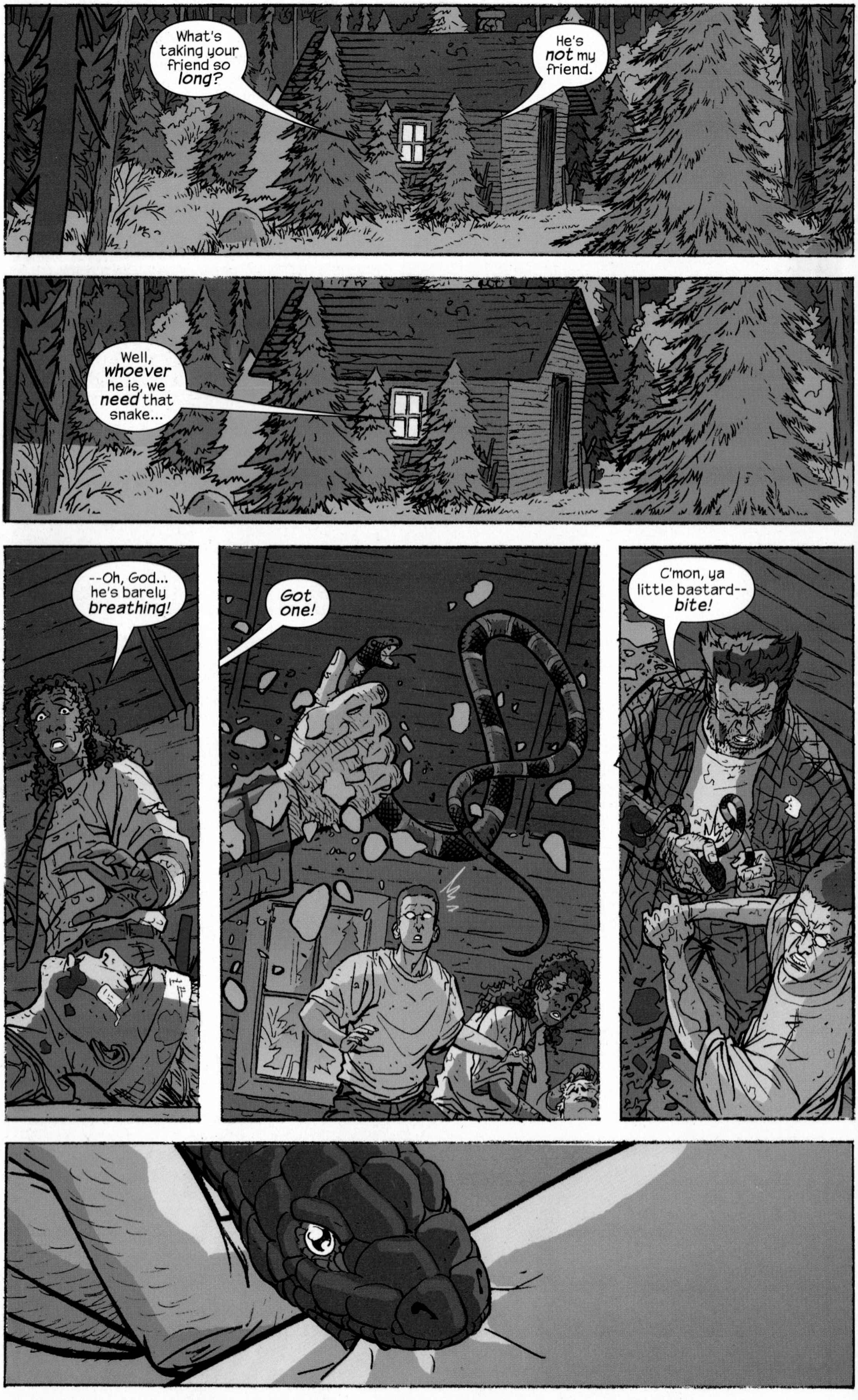
What's taking your friend so *long?*
He's *not* my friend.
Well, *whoever* he is, we *need* that snake...
--Oh, God... he's barely *breathing!*
Got one!
C'mon, ya little bastard-- *bite!*

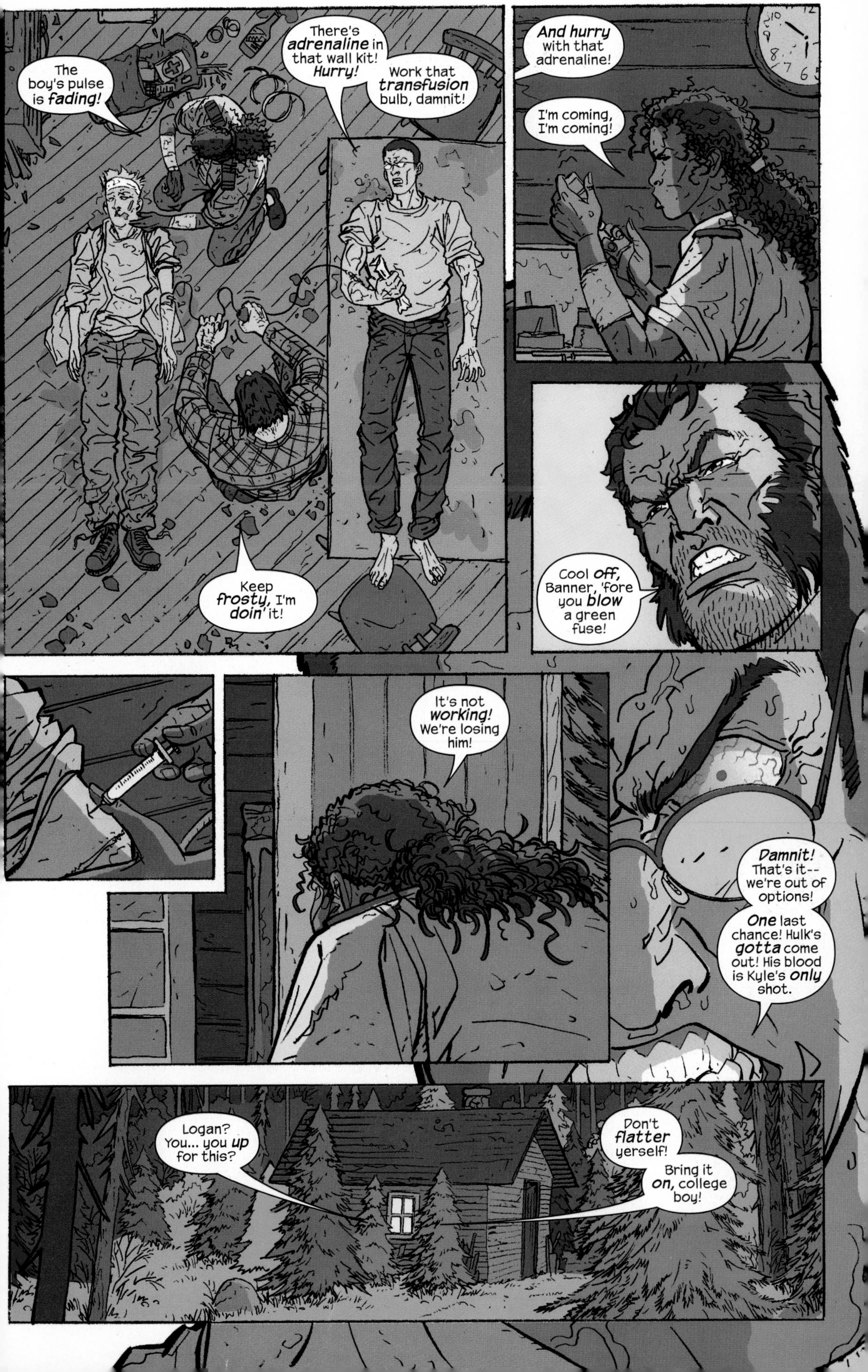

The boy's pulse is fading!
There's adrenaline in that wall kit! Hurry!
Work that transfusion bulb, damnit!
Keep frosty, I'm doin' it!
And hurry with that adrenaline!
I'm coming, I'm coming!
Cool off, Banner, 'fore you blow a green fuse!
It's not working! We're losing him!
Damnit! That's it-- we're out of options!
One last chance! Hulk's gotta come out! His blood is Kyle's only shot.
Logan? You... you up for this?
Don't flatter yerself!
Bring it on, college boy!

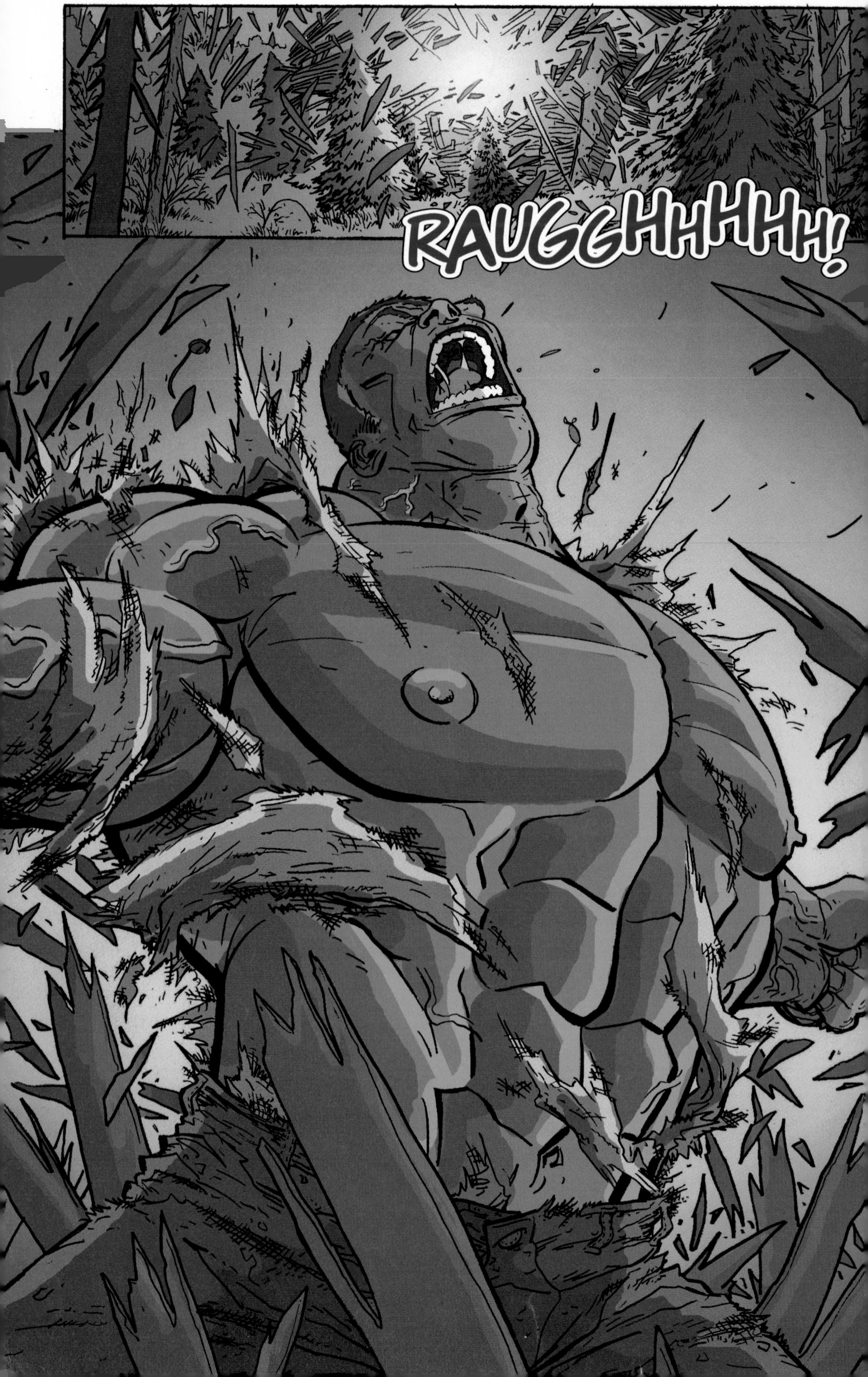
RAUGGHHHHH!

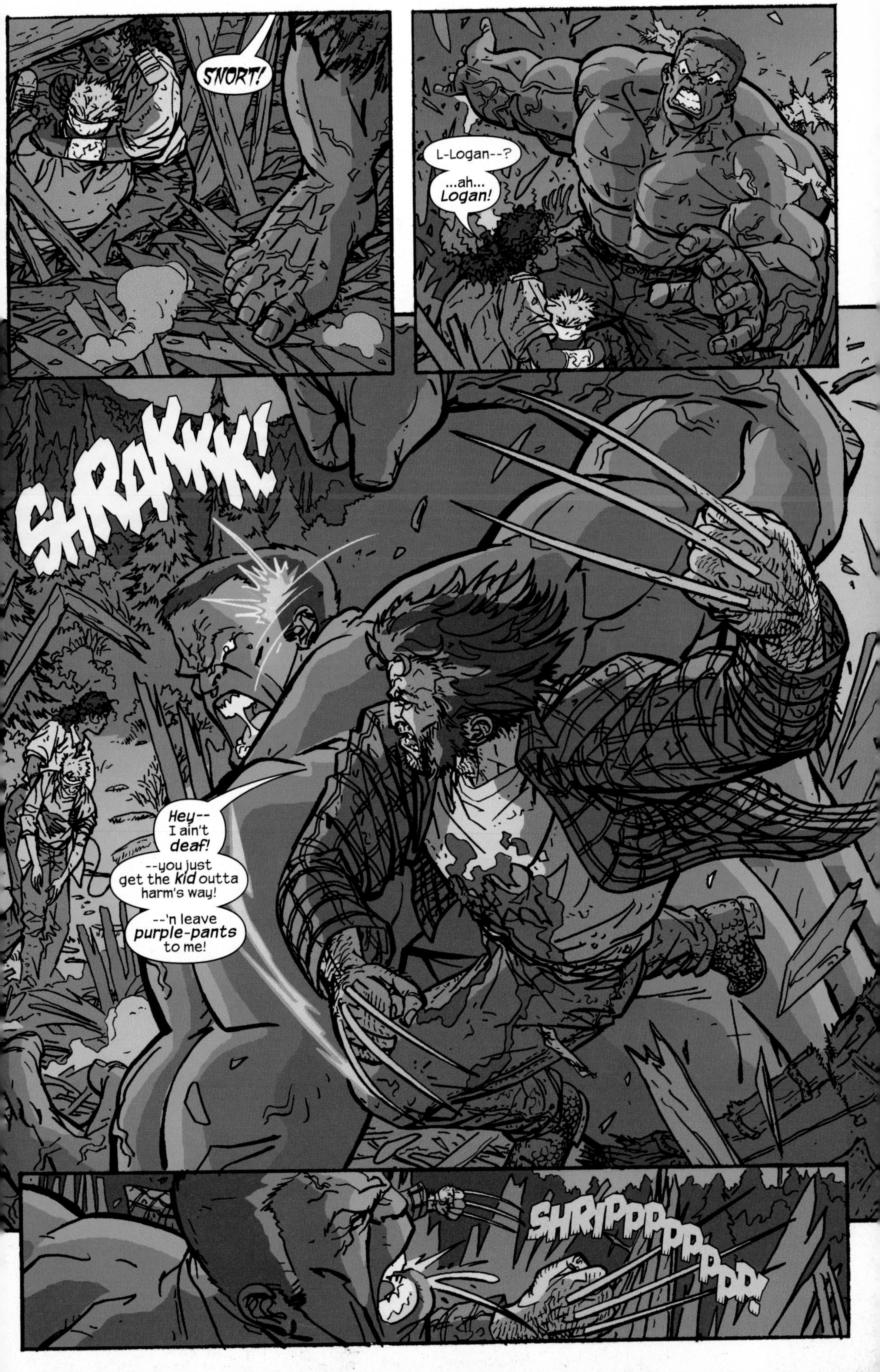
SNORT!
L-Logan--?
...ah... Logan!
SHRAKKK!
Hey-- I ain't deaf!
--you just get the kid outta harm's way!
--'n leave purple-pants to me!
SHRIPPPPPPPPPP!

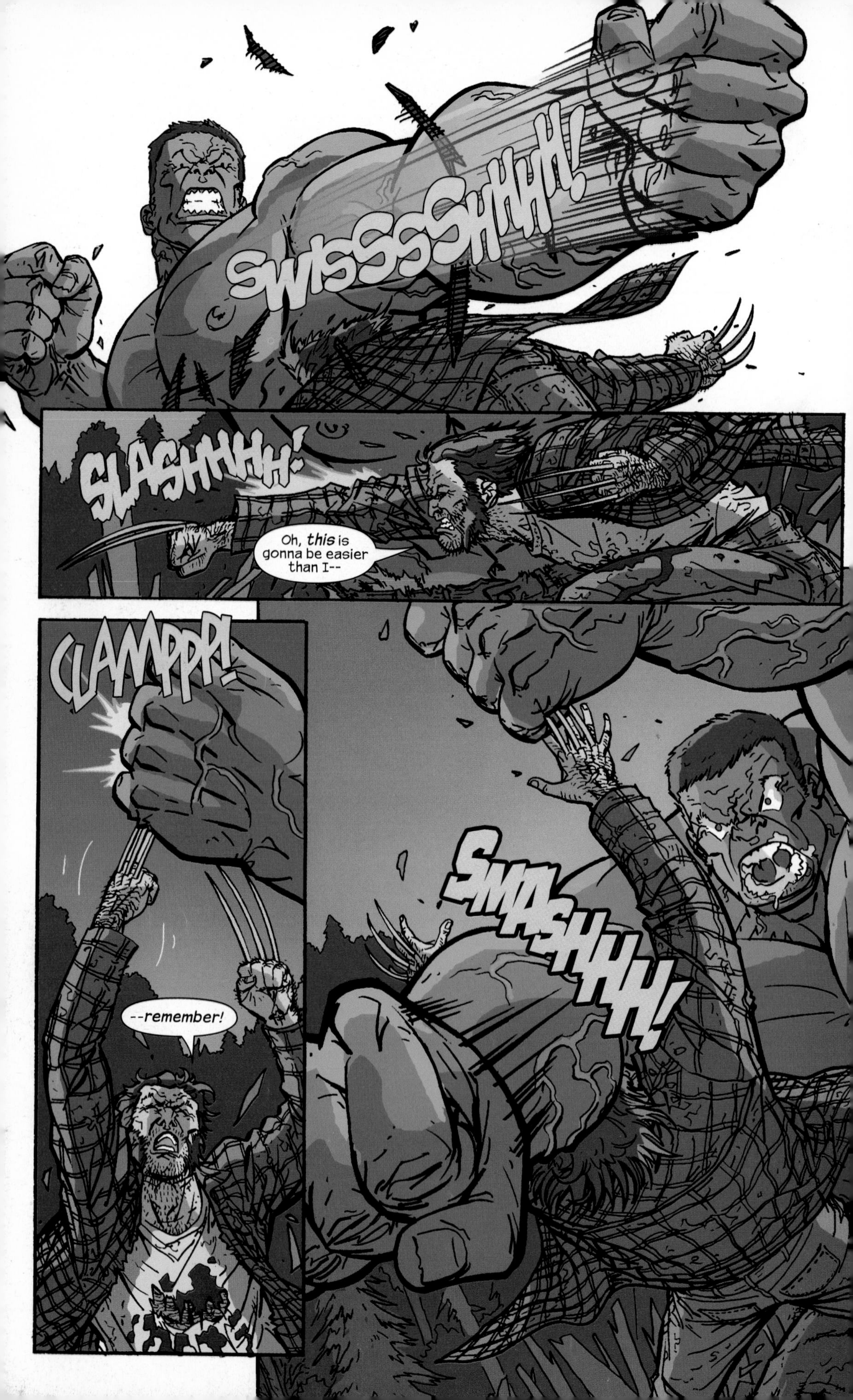
SWISSSSHHHH!
SLASHHHHH!
Oh, this is gonna be easier than I--
CLAMPPP!
--remember!
SMASHHHH!

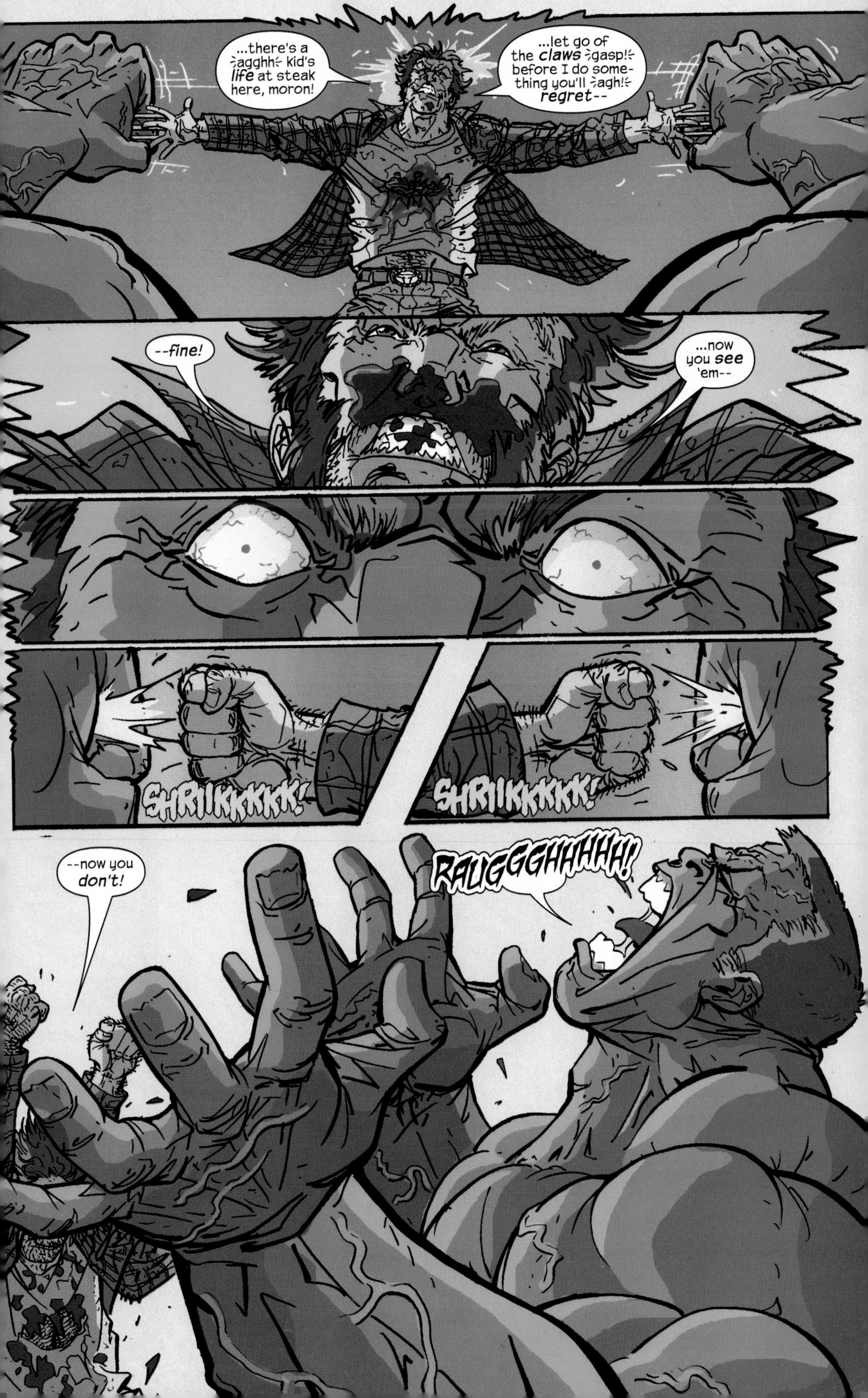
...there's a -agghh- kid's *life* at steak here, moron!
...let go of the **claws** -gasp!- before I do some-thing you'll -agh!- **regret**--
--*fine!*
...now you **see** 'em--
SHRIIKKKKK!
SHRIIKKKKK!
--now you **don't!**
RAUGGGHHHHH!

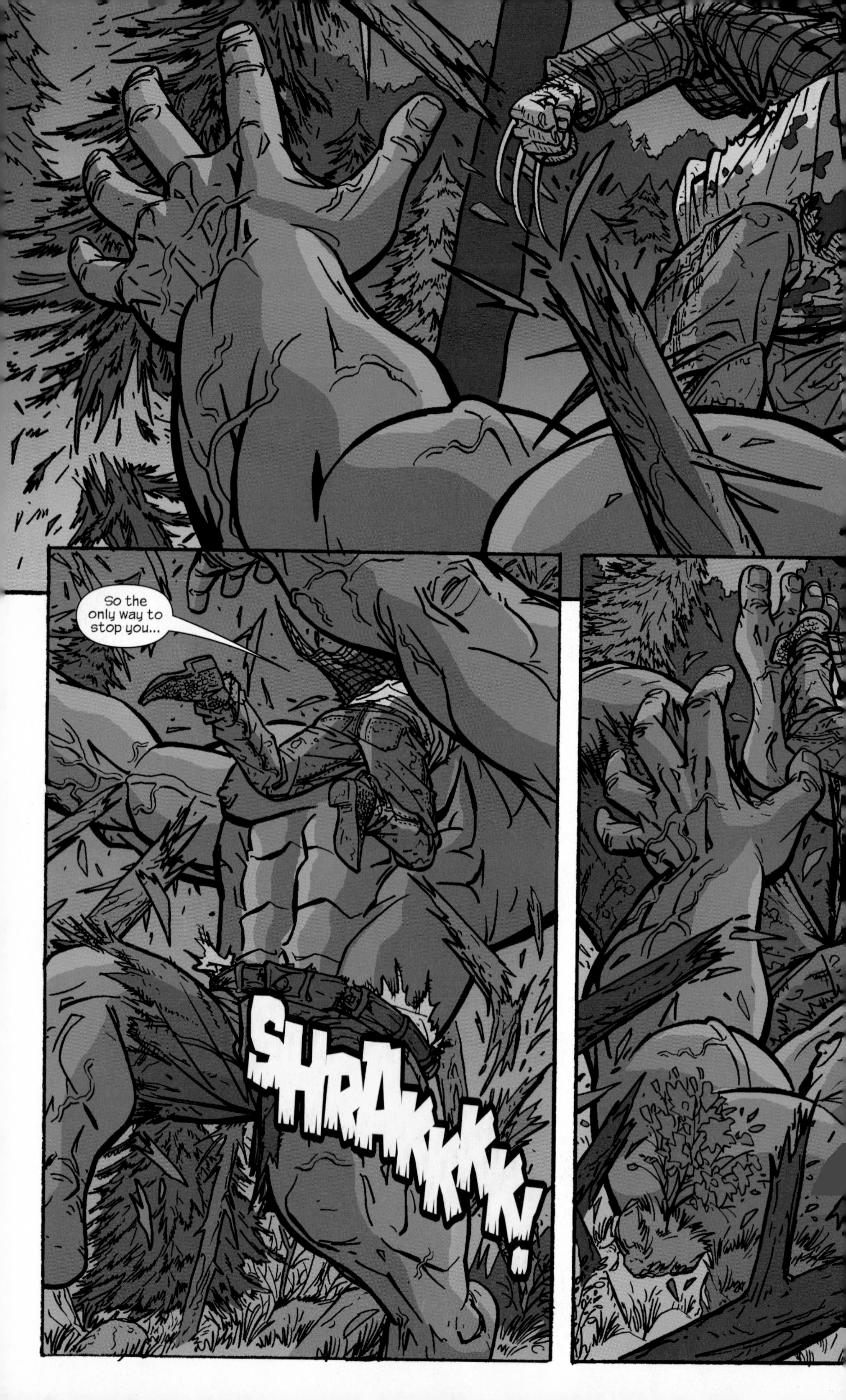
So the only way to stop you...
SHRAKKKK!

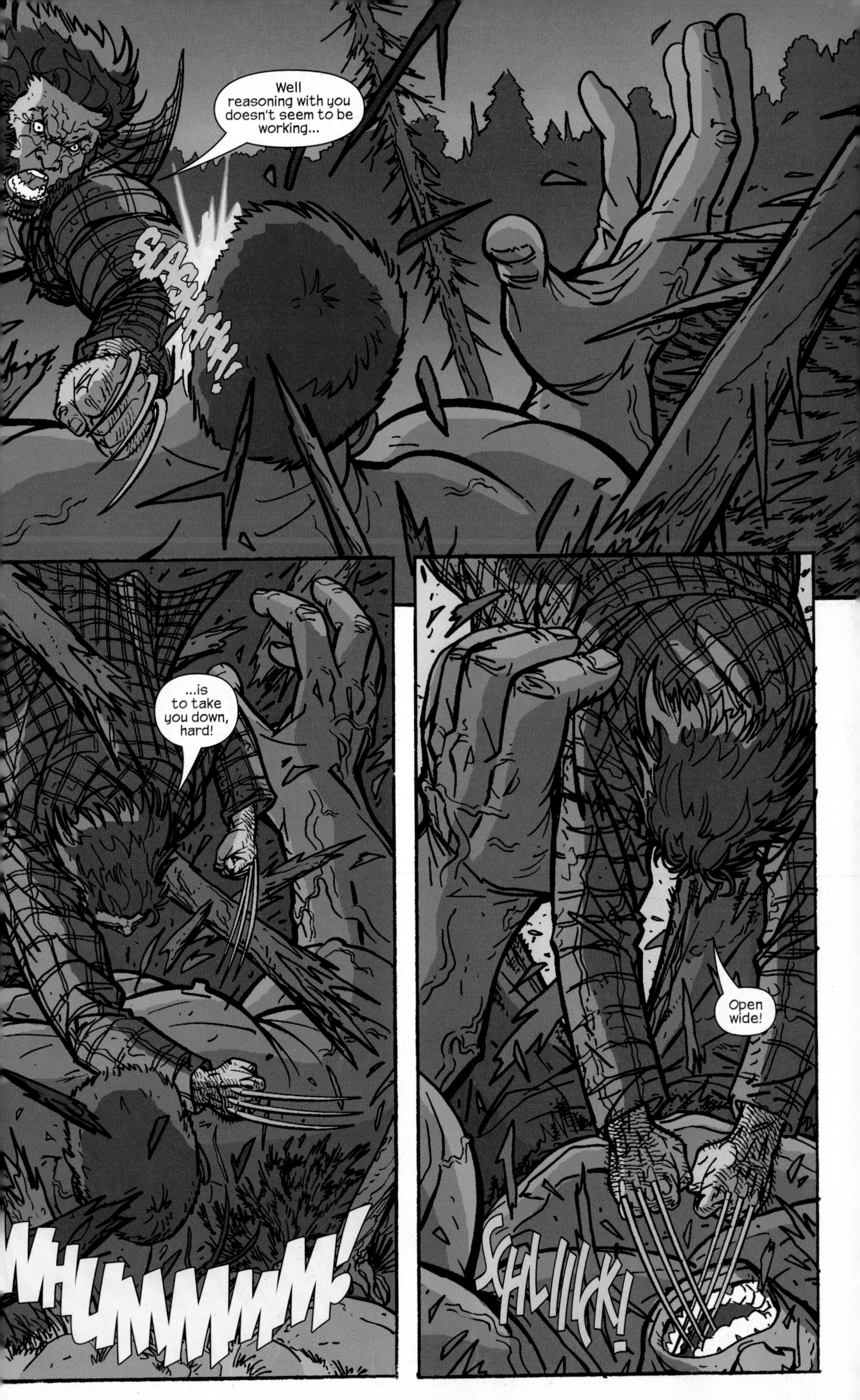
Well reasoning with you doesn't seem to be working...
SLASHHH!
...is to take you down, hard!
WHUMMMM!
Open wide!
SCHLIIIK!

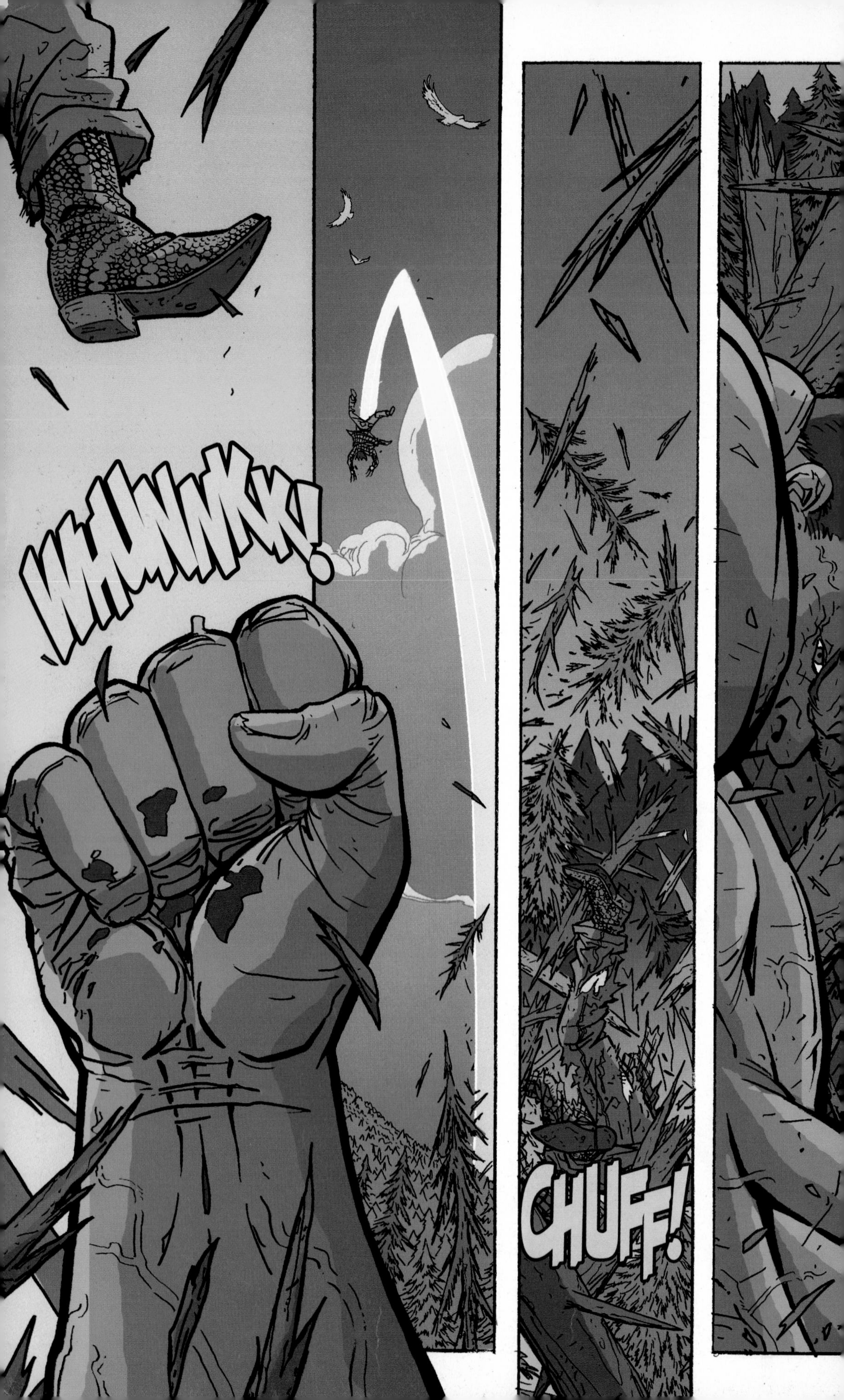
WHUNNKK!
CHUFF!

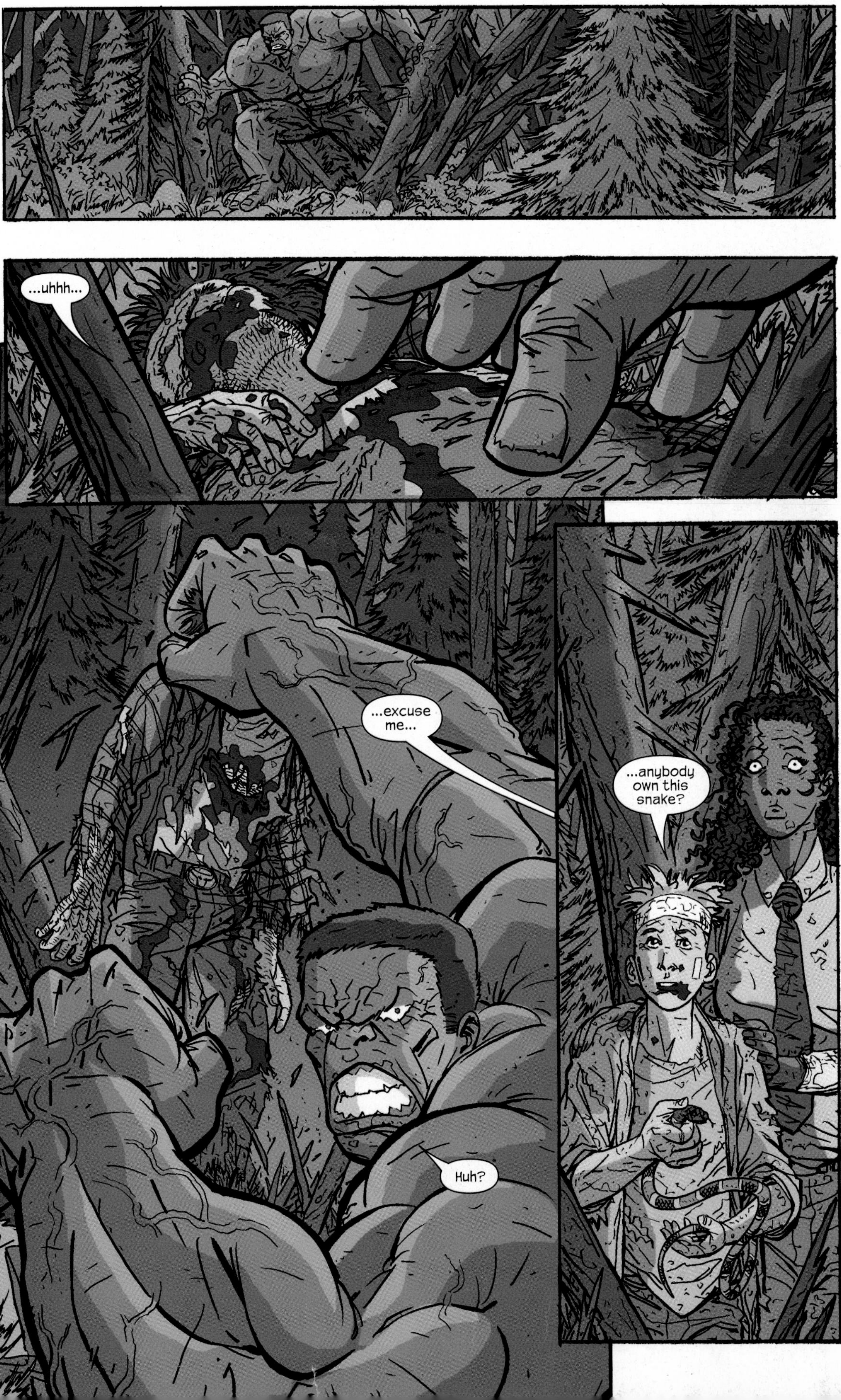
...uhhh...
...excuse me...
Huh?
...anybody own this snake?

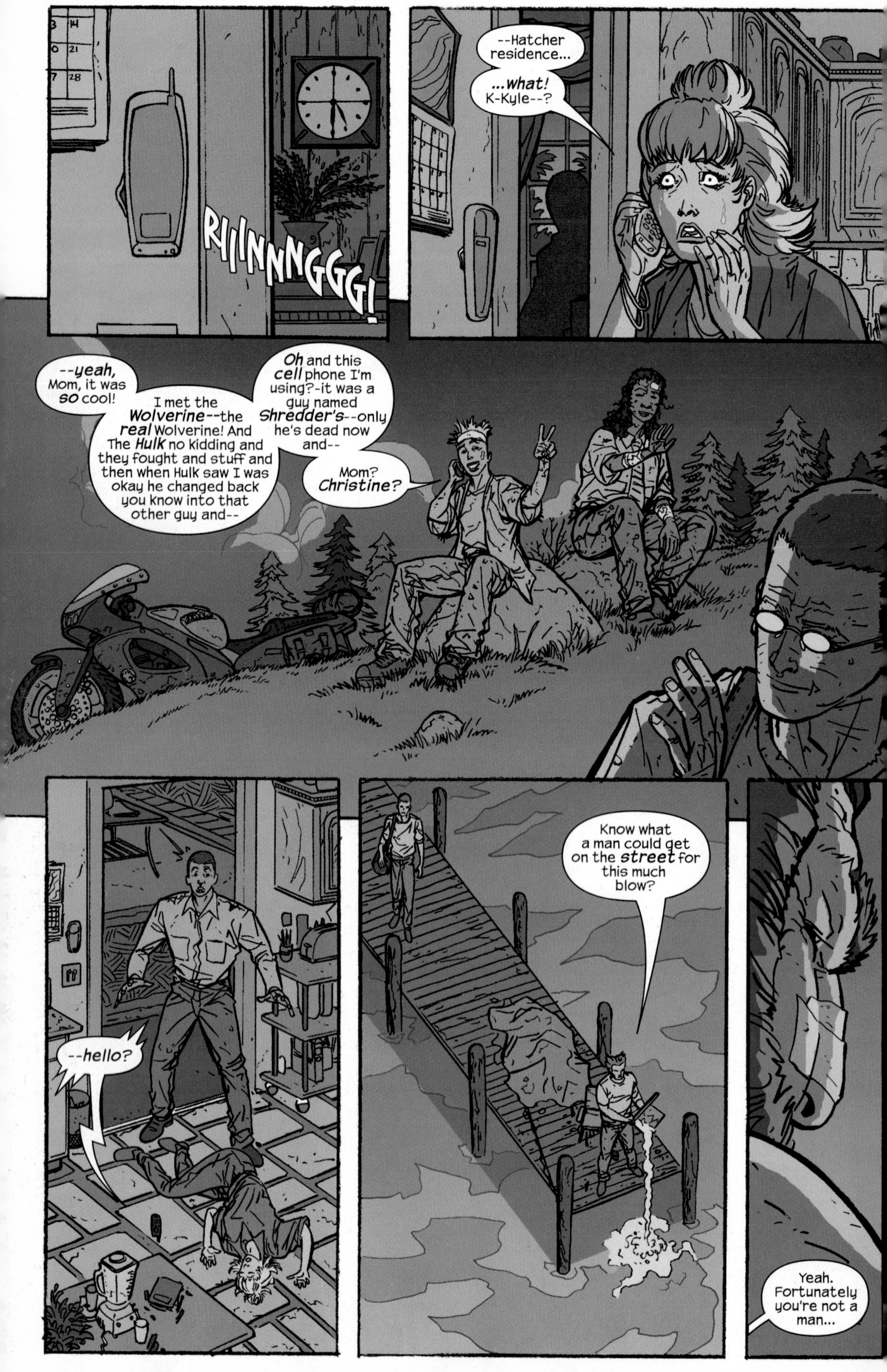
RIIINNNGGG!
--Hatcher residence...
...what! K-Kyle--?
--yeah, Mom, it was so cool!
I met the Wolverine--the real Wolverine! And The Hulk no kidding and they fought and stuff and then when Hulk saw I was okay he changed back you know into that other guy and--
Oh and this cell phone I'm using?-it was a guy named Shredder's--only he's dead now and--
Mom? Christine?
--hello?
Know what a man could get on the street for this much blow?
Yeah. Fortunately you're not a man...

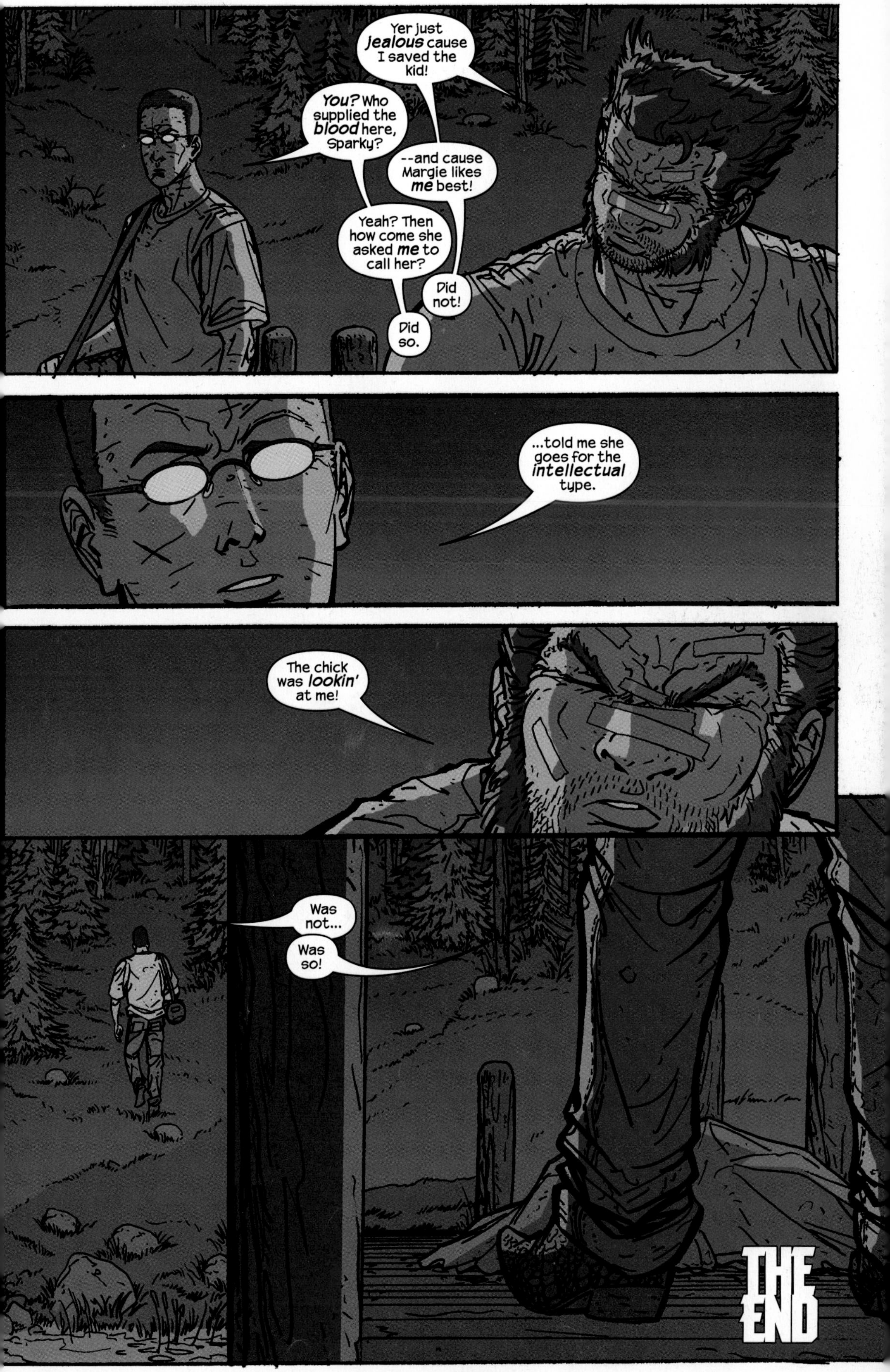
Yer just jealous cause I saved the kid!
You? Who supplied the blood here, Sparky?
--and cause Margie likes me best!
Yeah? Then how come she asked me to call her?
Did not!
Did so.
...told me she goes for the intellectual type.
The chick was lookin' at me!
Was not...
Was so!
THE END

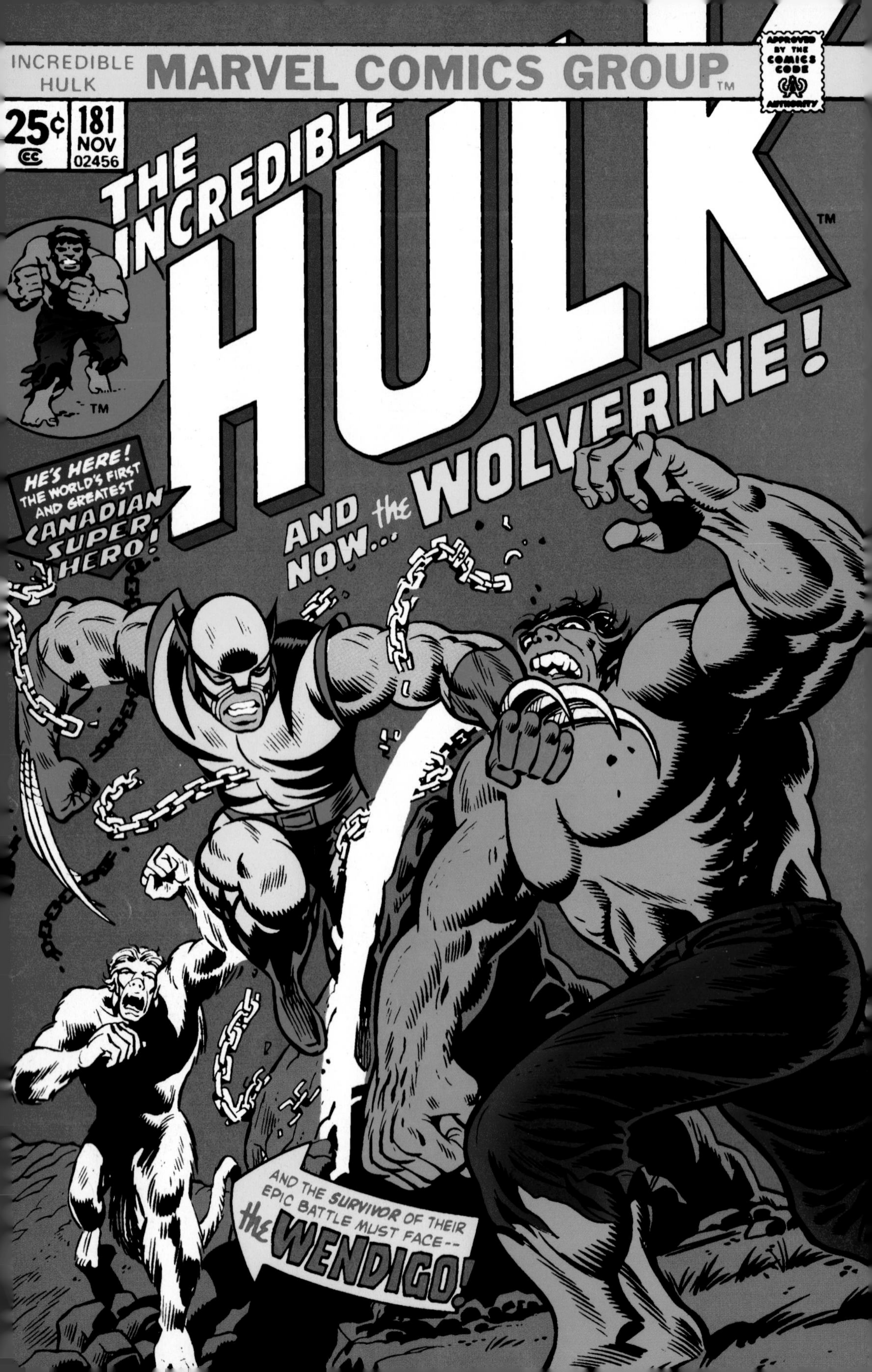
INCREDIBLE HULK
MARVEL COMICS GROUP
APPROVED BY THE COMICS CODE AUTHORITY
25¢
181 NOV 02456
THE INCREDIBLE HULK
HE'S HERE! THE WORLD'S FIRST AND GREATEST CANADIAN SUPER-HERO!
AND NOW... THE WOLVERINE!
AND THE SURVIVOR OF THEIR EPIC BATTLE MUST FACE-- THE WENDIGO!

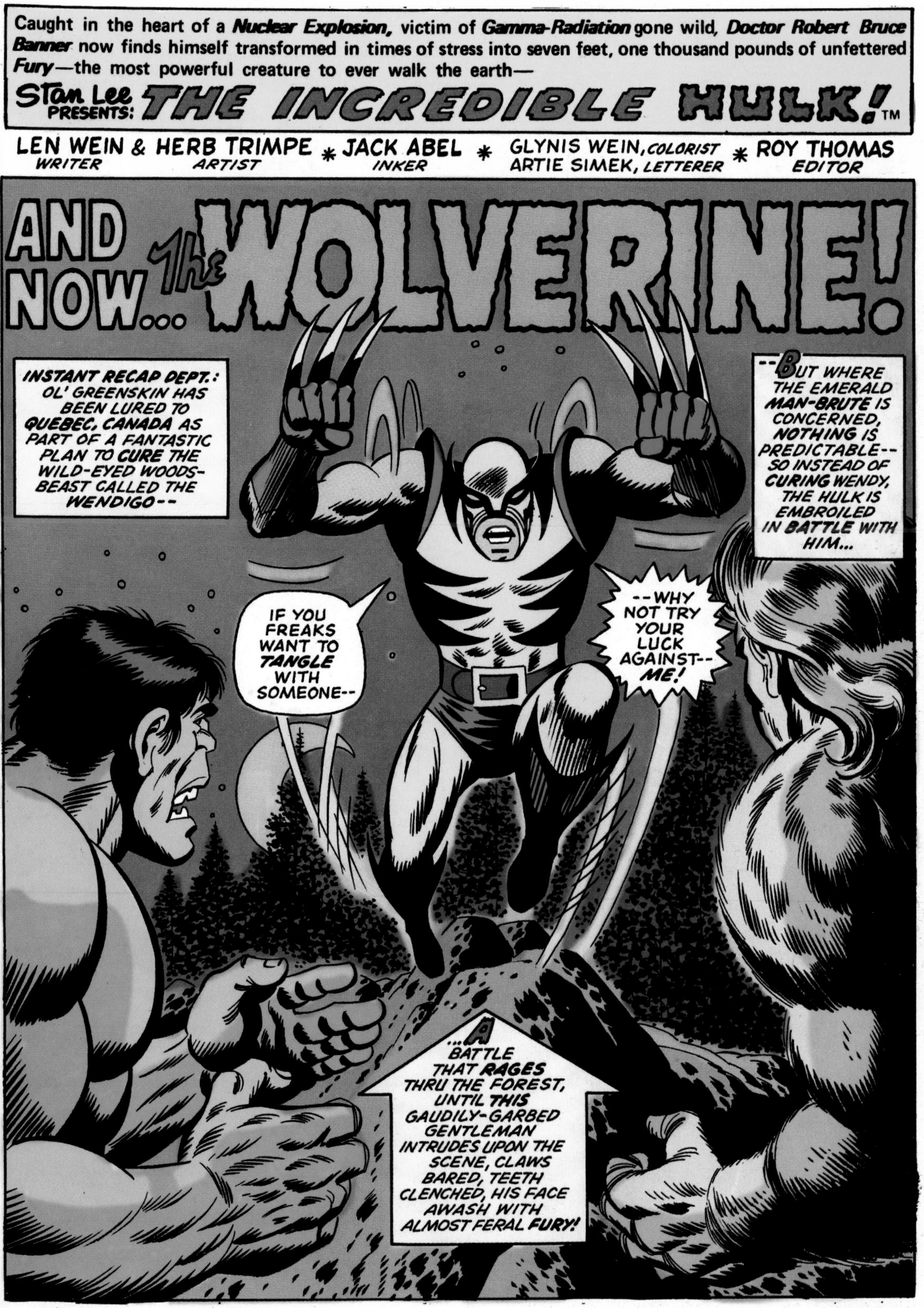
Caught in the heart of a Nuclear Explosion, victim of Gamma-Radiation gone wild, Doctor Robert Bruce Banner now finds himself transformed in times of stress into seven feet, one thousand pounds of unfettered Fury—the most powerful creature to ever walk the earth—
Stan Lee PRESENTS: THE INCREDIBLE HULK! TM
LEN WEIN & HERB TRIMPE WRITER ARTIST * JACK ABEL INKER * GLYNIS WEIN, COLORIST ARTIE SIMEK, LETTERER * ROY THOMAS EDITOR
AND NOW... The WOLVERINE!
INSTANT RECAP DEPT.: OL' GREENSKIN HAS BEEN LURED TO QUEBEC, CANADA AS PART OF A FANTASTIC PLAN TO CURE THE WILD-EYED WOODS-BEAST CALLED THE WENDIGO--
--BUT WHERE THE EMERALD MAN-BRUTE IS CONCERNED, NOTHING IS PREDICTABLE--SO INSTEAD OF CURING WENDY, THE HULK IS EMBROILED IN BATTLE WITH HIM...
IF YOU FREAKS WANT TO TANGLE WITH SOMEONE--
--WHY NOT TRY YOUR LUCK AGAINST--ME!
...A BATTLE THAT RAGES THRU THE FOREST, UNTIL THIS GAUDILY-GARBED GENTLEMAN INTRUDES UPON THE SCENE, CLAWS BARED, TEETH CLENCHED, HIS FACE AWASH WITH ALMOST FERAL FURY!

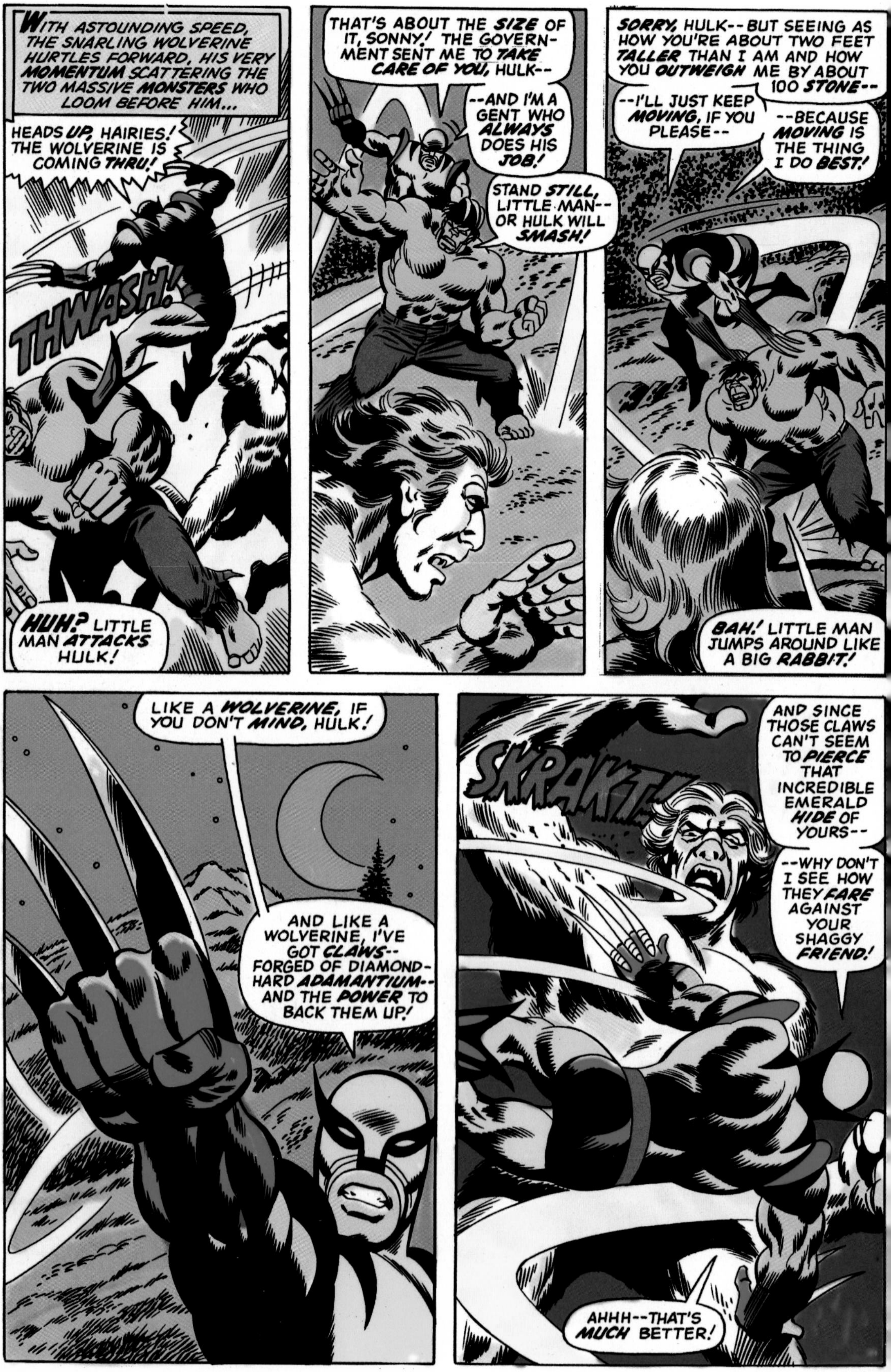

WITH ASTOUNDING SPEED, THE SNARLING WOLVERINE HURTLES FORWARD, HIS VERY MOMENTUM SCATTERING THE TWO MASSIVE MONSTERS WHO LOOM BEFORE HIM...
HEADS UP, HAIRIES! THE WOLVERINE IS COMING THRU!
THWASH!
HUH? LITTLE MAN ATTACKS HULK!
THAT'S ABOUT THE SIZE OF IT, SONNY! THE GOVERNMENT SENT ME TO TAKE CARE OF YOU, HULK--
--AND I'M A GENT WHO ALWAYS DOES HIS JOB!
STAND STILL, LITTLE MAN--OR HULK WILL SMASH!
SORRY, HULK--BUT SEEING AS HOW YOU'RE ABOUT TWO FEET TALLER THAN I AM AND HOW YOU OUTWEIGH ME BY ABOUT 100 STONE--
--I'LL JUST KEEP MOVING, IF YOU PLEASE--
--BECAUSE MOVING IS THE THING I DO BEST!
BAH! LITTLE MAN JUMPS AROUND LIKE A BIG RABBIT!
LIKE A WOLVERINE, IF YOU DON'T MIND, HULK!
AND LIKE A WOLVERINE, I'VE GOT CLAWS--FORGED OF DIAMOND-HARD ADAMANTIUM--AND THE POWER TO BACK THEM UP!
SKRAKT!
AND SINCE THOSE CLAWS CAN'T SEEM TO PIERCE THAT INCREDIBLE EMERALD HIDE OF YOURS--
--WHY DON'T I SEE HOW THEY FARE AGAINST YOUR SHAGGY FRIEND!
AHHH--THAT'S MUCH BETTER!

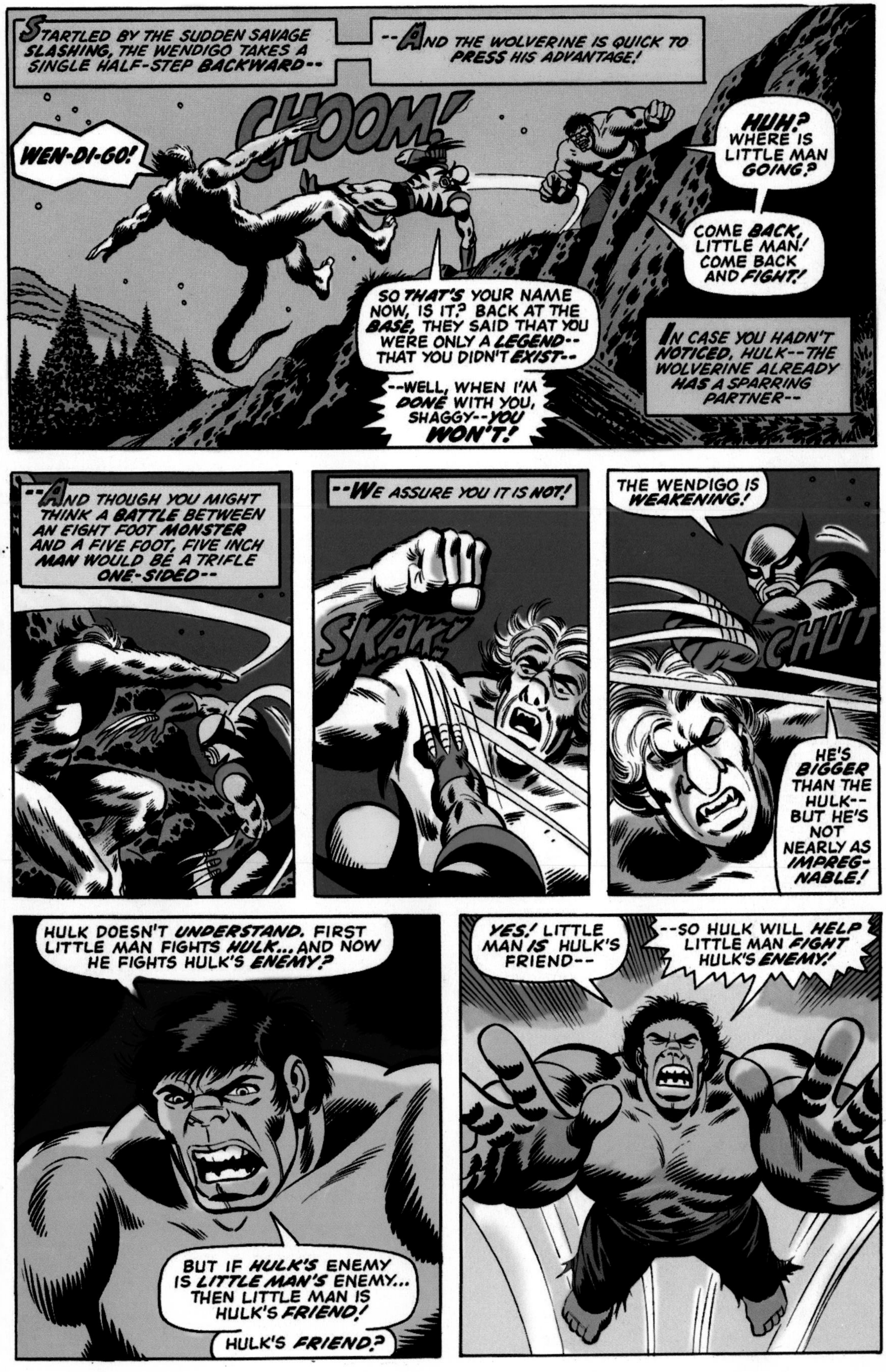

STARTLED BY THE SUDDEN SAVAGE SLASHING, THE WENDIGO TAKES A SINGLE HALF-STEP BACKWARD--
--AND THE WOLVERINE IS QUICK TO PRESS HIS ADVANTAGE!
CHOOM!
WEN-DI-GO!
HUH? WHERE IS LITTLE MAN GOING?
COME BACK, LITTLE MAN! COME BACK AND FIGHT!
SO THAT'S YOUR NAME NOW, IS IT? BACK AT THE BASE, THEY SAID THAT YOU WERE ONLY A LEGEND-- THAT YOU DIDN'T EXIST--
--WELL, WHEN I'M DONE WITH YOU, SHAGGY--YOU WON'T!
IN CASE YOU HADN'T NOTICED, HULK--THE WOLVERINE ALREADY HAS A SPARRING PARTNER--
--AND THOUGH YOU MIGHT THINK A BATTLE BETWEEN AN EIGHT FOOT MONSTER AND A FIVE FOOT, FIVE INCH MAN WOULD BE A TRIFLE ONE-SIDED--
--WE ASSURE YOU IT IS NOT!
SKAK!
THE WENDIGO IS WEAKENING!
CHUT
HE'S BIGGER THAN THE HULK--BUT HE'S NOT NEARLY AS IMPREGNABLE!
HULK DOESN'T UNDERSTAND. FIRST LITTLE MAN FIGHTS HULK... AND NOW HE FIGHTS HULK'S ENEMY?
BUT IF HULK'S ENEMY IS LITTLE MAN'S ENEMY... THEN LITTLE MAN IS HULK'S FRIEND!
HULK'S FRIEND?
YES! LITTLE MAN IS HULK'S FRIEND--
--SO HULK WILL HELP LITTLE MAN FIGHT HULK'S ENEMY!

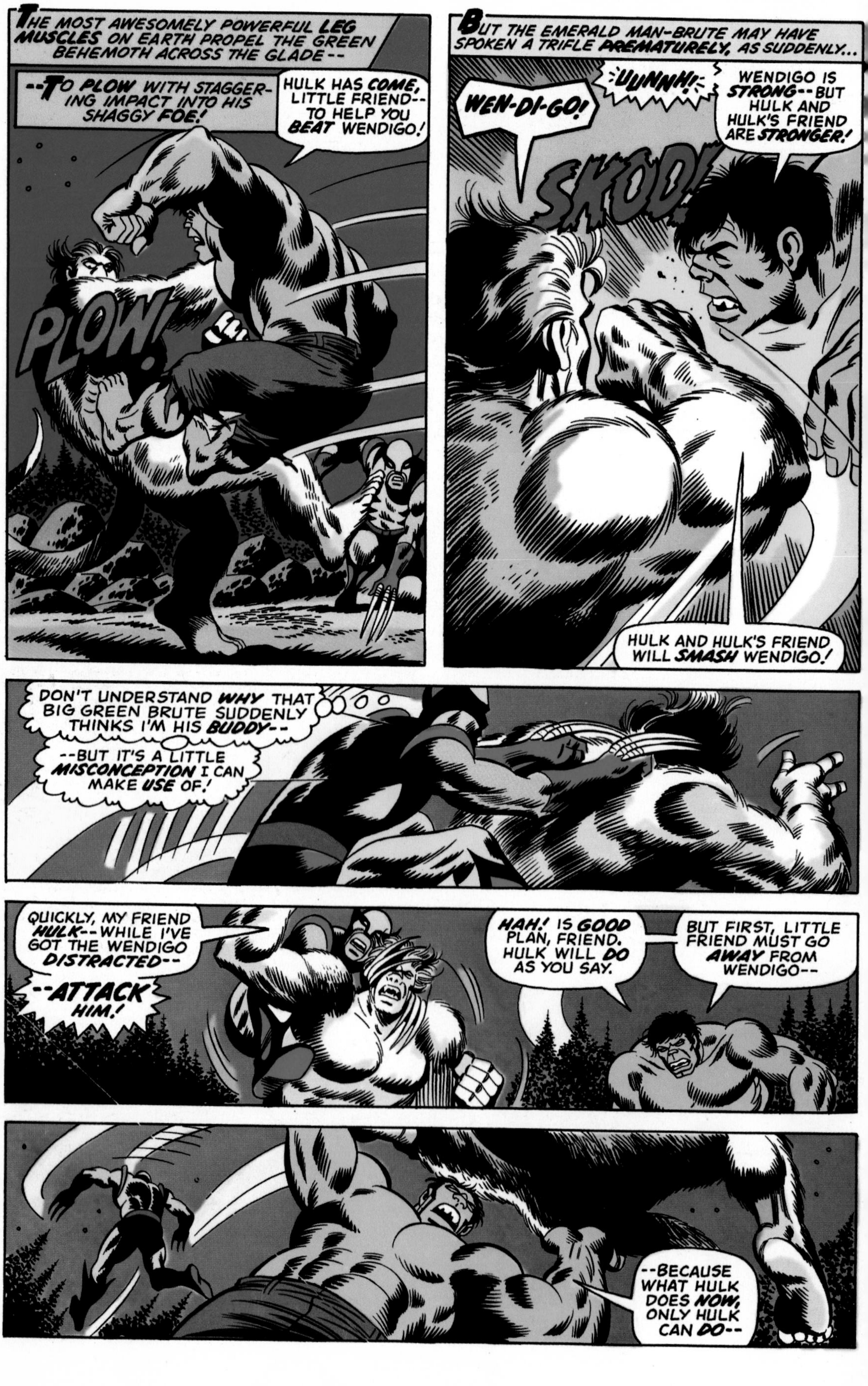
THE MOST AWESOMELY POWERFUL LEG MUSCLES ON EARTH PROPEL THE GREEN BEHEMOTH ACROSS THE GLADE--
--TO PLOW WITH STAGGERING IMPACT INTO HIS SHAGGY FOE!
HULK HAS COME, LITTLE FRIEND-- TO HELP YOU BEAT WENDIGO!
PLOW!
BUT THE EMERALD MAN-BRUTE MAY HAVE SPOKEN A TRIFLE PREMATURELY, AS SUDDENLY...
WEN-DI-GO!
UUNNH!
WENDIGO IS STRONG--BUT HULK AND HULK'S FRIEND ARE STRONGER!
SKOD!
HULK AND HULK'S FRIEND WILL SMASH WENDIGO!
DON'T UNDERSTAND WHY THAT BIG GREEN BRUTE SUDDENLY THINKS I'M HIS BUDDY--
--BUT IT'S A LITTLE MISCONCEPTION I CAN MAKE USE OF!
QUICKLY, MY FRIEND HULK--WHILE I'VE GOT THE WENDIGO DISTRACTED--
--ATTACK HIM!
HAH! IS GOOD PLAN, FRIEND. HULK WILL DO AS YOU SAY.
BUT FIRST, LITTLE FRIEND MUST GO AWAY FROM WENDIGO--
--BECAUSE WHAT HULK DOES NOW, ONLY HULK CAN DO--

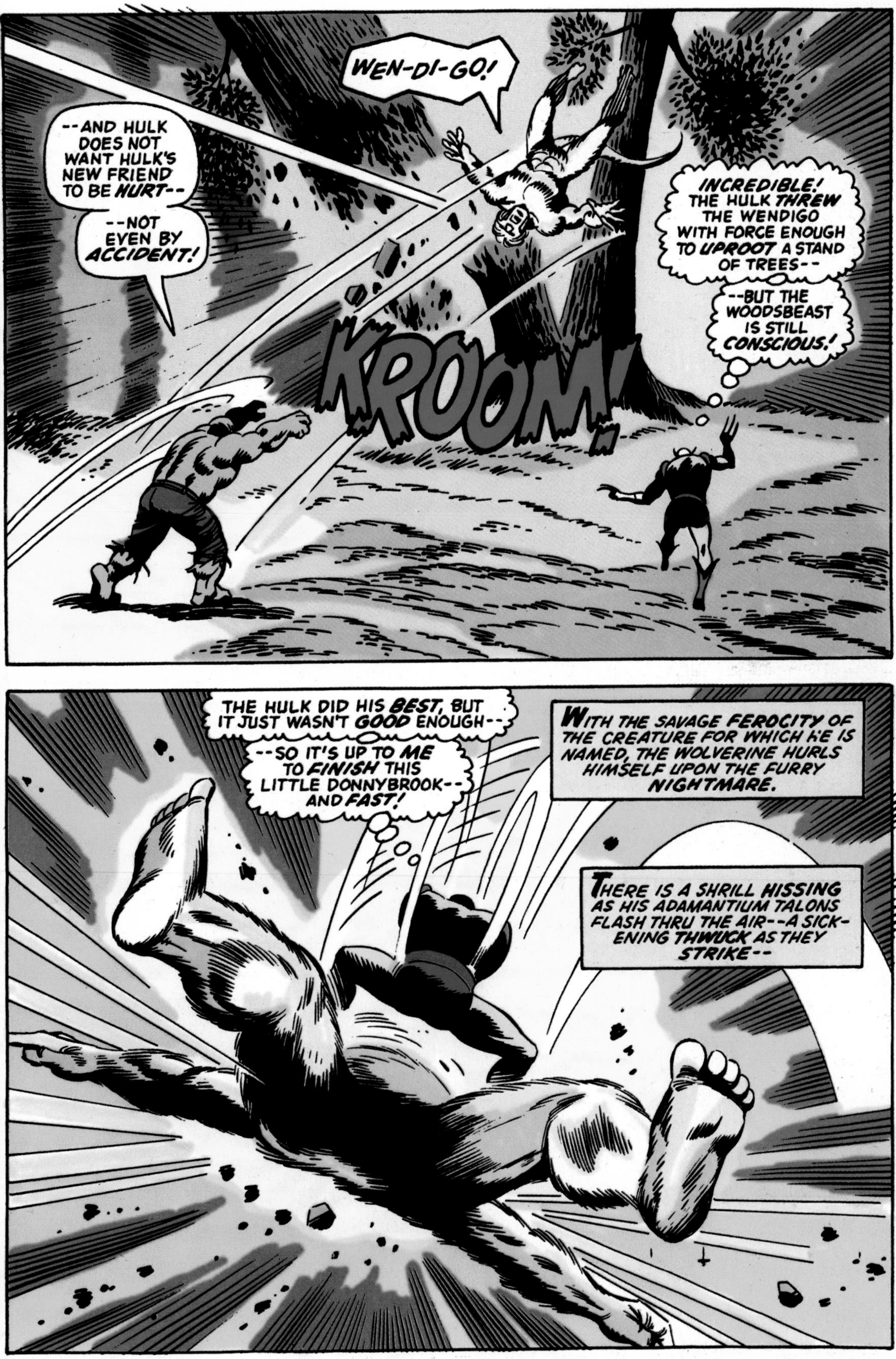
--AND HULK DOES NOT WANT HULK'S NEW FRIEND TO BE HURT--
--NOT EVEN BY ACCIDENT!
WEN-DI-GO!
INCREDIBLE! THE HULK THREW THE WENDIGO WITH FORCE ENOUGH TO UPROOT A STAND OF TREES--
--BUT THE WOODSBEAST IS STILL CONSCIOUS!
KROOM!
THE HULK DID HIS BEST, BUT IT JUST WASN'T GOOD ENOUGH--
--SO IT'S UP TO ME TO FINISH THIS LITTLE DONNYBROOK--AND FAST!
WITH THE SAVAGE FEROCITY OF THE CREATURE FOR WHICH HE IS NAMED, THE WOLVERINE HURLS HIMSELF UPON THE FURRY NIGHTMARE.
THERE IS A SHRILL HISSING AS HIS ADAMANTIUM TALONS FLASH THRU THE AIR--A SICKENING THWUCK AS THEY STRIKE--

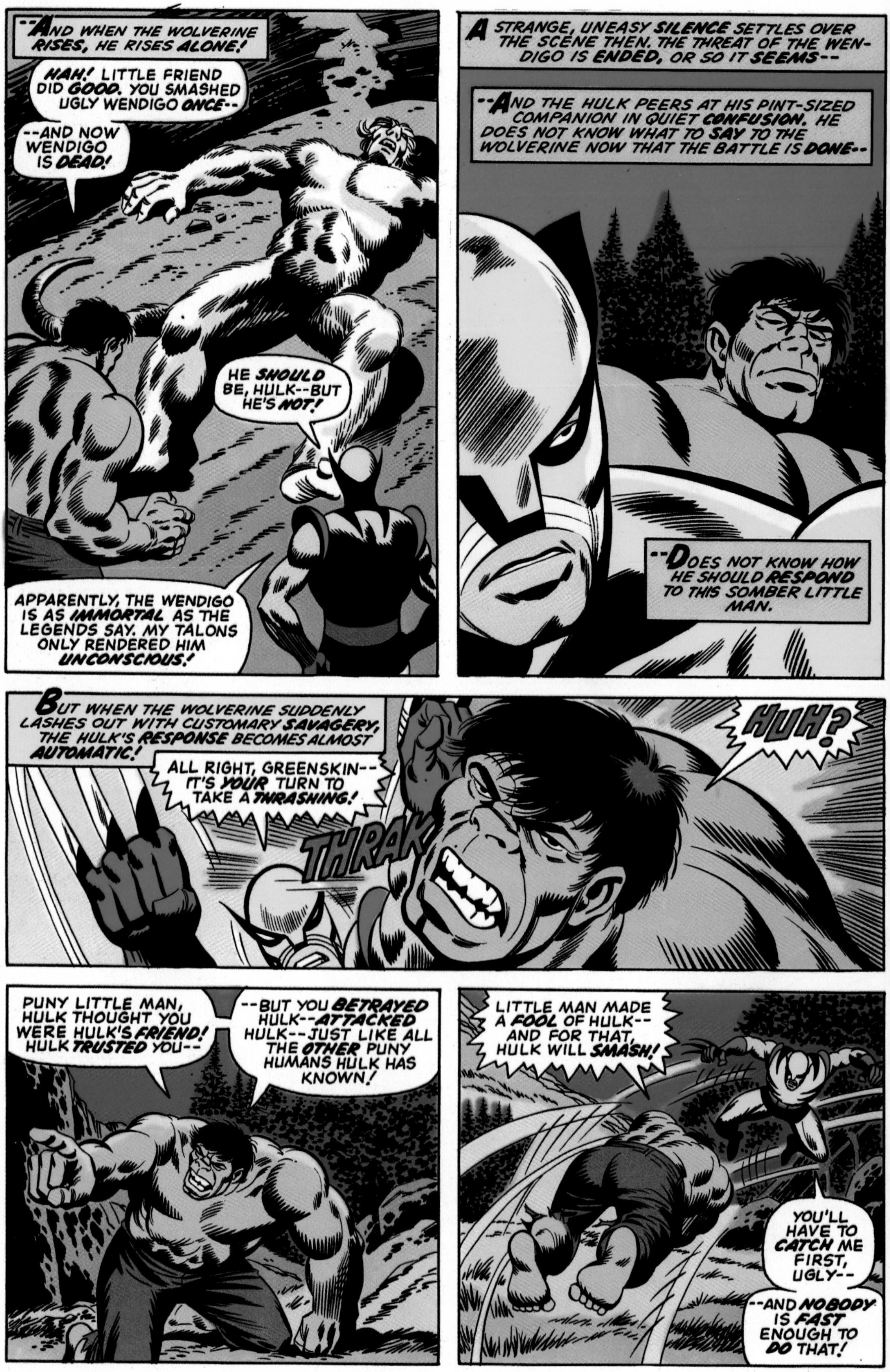
--AND WHEN THE WOLVERINE RISES, HE RISES ALONE!
HAH! LITTLE FRIEND DID GOOD. YOU SMASHED UGLY WENDIGO ONCE--
--AND NOW WENDIGO IS DEAD!
HE SHOULD BE, HULK--BUT HE'S NOT!
APPARENTLY, THE WENDIGO IS AS IMMORTAL AS THE LEGENDS SAY. MY TALONS ONLY RENDERED HIM UNCONSCIOUS!
A STRANGE, UNEASY SILENCE SETTLES OVER THE SCENE THEN. THE THREAT OF THE WENDIGO IS ENDED, OR SO IT SEEMS--
--AND THE HULK PEERS AT HIS PINT-SIZED COMPANION IN QUIET CONFUSION. HE DOES NOT KNOW WHAT TO SAY TO THE WOLVERINE NOW THAT THE BATTLE IS DONE--
--DOES NOT KNOW HOW HE SHOULD RESPOND TO THIS SOMBER LITTLE MAN.
BUT WHEN THE WOLVERINE SUDDENLY LASHES OUT WITH CUSTOMARY SAVAGERY, THE HULK'S RESPONSE BECOMES ALMOST AUTOMATIC!
ALL RIGHT, GREENSKIN--IT'S YOUR TURN TO TAKE A THRASHING!
HUH?
THRAK
PUNY LITTLE MAN, HULK THOUGHT YOU WERE HULK'S FRIEND! HULK TRUSTED YOU--
--BUT YOU BETRAYED HULK--ATTACKED HULK--JUST LIKE ALL THE OTHER PUNY HUMANS HULK HAS KNOWN!
LITTLE MAN MADE A FOOL OF HULK--AND FOR THAT, HULK WILL SMASH!
YOU'LL HAVE TO CATCH ME FIRST, UGLY--
--AND NOBODY IS FAST ENOUGH TO DO THAT!

HIDDEN IN THE PRE-DAWN SHADOWS NEARBY, AN UNCOMFORTABLE *GEORGES BAPTISTE* AND A GRIM *MARIE CARTIER*--THE GIRL WHO *LURED* THE HULK TO QUEBEC--WATCH THE RAGING BATTLE WITH A MIXTURE OF HORROR AND ANXIOUS *ANTICIPATION.*

THERE, MARIE. DO YOU SEE WHAT YOUR MADNESS HAS *WROUGHT?* YOUR BROTHER HAS *FALLEN*--PERHAPS MORTALLY *WOUNDED*--AND IT IS ALL *YOUR* FAULT!

NONSENSE, GEORGES--EVERY-THING GOES EVEN *BETTER* THAN EXPECTED!

THE WENDIGO CAN'T BE *HARMED*--YOU *KNOW* THAT.

THE HULK AND THE ONE CALLED *WOLVERINE* MERELY SAVED US THE TASK OF *OVERCOMING* PAUL ALL BY OURSELVES!

NOW *QUICKLY*--WHILE THEY'RE STILL *DIS-TRACTED*--HELP ME *CARRY* PAUL'S BODY INSIDE.

THE SOONER THINGS ARE *PREPARED,* THE SOONER WE'LL BE READY TO BEGIN THE *TRANSFORMA-TION!*

MOMENTS LATER, *WITHIN THE STONE-SLAB HOVEL NEARBY...*

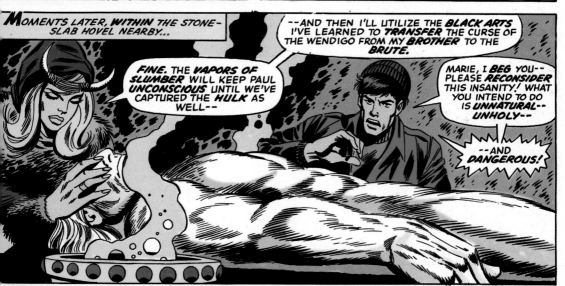

FINE. THE *VAPORS OF SLUMBER* WILL KEEP PAUL UNCONSCIOUS UNTIL WE'VE CAPTURED THE *HULK* AS WELL--

--AND THEN I'LL UTILIZE THE *BLACK ARTS* I'VE LEARNED TO *TRANSFER* THE CURSE OF THE WENDIGO FROM MY *BROTHER* TO THE *BRUTE.*

MARIE, I *BEG* YOU-- PLEASE *RECONSIDER* THIS INSANITY! WHAT YOU INTEND TO DO IS *UNNATURAL*-- *UNHOLY*--

--AND *DANGEROUS!*

OUTSIDE, THE JADE-HUED JUGGERNAUT FIGHTS ON, *UNAWARE* OF THE TERRIBLE *FATE* THE MANIACALLY OBSESSED GIRL HAS PLANNED FOR HIM--

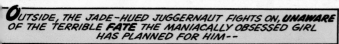

--*U*NAWARE OF THE GOLD-AND-CRIMSON *SPLENDOR* SPREAD ACROSS HIS BATTLE-FIELD BY THE SWIFTLY RISING *SUN*--

--*A* SUN ALSO RISING BEHIND A SECRET CANADIAN *MILITARY COM-PLEX* NESTLED DEEP IN THE SHELTERING HILLS NOT TOO VERY FAR *AWAY.*

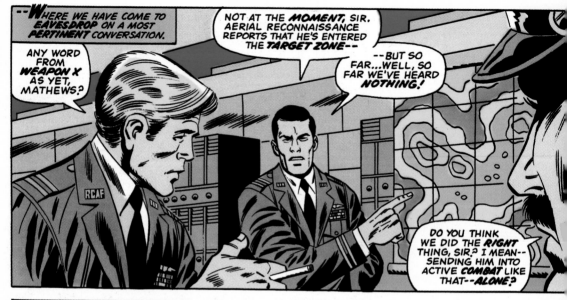

--WHERE WE HAVE COME TO EAVESDROP ON A MOST PERTINENT CONVERSATION.

ANY WORD FROM **WEAPON X** AS YET, MATHEWS?

NOT AT THE **MOMENT**, SIR. AERIAL RECONNAISSANCE REPORTS THAT HE'S ENTERED THE **TARGET ZONE**--

--BUT SO FAR...WELL, SO FAR WE'VE HEARD **NOTHING!**

DO YOU THINK WE DID THE **RIGHT** THING, SIR? I MEAN-- SENDING HIM INTO ACTIVE **COMBAT** LIKE THAT--**ALONE?**

WE WOULDN'T HAVE **SENT** HIM IF WE DIDN'T THINK HE WAS **READY,** HOLDERIDGE!

THE GOVERNMENT HAS SPENT A GREAT DEAL OF TIME, EFFORT, AND **MONEY,** DEVELOPING THAT MUTANT'S NATURAL-BORN **SPEED, STRENGTH** AND **SAVAGERY** INTO THE **SKILLS** OF A PROFESSIONAL **WARRIOR**--

--AND DESPITE THE FEW **KINKS** STILL REMAINING IN HIS PSYCHO-LOGICAL MAKEUP, I THINK WE'VE DONE A PRETTY GOOD **JOB!**

THE WOLVERINE ASKED FOR **SIX HOURS** TO BRING IN THE HULK **SINGLE-HANDED**--AND HE'S GOING TO HAVE THOSE SIX HOURS.

THEN, IF HE **FAILS**--AND, MIND YOU, I DON'T THINK HE **WILL**--THEN WE WILL TAKE **OTHER** ACTION!

CONTINGENCY MEASURES HAVE ALREADY BEEN PUT INTO **ACTIVE** OPERATION OUTSIDE!

THAT SPECIALLY-DESIGNED **CHOPPER** IS READY TO DROP A CRACK TEAM OF TOP **COMMANDOES** INTO THE AREA IF NECESSARY!

BELIEVE ME, GENTLEMEN, **ONE** WAY OR THE **OTHER**--THE **HULK** IS AS GOOD AS **FINISHED!**

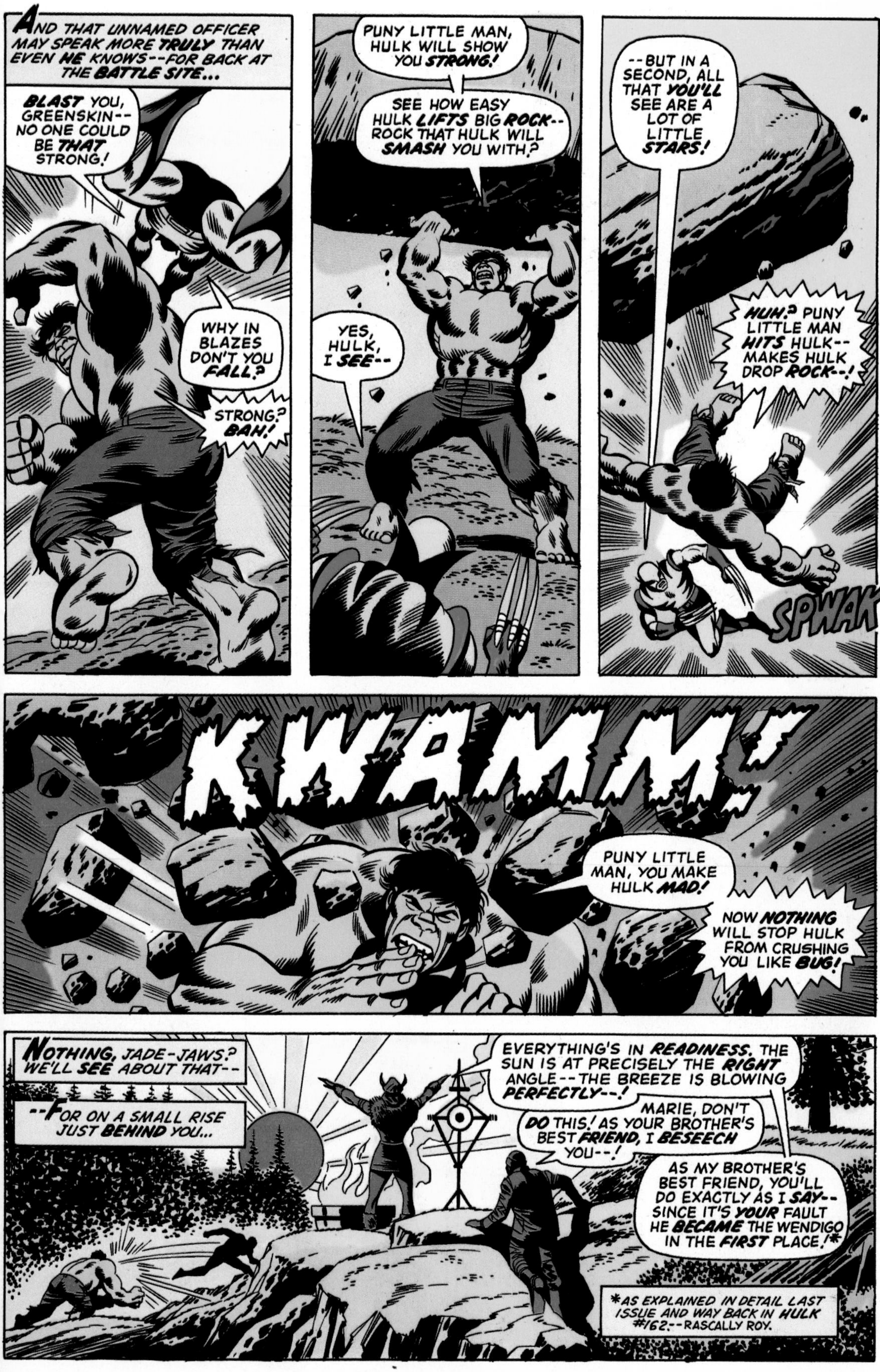

AND THAT UNNAMED OFFICER MAY SPEAK MORE TRULY THAN EVEN HE KNOWS--FOR BACK AT THE BATTLE SITE...
BLAST YOU, GREENSKIN--NO ONE COULD BE THAT STRONG!
WHY IN BLAZES DON'T YOU FALL?
STRONG? BAH!
PUNY LITTLE MAN, HULK WILL SHOW YOU STRONG!
SEE HOW EASY HULK LIFTS BIG ROCK--ROCK THAT HULK WILL SMASH YOU WITH?
YES, HULK, I SEE--
--BUT IN A SECOND, ALL THAT YOU'LL SEE ARE A LOT OF LITTLE STARS!
HUH? PUNY LITTLE MAN HITS HULK--MAKES HULK DROP ROCK--!
SPWAK
KWAMM!
PUNY LITTLE MAN, YOU MAKE HULK MAD!
NOW NOTHING WILL STOP HULK FROM CRUSHING YOU LIKE BUG!
NOTHING, JADE-JAWS? WE'LL SEE ABOUT THAT--
--FOR ON A SMALL RISE JUST BEHIND YOU...
EVERYTHING'S IN READINESS. THE SUN IS AT PRECISELY THE RIGHT ANGLE--THE BREEZE IS BLOWING PERFECTLY--!
MARIE, DON'T DO THIS! AS YOUR BROTHER'S BEST FRIEND, I BESEECH YOU--!
AS MY BROTHER'S BEST FRIEND, YOU'LL DO EXACTLY AS I SAY--SINCE IT'S YOUR FAULT HE BECAME THE WENDIGO IN THE FIRST PLACE!*
*AS EXPLAINED IN DETAIL LAST ISSUE AND WAY BACK IN HULK #162.--RASCALLY ROY.

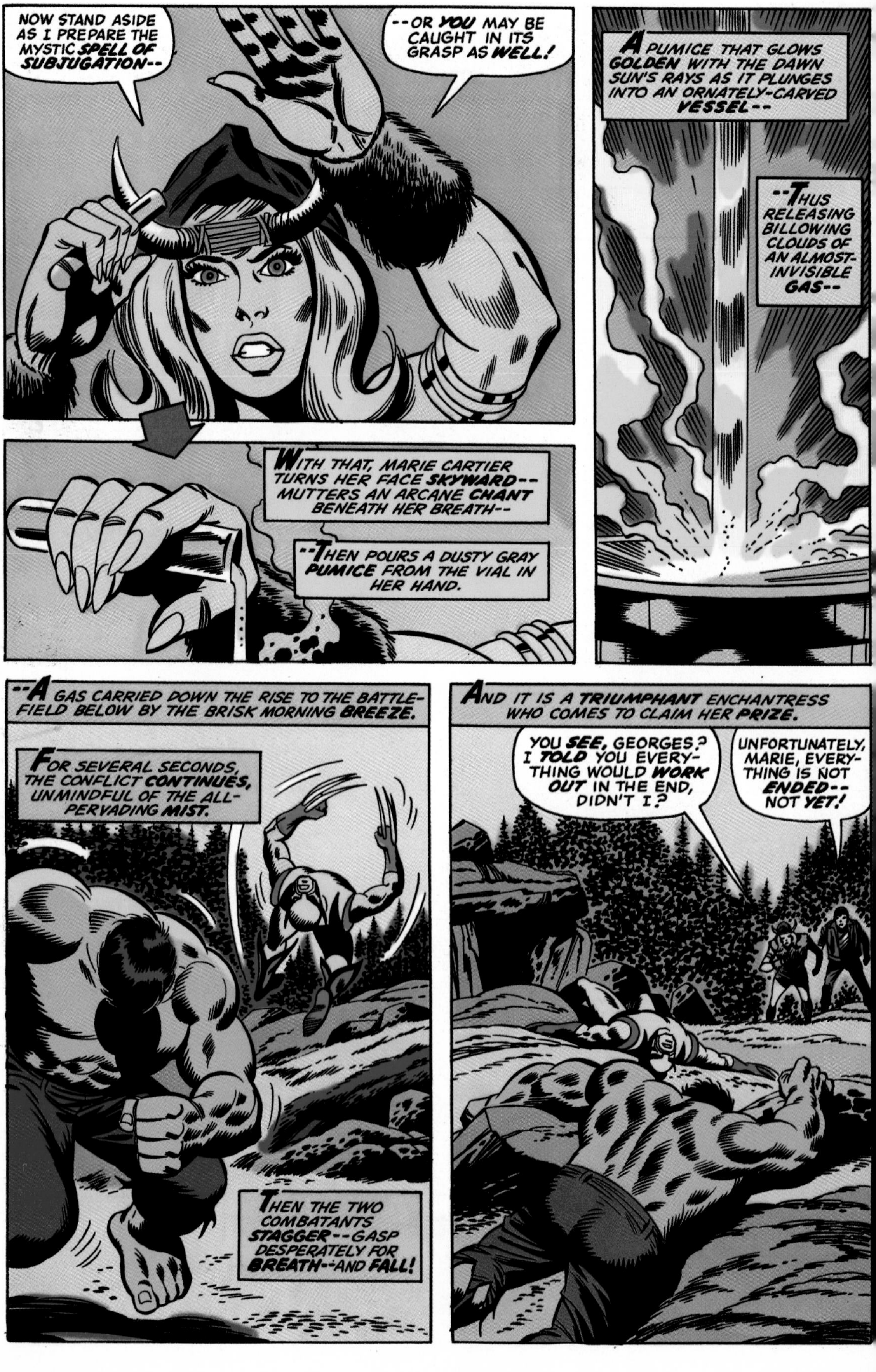
NOW STAND ASIDE AS I PREPARE THE MYSTIC SPELL OF SUBJUGATION--
--OR YOU MAY BE CAUGHT IN ITS GRASP AS WELL!
WITH THAT, MARIE CARTIER TURNS HER FACE SKYWARD--MUTTERS AN ARCANE CHANT BENEATH HER BREATH--
--THEN POURS A DUSTY GRAY PUMICE FROM THE VIAL IN HER HAND.
A PUMICE THAT GLOWS GOLDEN WITH THE DAWN SUN'S RAYS AS IT PLUNGES INTO AN ORNATELY-CARVED VESSEL--
--THUS RELEASING BILLOWING CLOUDS OF AN ALMOST-INVISIBLE GAS--
--A GAS CARRIED DOWN THE RISE TO THE BATTLE-FIELD BELOW BY THE BRISK MORNING BREEZE.
FOR SEVERAL SECONDS, THE CONFLICT CONTINUES, UNMINDFUL OF THE ALL-PERVADING MIST.
THEN THE TWO COMBATANTS STAGGER--GASP DESPERATELY FOR BREATH--AND FALL!
AND IT IS A TRIUMPHANT ENCHANTRESS WHO COMES TO CLAIM HER PRIZE.
YOU SEE, GEORGES? I TOLD YOU EVERY-THING WOULD WORK OUT IN THE END, DIDN'T I?
UNFORTUNATELY, MARIE, EVERY-THING IS NOT ENDED--NOT YET!

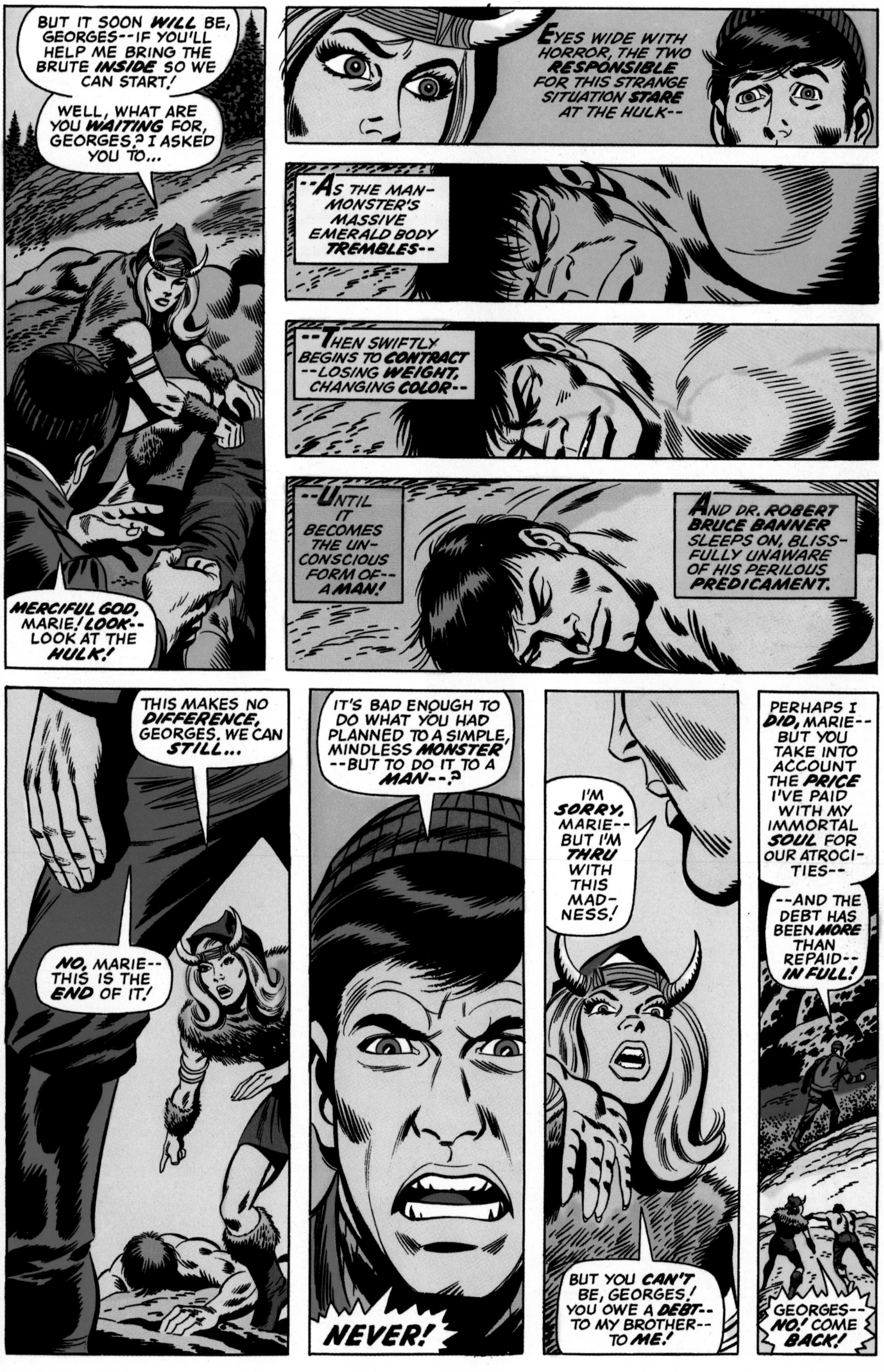
BUT IT SOON WILL BE, GEORGES--IF YOU'LL HELP ME BRING THE BRUTE INSIDE SO WE CAN START!
WELL, WHAT ARE YOU WAITING FOR, GEORGES? I ASKED YOU TO...
MERCIFUL GOD, MARIE! LOOK-- LOOK AT THE HULK!
EYES WIDE WITH HORROR, THE TWO RESPONSIBLE FOR THIS STRANGE SITUATION STARE AT THE HULK--
--AS THE MAN-MONSTER'S MASSIVE EMERALD BODY TREMBLES--
--THEN SWIFTLY BEGINS TO CONTRACT --LOSING WEIGHT, CHANGING COLOR--
--UNTIL IT BECOMES THE UN-CONSCIOUS FORM OF-- A MAN!
AND DR. ROBERT BRUCE BANNER SLEEPS ON, BLISS-FULLY UNAWARE OF HIS PERILOUS PREDICAMENT.
THIS MAKES NO DIFFERENCE, GEORGES. WE CAN STILL...
NO, MARIE-- THIS IS THE END OF IT!
IT'S BAD ENOUGH TO DO WHAT YOU HAD PLANNED TO A SIMPLE, MINDLESS MONSTER --BUT TO DO IT TO A MAN--?
NEVER!
I'M SORRY, MARIE-- BUT I'M THRU WITH THIS MAD-NESS!
BUT YOU CAN'T BE, GEORGES! YOU OWE A DEBT-- TO MY BROTHER-- TO ME!
PERHAPS I DID, MARIE-- BUT YOU TAKE INTO ACCOUNT THE PRICE I'VE PAID WITH MY IMMORTAL SOUL FOR OUR ATROCI-TIES--
--AND THE DEBT HAS BEEN MORE THAN REPAID-- IN FULL!
GEORGES-- NO! COME BACK!

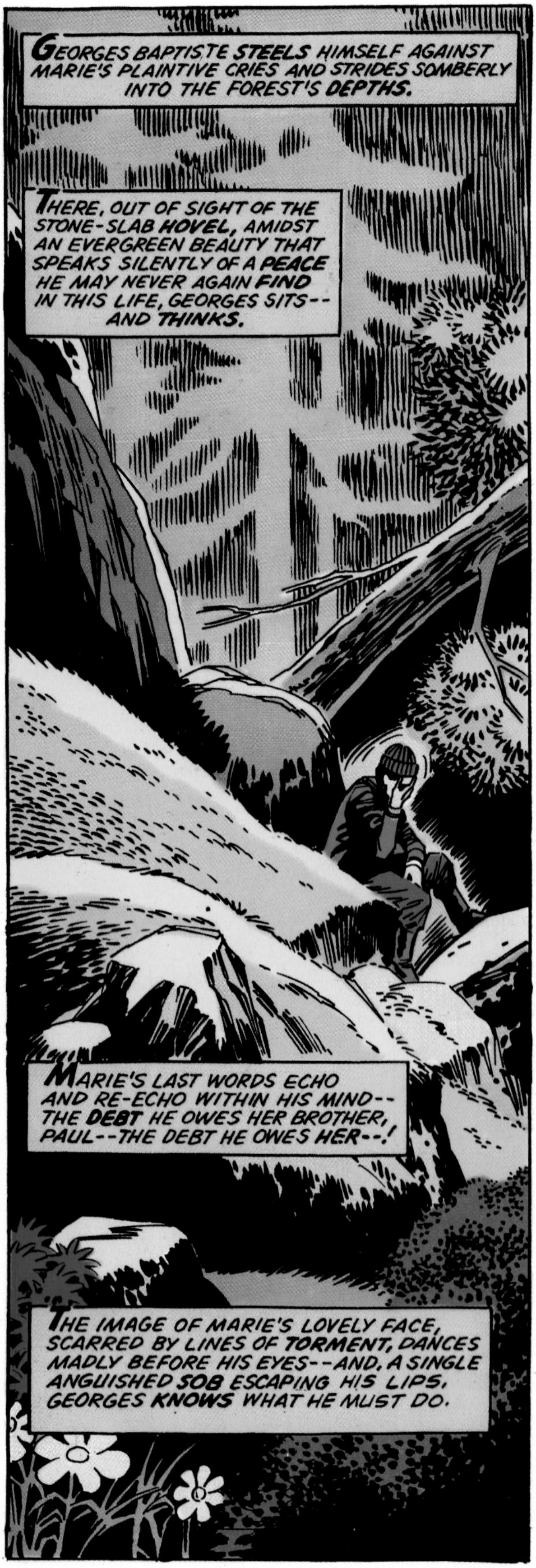
GEORGES BAPTISTE STEELS HIMSELF AGAINST MARIE'S PLAINTIVE CRIES AND STRIDES SOMBERLY INTO THE FOREST'S DEPTHS.
THERE, OUT OF SIGHT OF THE STONE-SLAB HOVEL, AMIDST AN EVERGREEN BEAUTY THAT SPEAKS SILENTLY OF A PEACE HE MAY NEVER AGAIN FIND IN THIS LIFE, GEORGES SITS-- AND THINKS.
MARIE'S LAST WORDS ECHO AND RE-ECHO WITHIN HIS MIND-- THE DEBT HE OWES HER BROTHER, PAUL--THE DEBT HE OWES HER--!
THE IMAGE OF MARIE'S LOVELY FACE, SCARRED BY LINES OF TORMENT, DANCES MADLY BEFORE HIS EYES--AND, A SINGLE ANGUISHED SOB ESCAPING HIS LIPS, GEORGES KNOWS WHAT HE MUST DO.
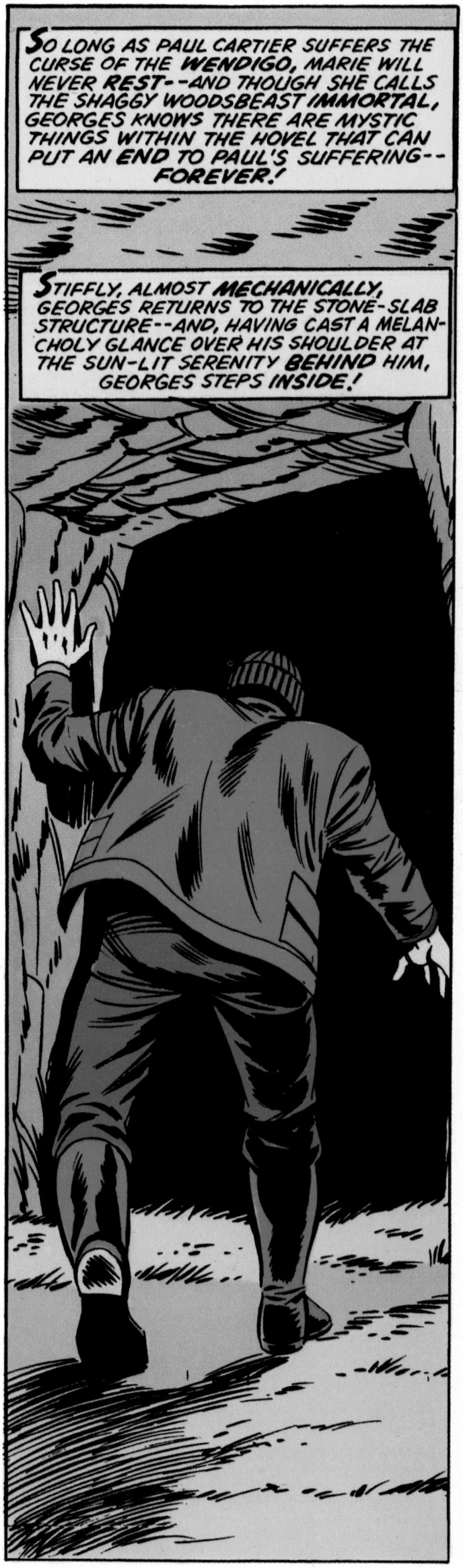
SO LONG AS PAUL CARTIER SUFFERS THE CURSE OF THE WENDIGO, MARIE WILL NEVER REST--AND THOUGH SHE CALLS THE SHAGGY WOODSBEAST IMMORTAL, GEORGES KNOWS THERE ARE MYSTIC THINGS WITHIN THE HOVEL THAT CAN PUT AN END TO PAUL'S SUFFERING-- FOREVER!
STIFFLY, ALMOST MECHANICALLY, GEORGES RETURNS TO THE STONE-SLAB STRUCTURE--AND, HAVING CAST A MELANCHOLY GLANCE OVER HIS SHOULDER AT THE SUN-LIT SERENITY BEHIND HIM, GEORGES STEPS INSIDE!

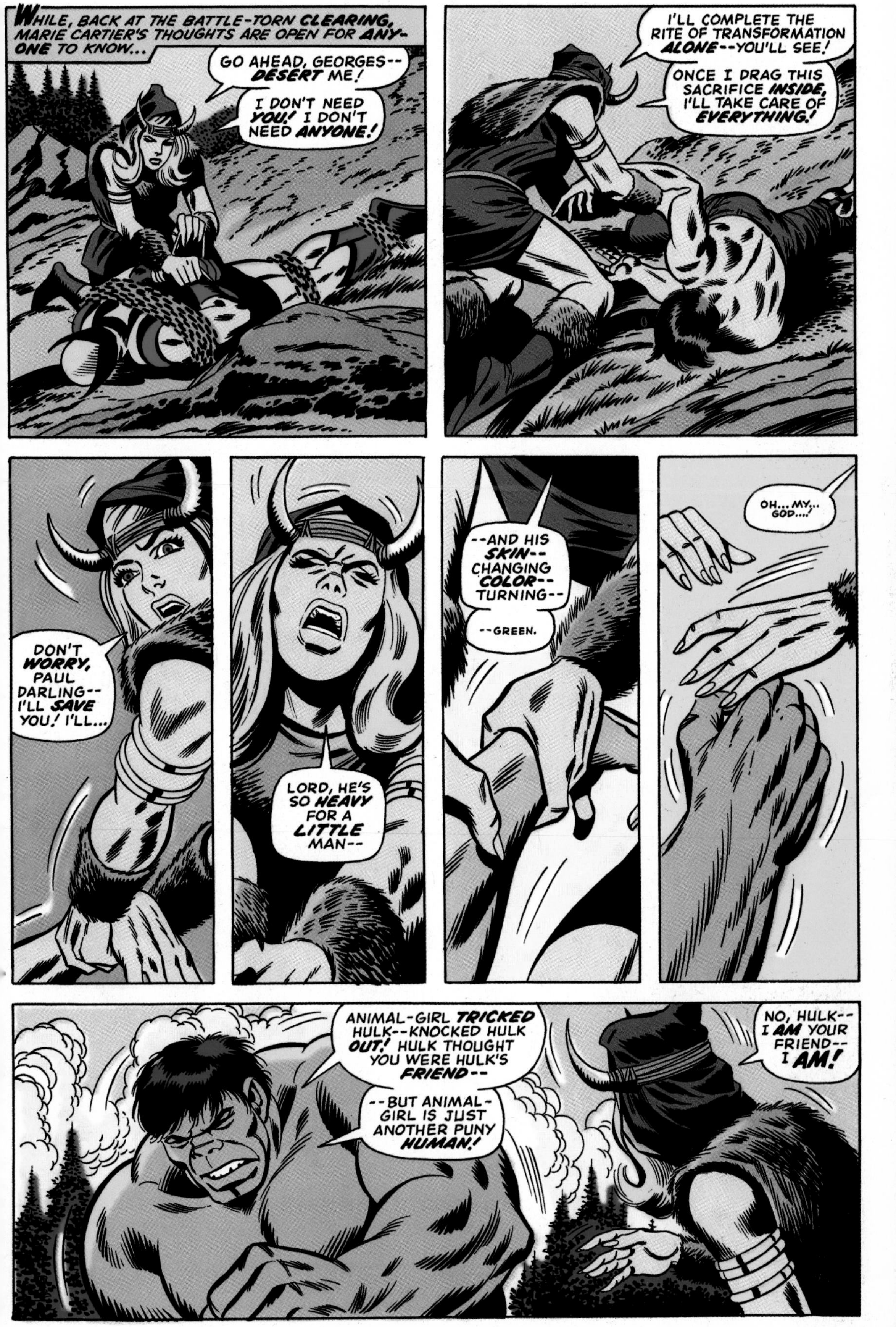
WHILE, BACK AT THE BATTLE-TORN CLEARING, MARIE CARTIER'S THOUGHTS ARE OPEN FOR ANYONE TO KNOW...
GO AHEAD, GEORGES-- DESERT ME!
I DON'T NEED YOU! I DON'T NEED ANYONE!
I'LL COMPLETE THE RITE OF TRANSFORMATION ALONE--YOU'LL SEE!
ONCE I DRAG THIS SACRIFICE INSIDE, I'LL TAKE CARE OF EVERYTHING!
DON'T WORRY, PAUL DARLING-- I'LL SAVE YOU! I'LL...
LORD, HE'S SO HEAVY FOR A LITTLE MAN--
--AND HIS SKIN-- CHANGING COLOR-- TURNING--
--GREEN.
OH... MY... GOD...!
ANIMAL-GIRL TRICKED HULK--KNOCKED HULK OUT! HULK THOUGHT YOU WERE HULK'S FRIEND--
--BUT ANIMAL-GIRL IS JUST ANOTHER PUNY HUMAN!
NO, HULK-- I AM YOUR FRIEND-- I AM!

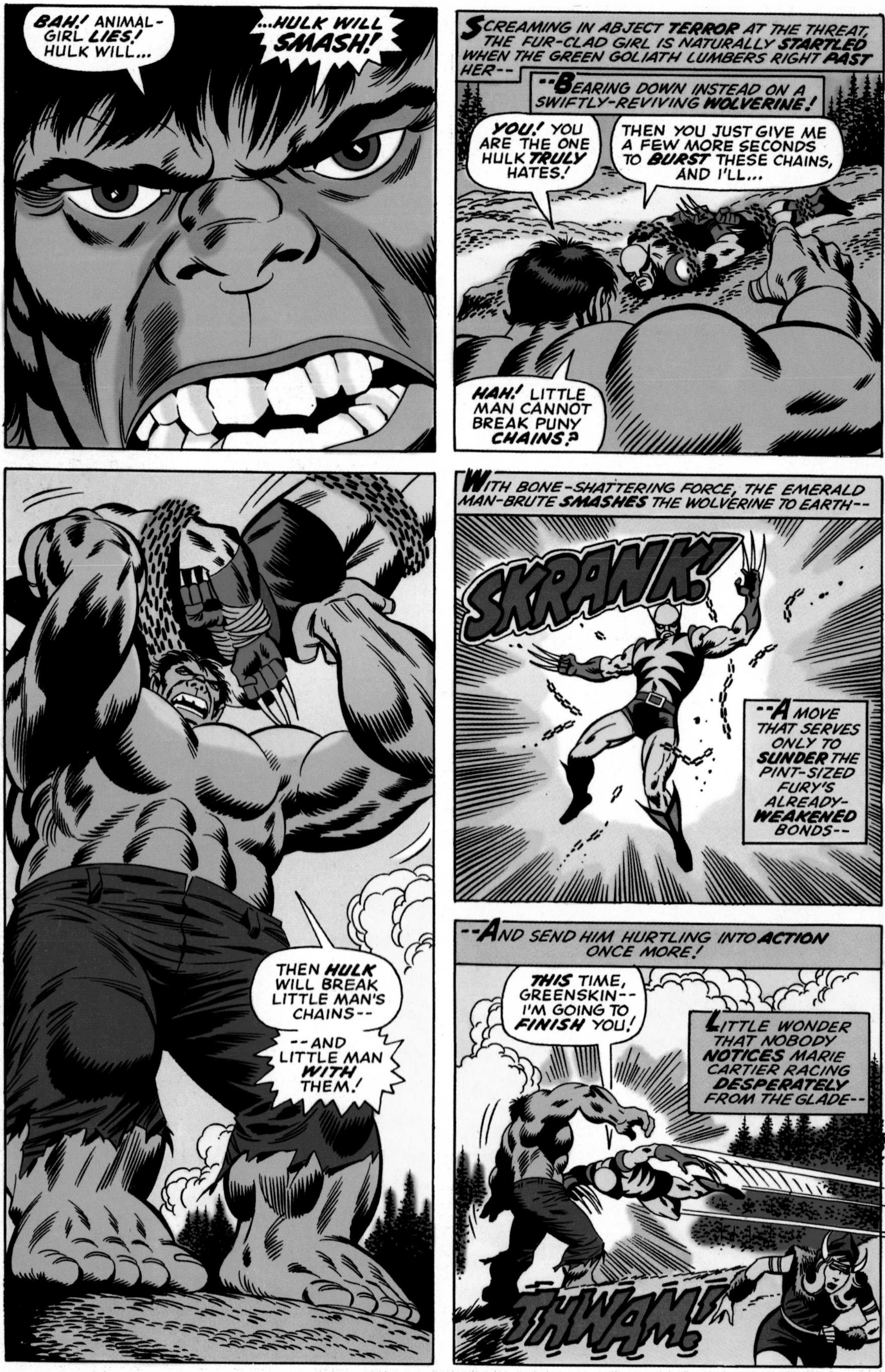
BAH! ANIMAL-GIRL LIES! HULK WILL...
...HULK WILL SMASH!
SCREAMING IN ABJECT TERROR AT THE THREAT, THE FUR-CLAD GIRL IS NATURALLY STARTLED WHEN THE GREEN GOLIATH LUMBERS RIGHT PAST HER--
--BEARING DOWN INSTEAD ON A SWIFTLY-REVIVING WOLVERINE!
YOU! YOU ARE THE ONE HULK TRULY HATES!
THEN YOU JUST GIVE ME A FEW MORE SECONDS TO BURST THESE CHAINS, AND I'LL...
HAH! LITTLE MAN CANNOT BREAK PUNY CHAINS?
THEN HULK WILL BREAK LITTLE MAN'S CHAINS--
--AND LITTLE MAN WITH THEM!
WITH BONE-SHATTERING FORCE, THE EMERALD MAN-BRUTE SMASHES THE WOLVERINE TO EARTH--
SKRANK!
--A MOVE THAT SERVES ONLY TO SUNDER THE PINT-SIZED FURY'S ALREADY-WEAKENED BONDS--
--AND SEND HIM HURTLING INTO ACTION ONCE MORE!
THIS TIME, GREENSKIN-- I'M GOING TO FINISH YOU!
LITTLE WONDER THAT NOBODY NOTICES MARIE CARTIER RACING DESPERATELY FROM THE GLADE--
THWAM!

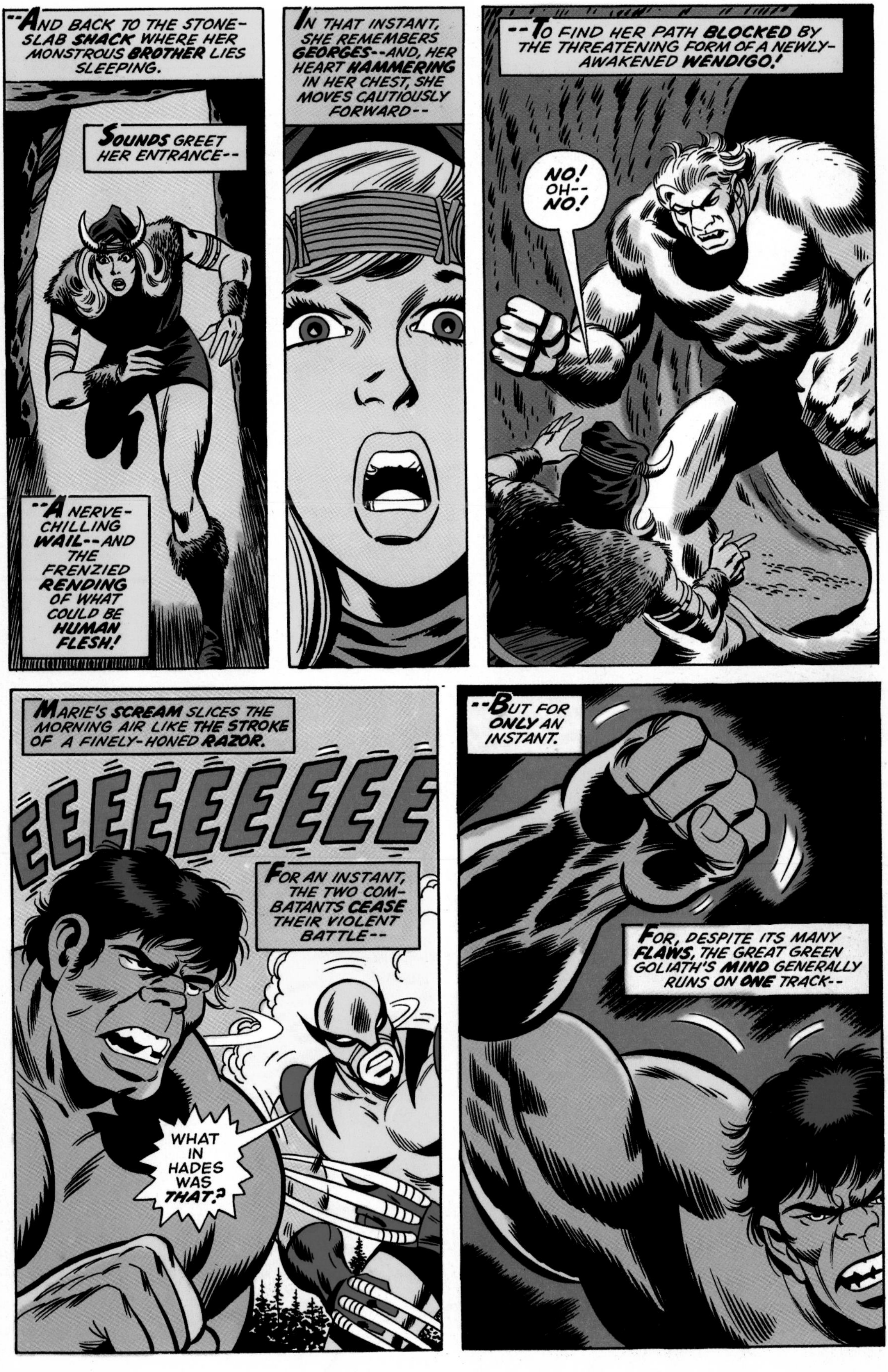
--AND BACK TO THE STONE-SLAB SHACK WHERE HER MONSTROUS BROTHER LIES SLEEPING.
SOUNDS GREET HER ENTRANCE--
--A NERVE-CHILLING WAIL--AND THE FRENZIED RENDING OF WHAT COULD BE HUMAN FLESH!
IN THAT INSTANT, SHE REMEMBERS GEORGES--AND, HER HEART HAMMERING IN HER CHEST, SHE MOVES CAUTIOUSLY FORWARD--
--TO FIND HER PATH BLOCKED BY THE THREATENING FORM OF A NEWLY-AWAKENED WENDIGO!
NO! OH-- NO!
MARIE'S SCREAM SLICES THE MORNING AIR LIKE THE STROKE OF A FINELY-HONED RAZOR.
EEEEEEEEEE
FOR AN INSTANT, THE TWO COMBATANTS CEASE THEIR VIOLENT BATTLE--
WHAT IN HADES WAS THAT?
--BUT FOR ONLY AN INSTANT.
FOR, DESPITE ITS MANY FLAWS, THE GREAT GREEN GOLIATH'S MIND GENERALLY RUNS ON ONE TRACK--

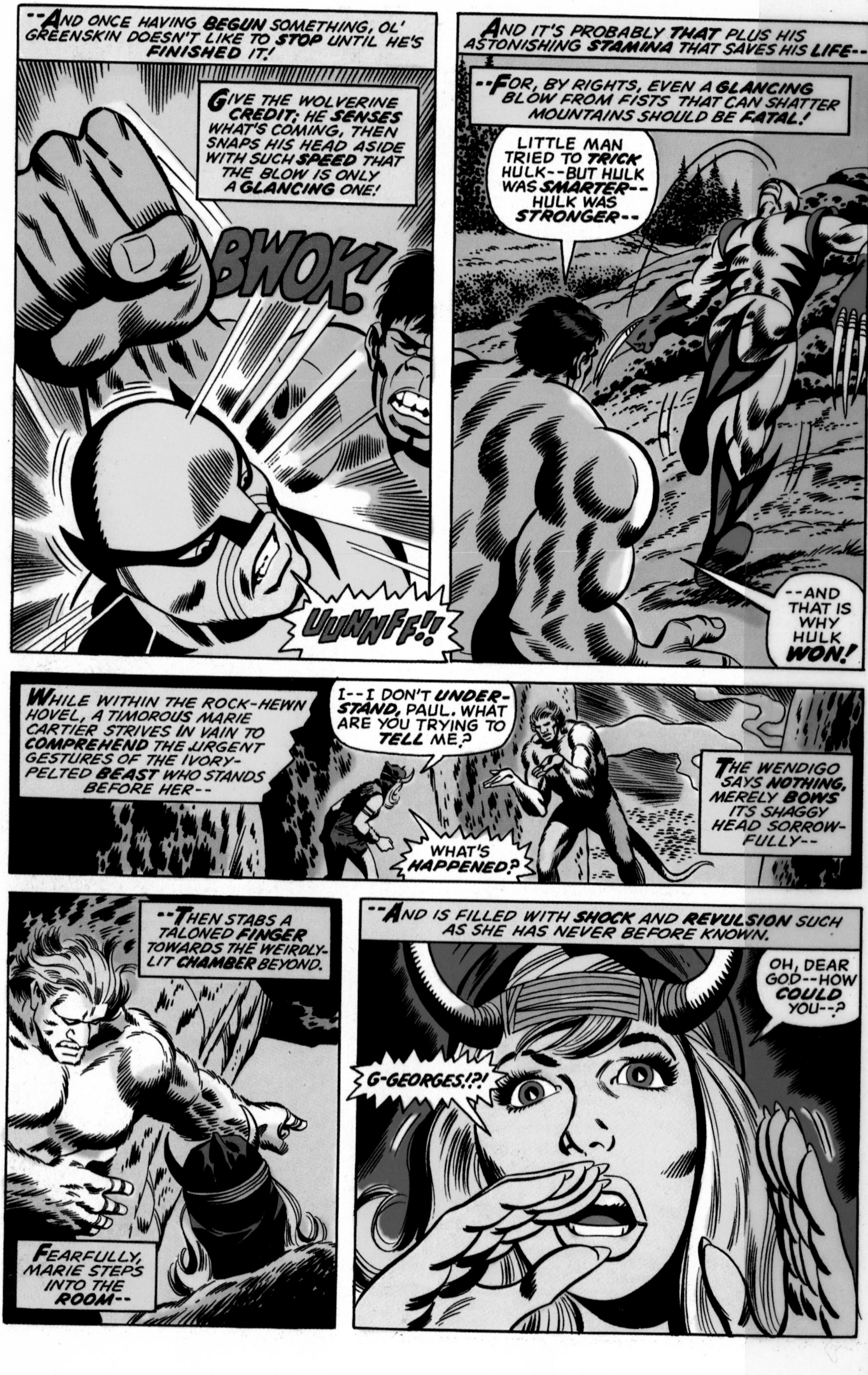
--AND ONCE HAVING BEGUN SOMETHING, OL' GREENSKIN DOESN'T LIKE TO STOP UNTIL HE'S FINISHED IT!
GIVE THE WOLVERINE CREDIT; HE SENSES WHAT'S COMING, THEN SNAPS HIS HEAD ASIDE WITH SUCH SPEED THAT THE BLOW IS ONLY A GLANCING ONE!
BWOK!
UUNNFF!!
AND IT'S PROBABLY THAT PLUS HIS ASTONISHING STAMINA THAT SAVES HIS LIFE--
--FOR, BY RIGHTS, EVEN A GLANCING BLOW FROM FISTS THAT CAN SHATTER MOUNTAINS SHOULD BE FATAL!
LITTLE MAN TRIED TO TRICK HULK--BUT HULK WAS SMARTER--HULK WAS STRONGER--
--AND THAT IS WHY HULK WON!
WHILE WITHIN THE ROCK-HEWN HOVEL, A TIMOROUS MARIE CARTIER STRIVES IN VAIN TO COMPREHEND THE URGENT GESTURES OF THE IVORY-PELTED BEAST WHO STANDS BEFORE HER--
I--I DON'T UNDERSTAND, PAUL. WHAT ARE YOU TRYING TO TELL ME?
WHAT'S HAPPENED?
THE WENDIGO SAYS NOTHING, MERELY BOWS ITS SHAGGY HEAD SORROWFULLY--
--THEN STABS A TALONED FINGER TOWARDS THE WEIRDLY-LIT CHAMBER BEYOND.
FEARFULLY, MARIE STEPS INTO THE ROOM--
--AND IS FILLED WITH SHOCK AND REVULSION SUCH AS SHE HAS NEVER BEFORE KNOWN.
OH, DEAR GOD--HOW COULD YOU--?
G-GEORGES!?!

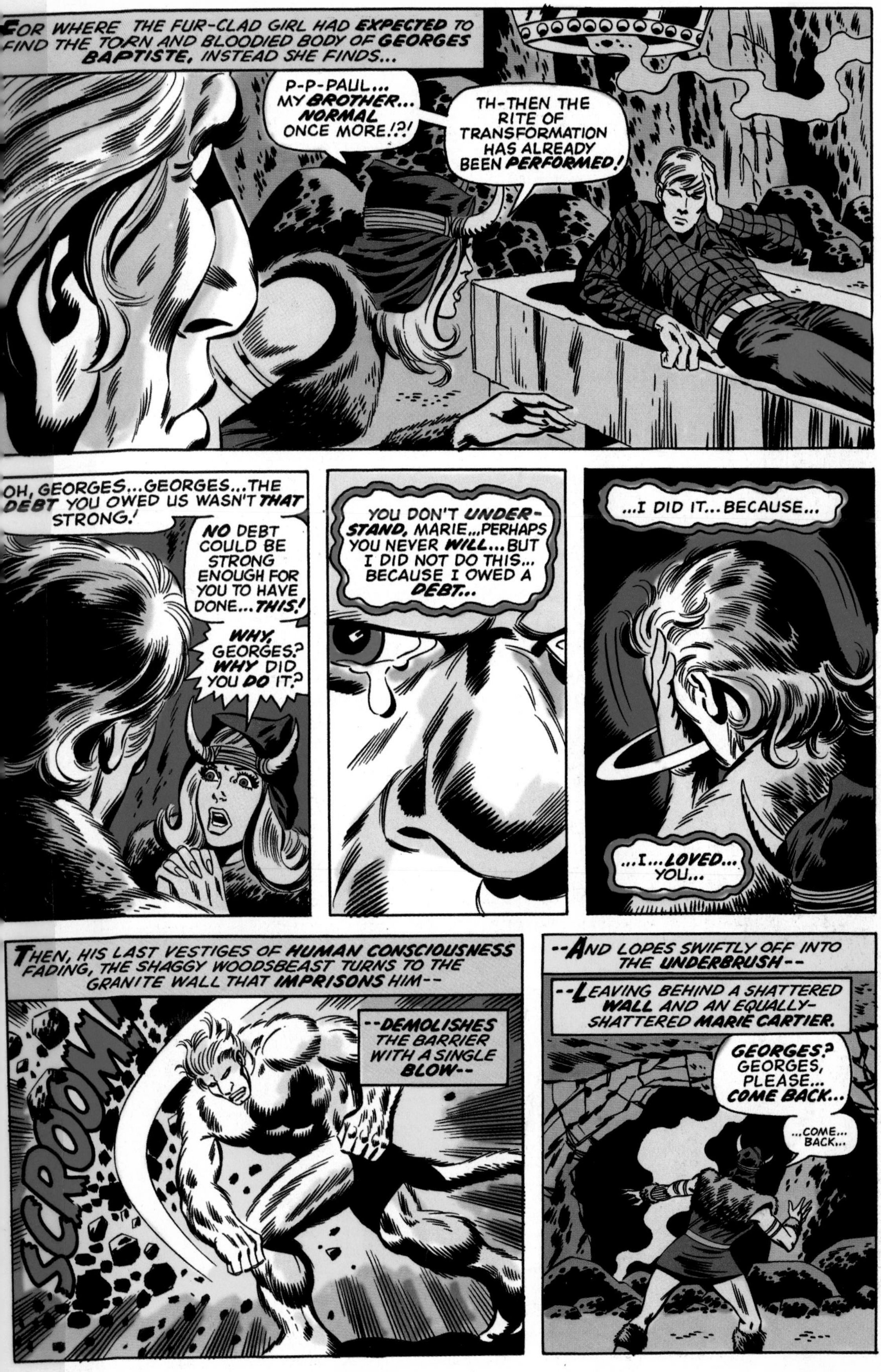
FOR WHERE THE FUR-CLAD GIRL HAD EXPECTED TO FIND THE TORN AND BLOODIED BODY OF GEORGES BAPTISTE, INSTEAD SHE FINDS...
P-P-PAUL... MY BROTHER... NORMAL ONCE MORE!?!
TH-THEN THE RITE OF TRANSFORMATION HAS ALREADY BEEN PERFORMED!
OH, GEORGES...GEORGES...THE DEBT YOU OWED US WASN'T THAT STRONG!
NO DEBT COULD BE STRONG ENOUGH FOR YOU TO HAVE DONE...THIS!
WHY, GEORGES? WHY DID YOU DO IT?
YOU DON'T UNDERSTAND, MARIE...PERHAPS YOU NEVER WILL...BUT I DID NOT DO THIS... BECAUSE I OWED A DEBT...
...I DID IT...BECAUSE...
...I...LOVED... YOU...
THEN, HIS LAST VESTIGES OF HUMAN CONSCIOUSNESS FADING, THE SHAGGY WOODSBEAST TURNS TO THE GRANITE WALL THAT IMPRISONS HIM--
--DEMOLISHES THE BARRIER WITH A SINGLE BLOW--
SCROOM!
--AND LOPES SWIFTLY OFF INTO THE UNDERBRUSH--
--LEAVING BEHIND A SHATTERED WALL AND AN EQUALLY-SHATTERED MARIE CARTIER.
GEORGES? GEORGES, PLEASE... COME BACK...
...COME... BACK...

OUTSIDE, THE HULK STARES IN CONFUSION FOR AN INSTANT AS A HUGE WHITE-MANED FORM LUMBERS OFF INTO THE SPRAWLING *FOREST*--

--THEN THE SOUND OF SOFT *WHIMPERING* REACHES HIS EMERALD EARS--

--AND, HIS CURIOSITY *PIQUED* BY THE SOUND, THE GREEN GOLIATH SHAMBLES HEAVILY TOWARDS THE RUINS OF THE STONE-SLAB *HOVEL.*

SOUNDS LIKE SOMEONE... *CRYING.*

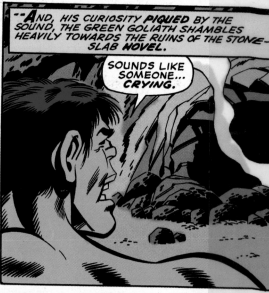

INSIDE, MARIE CARTIER STANDS ALMOST *MOTIONLESS,* HER THOUGHTS WHIRLING AIMLESSLY THRU RAGING POOLS OF DEEP CHAOTIC *BLACK.*

TOO MUCH HAS HAPPENED TOO QUICKLY FOR HER POOR MIND TO *COMPREHEND.*

THUS, IN *SELF-DEFENSE,* SHE HAS RETREATED INTO THE SHELTER OF *TENDER MADNESS.*

SHE STARES BLANKLY AT HER RAPIDLY REVIVING *BROTHER,* AT THE UNINTENTIONAL *CAUSE* OF ALL THIS--

--AND SHE DOES NOT EVEN *FEEL* THE HEAVY EMERALD HAND LAID EVER SO *GENTLY* UPON HER SHOULDER.

HE IS A *SIMPLE* CREATURE, THIS INCREDIBLE HULK; THERE IS SO MUCH HE DOESN'T *UNDERSTAND*--

--BUT GRIEF, *DESPAIR,* THESE ARE EMOTIONS HE CAN *RECOGNIZE*--

--AND, IN HIS OWN CLUMSY WAY, TRY TO *SOOTHE.*

SO THEY STAND *TOGETHER,* THE MONSTER AND THE GIRL--

--*BOTH* THE VICTIMS OF CIRCUMSTANCES THEY COULD NOT HOPE TO *CONTROL*--

--AND BOTH OF THEM SO *TERRIBLY, TERRIBLY ALONE.*

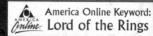

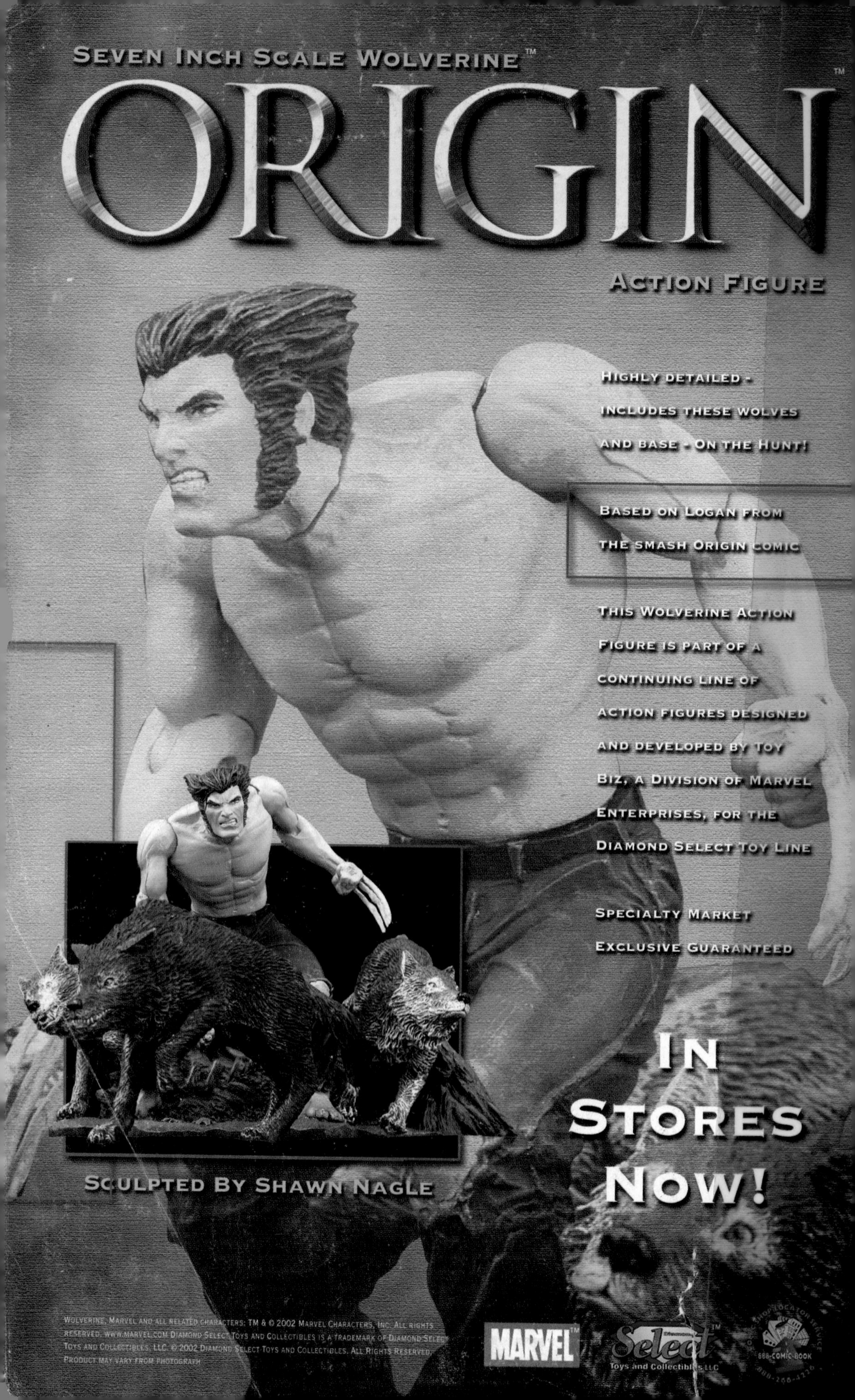
SEVEN INCH SCALE WOLVERINE™
ORIGIN™
ACTION FIGURE
HIGHLY DETAILED - INCLUDES THESE WOLVES AND BASE - ON THE HUNT!
BASED ON LOGAN FROM THE SMASH ORIGIN COMIC
THIS WOLVERINE ACTION FIGURE IS PART OF A CONTINUING LINE OF ACTION FIGURES DESIGNED AND DEVELOPED BY TOY BIZ, A DIVISION OF MARVEL ENTERPRISES, FOR THE DIAMOND SELECT TOY LINE
SPECIALTY MARKET EXCLUSIVE GUARANTEED
IN STORES NOW!
SCULPTED BY SHAWN NAGLE
WOLVERINE, MARVEL AND ALL RELATED CHARACTERS: TM & © 2002 MARVEL CHARACTERS, INC. ALL RIGHTS RESERVED. WWW.MARVEL.COM DIAMOND SELECT TOYS AND COLLECTIBLES IS A TRADEMARK OF DIAMOND SELECT TOYS AND COLLECTIBLES, LLC. © 2002 DIAMOND SELECT TOYS AND COLLECTIBLES. ALL RIGHTS RESERVED. PRODUCT MAY VARY FROM PHOTOGRAPH
MARVEL™
Select™
Toys and Collectibles LLC
888-COMIC-BOOK